her master's voice
concert register and discography of dame elisabeth schwarzkopf 1915-2006

compiled by john hunt

Her Master's voice
Having twice previously surveyed the recorded legacy of this unforgettable soprano voice, firstly in 1991 in the company of a group of her coevals on the post-war Vienna opera scene (Viennese sopranos ISBN 0 951026 83 6) and again in 1996, when she was grouped with other soprano voices of similar schooling or background (Teachers and pupils ISBN 0 952582 73 2), it was almost inevitable that this devout admirer would return to the matter for a third time. This volume, celebrating both Schwarzkopf's ninetieth birthday in December 2005 as well as marking her passing from the scene in August 2006, embraces not only the recordings but also the complete listing of her public performances between April 1938 and March 1979. These 41 years represent a period of almost unprecedented artistic activity, noteworthy both for its fertility and its industrious devotion to the cause of German music. The singer herself abhorred epithets like *diva* or *prima donna*, choosing unswervingly to describe herself as the composer's obedient servant, guided as she was for almost all those years by the taste and discernment of her impresario husband Walter Legge: the title of *Her Master's voice* met with her full approval.

I have been lucky enough to draw on the scholarship of the Schwarzkopf scholars Alan Sanders and André Tubeuf, and additionally to obtain assistance in my research from Mathias Erhard, Brian Godfrey, Syd Gray, Marlen Hall, John Hancock, Roderick Krüsemann, Luis Luna and Malcolm Walker – not to mention various staff members in the National Sound Archive at the British Library.

It is very difficult to convey in mere words, and at a remove of thirty years or more, the pleasurable thrill of attending a Schwarzkopf recital. A *Times* critic wrote in 1958: "By the end of the evening her voice, her musical personality and her personal radiance had once again combined to reduce the large audience to a state of helpless, starry-eyed and wholly devoted admiration." And of her performance of Donna Elvira in Mozart's *Don Giovanni* Neville Cardus once wrote: "Personally I have never heard (or seen) a better. Maybe this Elvira is a shade too radiantly alive: Giovanni could never have tired of her looks or her spirit."

Copyright 2006 by John Hunt

Her Master's voice: concert register and discography of Dame Elisabeth Schwarzkopf
The concert register/*page 6*   The discography/*page 162*
Appendices/*page 290*

Her Master's Voice
Published by John Hunt.
© 2006 John Hunt
reprinted 2009
ISBN 978-1-901395-21-1

Sole distributors:
Travis & Emery,
17 Cecil Court,
London, WC2N 4EZ,
United Kingdom.
(+44) 20 7 459 2129.
sales@travis-and-emery.com

The concert register: an introduction

Prior to the official debut by the 23-year old Elisabeth Schwarzkopf in Berlin on 15 April 1938, she had of course taken part in a range of student performances both in the German capital and elsewhere. These included work both as soloist and chorus-member, the culmination of her activity in that latter capacity being with the Favres Solistenvereingung for Sir Thomas Beecham's 1937 recording of *Zauberflöte*.

The basis for this listing have been the various diary entries which were made available to Alan Sanders and André Tubeuf, containing as they did certain anomalies and omissions. I suspect that they were based on notes for future plans, as they include engagements which were subsequently cancelled or amended. I have striven to give an accurate picture of what actually took place, although in some cases doubts will remain.

In order to stress the important pioneering work which Schwarzkopf carried out as a *Lied* recitalist, I have from time to time included details of the programme contents. Although some of the earliest recitals with Michael Raucheisen were mixed programmes (in certain cases possibly shared with other artists) and although late in her career she returned on occasion to recital programmes which were grouped by subject matter rather than by composer, it was nevertheless the concerted effort (shared with her contemporaries Irmgard Seefried and Dietrich Fischer-Dieskau) to bring the German-language song composers, in particulat Hugo Wolf, to a world-wide audience that earns the greatest accolade.

For the many series of opera performances that Schwarzkopf gave in houses which up to the 1960s were operating a repertory system, conductor and other soloists are named for the first performance, but it is obvious that changes might well have occured for later performances of a run.

As well as public performances in front of an audience I have included numerous ones set up for broadcasting organisations, many of which stand a good chance of having survived in radio archives. Indeed, some have already seen the light of day in publications on LP or CD in both official and unauthorised versions, and these therefore reappear in the discography (in the concert register, those broadcasts which have been published are marked with an asterisk).

The scope and industry of this workload (almost 850 *Liederabende* and 400 appearances in orchestral and choral concerts over the 41-year period) cannot but be a source of wonderment. To these must be added the operatic performances which I have listed in an appendix at the end of the book.

John Hunt 2006

15 april 1938/berlin deutsches opernhaus
wagner parsifal/blumenmädchen
conductor arthur rother
principals included larcen/ laholm/ schirp/ reinmar/ baumann/ windisch
further performances on 16, 17, 18, 23 and 24 april 1938

20 april 1938/berlin deutsches opernhaus
wagner tannhäuser/junger hirt and edelknabe
conductor walter lutze
further performance on 17 may 1938

26 april 1938/berlin deutsches opernhaus
wagner das rheingold/wellgunde
conductor karl dammer

4 may 1938/berlin deutsches opernhaus
wagner götterdämmerung/wellgunde
conductor karl dammer

7 may 1938/berlin deutsches opernhaus
kienzl der evangelimann/lumpensämmlerin
conductor walter lutze

20 june 1938/berlin deutsches opernhaus
smetana bartered bride/esmeralda
conductor walter lutze

1 july 1938/berlin deutsches opernhaus
strauss die fledermaus/ida
conductor karl dammer
principals included pfahl/ beilke/ rudolph/ w.ludwig/ schmitt-walter/ reinmar/ kandl
further performances on 2 and 3 july and 21, 22, 23 and 24 august 1938

7 september 1938/berlin deutsches opernhaus
lortzing der waffenschmied/marie
conductor walter lutze

10 september 1938/berlin deutsches opernhaus
strauss die fledermaus/ida
further performance on 21 september 1938

14 september 1938/berlin deutsches opernhaus
weber euryanthe/bertha
conductor arthur rother
principals included nettesheim/ larcen/ fidesser/ nissen/ schirp
further performances on 17 and 25 september 1938, 1, 6, 9 and 28 october 1938,
7, 11 and 29 november 1938 and 12 december 1938

18 september 1938/berlin deutsches opernhaus
wagner tannhäuser/junger hirt and edelknabe
conductor meinhard von zallinger
principals included stetzler/ larcen/ laholm/ treptow/ reinmar/ schirp
further performance on 26 october 1938

5 october 1938/berlin deutsches opernhaus
d'albert tiefland/pepa
conductor karl dammer
further performances on 12 and 20 november 1938 and 19 december 1938

14 october 1938/berlin deutsches opernhaus
wagner das rheingold/wellgunde

19 october 1938/berlin deutsches opernhaus
lortzing prinz caramo/angela
conductor walter lutze
other principals included pfahl/ wocke/ wörle/ kandl
further performance on 27 october 1938

30 october 1938/schloss schönhausen
liedmatinee
pianist uve scharlan

30 october 1938/berlin deutsches opernhaus
wagner lohengrin/edelknabe
conductor karl dammer

1 november 1938/berlin reichssender
***verdi alzira**/title role
conductor heinrich steiner
other principals included glawitsch/ huebner/ garavello

17 november 1938/berlin deutsches opernhaus
bizet carmen/frasquita
conductor arthur rother
principals included beckmann/ stoska/ beinert/ reinmar/ lang
further performances on 22 and 26 november 1938 and 2, 10, 13 and 21 december 1938

19 november 1938
performance of 4 lieder by harald genzmer

6 december 1938/berlin deutsches opernhaus
verdi il trovatore/ines
conductor walter lutze
further performances on 15 february 1939 and 13 march 1939

14 december 1938/berlin deutsches opernhaus
strauss die fledermaus/ida

23 december 1938/berlin deutsches opernhaus
schultze der schwarze peter/erika
conductor norbert schultze
other principals included meinhardt/ schilp/ dörr/ kandl/ wocke
further performance on 27 december 1938

6 january 1939/berlin deutsches opernhaus
bizet carmen/frasquita
conductor arthur rother
further performances on 9, 16, 21, 22 and 29 january 1939 and 17 and 27 february 1939

18 january 1939/berlin deutsches opernhaus
weber euryanthe/bertha
further performances on 14 february 1939 and 17 april 1939

24 january 1939/berlin deutsches opernhaus
mozart die zauberflöte/1.knabe
conductor arthur rother
principals included nettesheim/ callam/ rudolph/ w.ludwig/ schmitt-walter/ lang/ nissen
further performances on 28 january 1939, 7, 19, 23 and 28 february 1939 and
12 march 1939

25 february 1939/berlin deutsches opernhaus
wagner tannhäuser/junger hirt and edelknabe

26 february 1939/berlin deutsches opernhaus
verdi rigoletto/page
conductor otto schäfer
further performance on 3 june 1939

2 march 1939/berlin deutsches opernhaus
puccini la boheme/musetta
conductor arthur rother
further performances on 27 march 1939, 9 and 12 may 1939 and
12 and 17 june 1939

3 march 1939/berlin deutsches opernhaus
strauss der rosenkavalier/adlige waise
conductor arthur rother
further performances on 22 march 1939, 22 april 1939, 25 may 1939 and
11 june 1939

7 march 1939/berlin deutsches opernhaus
d'albert tiefland/pepa
further performances on 23 march 1939 and 17 and 28 april 1939

28 march 1939/berlin deutsches opernhaus
bizet carmen/frasquita
conductor arthur rother
further performances on 8 and 28 may 1939 and 14 and 28 june 1939

3 april 1939/berlin deutsches opernhaus
mozart die zauberflöte/1.knabe
further performances on 23, 24 and 27 april 1939, 4, 13 and 19 may 1939
and 5 and 24 june 1939

4 april 1939/berlin deutsches opernhaus
smetana bartered bride/esmeralda
further performances on 11 april 1939, 7 may 1939 and 16 june 1939

7 april 1939/berlin deutsches opernhaus
wagner parsifal/blumenmädchen
further performances on 8, 9 and 10 april 1939

19 april 1939/berlin deutsches opernhaus
wagner lohengrin/edelknabe

14 may 1939/berlin deutsches opernhaus
kusterer katarina/1.page
conductor arthur rother
principals included rudolph/ larcen/ meinhardt/ hoffmann/ pistor/ reinmar/ schirp/ nissen
further performances on 17 and 23 may 1939

15 may 1939/berlin deutsches opernhaus
verdi il trovatore/ines

29 may 1939/berlin deutsches opernhaus
kusterer katarina/alexei
conductor arthur rother
other principals included rudolph/ larcen/ meinhardt/ pistor/ reinmar/ schirp/ nissen
further performance on 2 june 1939

8 june 1939/berlin deutsches opernhaus
strauss die fledermaus/ida

10 june 1939/berlin deutsches opernhaus
wagner tannhäuser/junger hirt and edelknabe
further performance on 26 june 1939

22 june 1939/berlin deutsches opernhaus
weber der freischütz/brautjungfer
conductor otto schäfer

2 september 1939/berlin deutsches opernhaus
wagner lohengrin/edelknabe
further performances on 27 october 1939 and 12 november 1939

4 september 1939/berlin deutsches opernhaus
strauss der zigeunerbaron/arsena
conductor arthur rother
further performances on 9 september 1939, 14 and 17 october 1939 and 7 and 26 december 1939

7 september 1939/berlin deutsches opernhaus
mascagni cavalleria rusticana/lola
conductor walter lutze
further performances on 22 september 1939 and 6 october 1939

8 september 1939/berlin deutsches opernhaus
strauss der rosenkavalier/adlige waise
further performances on 8 october 1939 and 6 december 1939

10 september 1939/berlin deutsches opernhaus
weber der freischütz/brautjungfer
further performance on 3 october 1939

14 september 1939/berlin deutsches opernhaus
verdi il trovatore/ines
further performances on 19 and 29 october 1939 and 1 november 1939

16 september 1939/berlin deutsches opernhaus
wagner tannhäuser/junger hirt and edelknabe
further performances on 24 october 1939 and 15 november 1939

17 september 1939/berlin deutsches opernhaus
mozart die zauberflöte/1.knabe
further performance on 25 december 1939

18 september 1939/berlin deutsches opernhaus
verdi rigoletto/page

25 september 1939/berlin deutsches opernhaus
smetana bartered bride/esmeralda
further performance on 9 october 1939

11 october 1939/berlin deutsches opernhaus
d'albert tiefland/pepa
further performances on 4 november 1939 and 13 december 1939

15 october 1939/berlin deutsches opernhaus
kusterer katarina/alexei

31 october 1939/berlin deutsches opernhaus
mozart la finta giardiniera/serpetta
conductor artur grüber
further performance on 10 november 1939

6 november 1939/berlin deutsches opernhaus
puccini la boheme/musetta
further performances on 17 november 1939 and 30 december 1939

19 november 1939/berlin deutsches opernhaus
wagner die walküre/ortlinde
conductor arthur rother

21 november 1939/berlin deutsches opernhaus
lortzing der waffenschmied/marie

22 november 1939/berlin deutsches opernhaus
wagner parsifal/blumenmädchen
further performances on 25 and 26 november 1939

28 november 1939/berlin deutsches opernhaus
lortzing der wildschütz/gretchen
conductor artur grüber
other principals included meinhardt/ pfahl/ tüscher/ wocke/ wörle/ kandl
further performances on 11 december 1939, 7 january 1940 and
15 february 1940

8 december 1939/berlin deutsches opernhaus
humperdinck hänsel und gretel/taumännchen
conductor arthur rother
principals included hoffmann/ tüscher/ carlsson/ nissen
further performances on 22, 23 and 29 december 1939 and 6, 8 and 10
january 1940

14

15 december 1939/berlin deutsches opernhaus
mozart le nozze di figaro/barbarina
conductor arthur rother
further performances on 20 and 28 december 1939, 20 january 1940 and
6 february 1940

31 december 1939/berlin deutsches opernhaus
strauss die fledermaus/ida
further performances on 1, 11 and 26 january 1940

2 january 1940/berlin deutsches opernhaus
wagner tannhäuser/junger hirt and edelknabe
further performance on 18 february 1940

4 january 1940/berlin deutsches opernhaus
carmen/frasquita
further performances on 14, 25 and 31 january 1940

13 january 1940/berlin deutsches opernhaus
strauss der zigeunerbaron/arsena
further performances on 21 january 1940 and 8, 16, 17 and 23 february 1940

16 january 1940/berlin deutsches opernhaus
mozart la finta giardiniera/serpetta
further performance on 19 february 1940

18 january 1940/berlin deutsches opernhaus
mozart die zauberflöte/1.knabe
further performance on 10 february 1940

19 january 1940/berlin deutsches opernhaus
d'albert tiefland/pepa

28 january 1940/berlin deutsches opernhaus
smetana bartered bride/esmeralda
further performance on 28 february 1940

27 february 1940/berlin deutsches opernhaus
donizetti l'elisir d'amore/gianetta
conductor walter lutze
principals included beilke/ w.ludwig/ wocke/ windisch
further performances on 1, 13 and 30 march 1940, 1, 19 and 28 april 1940,
5, 11 and 20 may 1940, 25 and 28 june 1940 and 2 july 1940

29 february 1940/berlin deutsches opernhaus
wagner das rheingold/wellgunde
further performance on 14 may 1940

3 march 1940/berlin deutsches opernhaus
mascagni cavalleria rusticana/lola
conductor walter lutze

5 march 1940/berlin deutsches opernhaus
strauss die fledermaus/ida

11 march 1940/berlin deutsches opernhaus
strauss der zigeunerbaron/arsena
conductor otto schäfer
further performances on 13 and 26 april 1940 and 8 and 27 may 1940

12 march 1940/berlin deutsches opernhaus
wagner götterdämmerung/wellgunde
conductor arthur rother
further performances on 20 april 1940 and 25 may 1940

14 march 1940/berlin deutsches opernhaus
bizet carmen/frasquita

15 march 1940/berlin deutsches opernhaus
mozart le nozze di figaro/barbarina
further performances on 20 march 1940 and 3 april 1940

21 march 1940/berlin deutsches opernhaus
verdi il trovatore/ines

22 march 1940/berlin deutsches opernhaus
wagner parsifal/blumenmädchen
further performance on 23 march 1940

16

30 march 1940/berlin deutsches opernhaus
puccini gianni schicchi/lauretta
conductor walter lutze
other principals included schilp/ haller/ schirp/ lang/ reinmar/ nissen
further performances on 1, 19 and 28 april 1940
performed on the above dates only as a double bill with l'elisir d'amore
(see 27 february 1940)

12 april 1940/berlin deutsches opernhaus
marinuzzi palla de mozzi/nun
conductor gino marinuzzi
principals included stetzler/ westenberger/ friedrich/ pistor/ noort/ nissen/ lang
further performances on 15, 18, 23, 25 and 29 april 1940 and 4, 9, 17 and 28 may 1940

21 april 1940/berlin deutsches opernhaus
bizet carmen/frasquita
conductor artur grüber

24 april 1940/berlin deutsches opernhaus
smetana bartered bride/esmeralda
further performance on 3 may 1940

30 april 1940/berlin deutsches opernhaus
strauss der rosenkavalier/adlige waise
further performance on 13 may 1940

1 may 1940/berlin deutsches opernhaus
strauss die fledermaus/adele
conductor otto schäfer
further performance on 12 may 1940

2 may 1940/berlin deutsches opernhaus
lortzing zar und zimmermann/marie

6 may 1940/berlin deutsches opernhaus
weber euryanthe/bertha
further performance on 18 may 1940

15 may 1940/berlin deutsches opernhaus
mozart die zauberflöte/1.knabe

24 may 1940/berlin deutsches opernhaus
mozart le nozze di figaro/barbarina

26 may 1940/berlin deutsches opernhaus
suppé boccaccio/isabella
conductor walter lutze
other principals included kerp/ wörle/ wocke/ kandl
further performances on 29 may 1940, 1 and 21 june 1940 and 1 and 3 july 1940

18 august 1940/berlin deutsches opernhaus
strauss der zigeunerbaron/arsena

11 september 1940/berlin deutsches opernhaus
wagner tannhäuser/junger hirt and edelknabe

12 september 1940/berlin deutsches opernhaus
mozart le nozze di figaro/barbarina
further performances on 22 and 29 october 1940 and 1 december 1940

13 september 1940/berlin deutsches opernhaus
mozart die zauberflöte/1.knabe
further performances on 10 and 11 october 1940 and 19 november 1940

28 september 1940/berlin deutsches opernhaus
strauss ariadne auf naxos/zerbinetta
conductor arthur rother
other principals included stetzler/ nettesheim/ noort/ nissen/ schmitt-walter
further performances on 30 september 1940, 5, 15 and 24 october 1940,
10 and 18 november 1940 and 9 december 1940

1 october 1940/berlin deutsches opernhaus
donizetti l'elisir d'amore/gianetta
further performances on 21 and 31 october 1940

4 october 1940/berlin deutsches opernhaus
strauss der zigeunerbaron/arsena
further performance on 13 october 1940

18

7 october 1940/berlin deutsches opernhaus
wagner das rheingold/wellgunde

9 october 1940/berlin deutsches opernhaus
wagner die walküre/ortlinde

30 october 1940/berlin deutsches opernhaus
puccini la boheme/musetta

11 november 1940/berlin deutsches opernhaus
d'albert tiefland/pepa
further performances on 13 november 1940 and 8 december 1940

17 november 1940/berlin deutsches opernhaus
strauss der rosenkavalier/adlige waise

27 november 1940/berlin deutsches opernhaus
mascagni cavalleria rusticana/lola
further performances on 30 november 1940 and 6, 12 and 18 december 1940

15 december 1940/berlin deutsches opernhaus
humperdinck hänsel und gretel/taumännchen
further performances on 17, 19, 22, 23 and 28 december 1940

16 december 1940/berlin deutsches opernhaus
lortzing undine/title role
conductor artur grüber
further performances on 27 december 1940 and 7 january 1941

20 december 1940/berlin deutsches opernhaus
weber der freischütz/brautjungfer
conductor arthur rother
further performance on 29 december 1940

9 january 1941/berlin deutsches opernhaus
weber der freischütz/ännchen
conductor arthur rother
other principals included stoska/ treptow/ schirp/ nissen/ wocke/ lang
further performances on 16 january 1941, 4 and 26 february 1941 and 11 may 1941

11 january 1941/berlin deutsches opernhaus
d'albert tiefland/pepa
further performances on 24 february 1941, 7 march 1941 and 7 april 1941

20 january 1941/berlin deutsches opernhaus
mozart le nozze di figaro/barbarina
further performance on 1 february 1941

23 january 1941/berlin deutsches opernhaus
mascagni cavalleria rusticana/lola
further performances on 10 february 1941, 18 may 1941 and 10 june 1941

26 january 1941/berlin deutsches opernhaus
wagner tannhäuser/junger hirt and edelknabe
further performances on 2 and 22 may 1941

28 january 1941/berlin deutsches opernhaus
puccini la boheme/musetta
further performance on 12 february 1941

5 february 1941/berlin deutsches opernhaus
lortzing der wildschütz/gretchen
further performances on 4 and 9 april 1941

20 february 1941/berlin deutsches opernhaus
wagner die walküre/ortlinde

14 march 1941/berlin deutsches opernhaus
strauss ariadne auf naxos/zerbinetta

20

15-16 march 1941/schloss dwasiden
liederabend
pianist michael raucheisen

18 march 1941/berlin deutsches opernhaus
lortzing undine/title role

11 april 1941/berlin deutsches opernhaus
wagner parsifal/blumenmädchen
further performances on 12, 13 and 14 april 1941

28 april 1941/berlin deutsches opernhaus
mozart le nozze di figaro/susanna

1 may 1941/berlin deutsches opernhaus
strauss der zigeunerbaron/arsena
further performance on 22 june 1941

7 may 1941/berlin deutsches opernhaus
mozart die zauberflöte/1.knabe
further performance on 30 may 1941

21 may 1941/berlin deutsches opernhaus
donizetti l'elisir d'amore/gianetta

24 may 1941/berlin deutsches opernhaus
wagner das rheingold/wellgunde

may 1941/berlin haus des rundfunks
*recording for reichsrundfunk of scenes from das rheingold
conductor arthur rother
other soloists included scheppan/ schilp/ aldenhoff/ zimmermann/ hann/ nissen

29 may 1941/berlin deutsches opernhaus
wagner götterdämmerung/wellgunde
further performance on 24 june 1941

13 june 1941/berlin deutsches opernhaus
mozart le nozze di figaro/barbarina
further performance on 7 july 1941

15 june 1941/berlin deutsches opernhaus
flotow alessandro stradella/leonore
conductor walter lutze
other principals included w.ludwig/ schirp/ kandl

8 september 1941/berlin deutsches opernhaus
puccini la boheme/musetta

13 september 1941/paris théatre de l'opéra
strauss die fledermaus/adele
conductor artur grüber
guest performance by deutsches opernhaus berlin
further performances on 14, 15, 16 and 17 september 1941

1 october 1941/berlin deutsches opernhaus
lortzing der wildschütz/gretchen
further performance on 14 december 1941

8 october 1941/berlin deutsches opernhaus
mozart le nozze di figaro/barbarina

9 october 1941/berlin deutsches opernhaus
donizetti l'elisir d'amore/gianetta
further performance on 13 november 1941

10 october 1941/berlin deutsches opernhaus
wagner tannhäuser/junger hirt and edelknabe
further performances on 26 october 1941, 16 november 1941 and 25 december 1941

31 october 1941/berlin deutsches opernhaus
weber der freischütz/ännchen
further performance on 4 november 1941

1 november 1941/berlin deutsches opernhaus
wagner siegfried/waldvogel
conductor arthur rother
further performances on 9 november 1941 and 22 december 1941

8 november 1941/berlin deutsches opernhaus
mascagni cavalleria rusticana/lola
further performance on 19 december 1941

17 november 1941/berlin deutsches opernhaus
mozart la finta giardiniera/serpetta
further performances on 9 and 27 december 1940

19 november 1941/berlin deutsches opernhaus
wagner parsifal/blumenmädchen
further performances on 20, 21, 22 and 23 november 1940

29 november 1941/berlin beethovensaal der philharmonie
liederabend
pianist michael raucheisen

9 december 1941/berlin haus des rundfunks
*radio recording of quartet from la boheme (addio dolce svegliare)
conductor hanns steinkopf
other soloists cebotari/ rosvaenge/ schmitt-walter

14 december 1941/berlin deutsches opernhaus
lortzing der wildschütz/gretchen
further performances on 10 and 13 january 1942

15 december 1941/berlin deutsches opernhaus
humperdinck hänsel und gretel/taumännchen
further performances on 17, 21, 23, 28 and 29 december 1941

26 december 1941/berlin beethovensaal der philharmonie
liederabend
pianist michael raucheisen

11 january 1942/berlin wilmersdorf
concert with arias from der freischütz and don pasquale

12 january 1942/berlin bachsaal der philharmonie
liederabend
pianist michael raucheisen

20 january 1942/berlin deutsches opernhaus
lortzing der waffenschmied/marie
further performances on 14 february 1942, 2 april 1942 and 3 may 1942

13 february 1942/berlin beethovensaal der philharmonie
liederabend
pianist michael raucheisen

28 february 1942/berlin deutsches opernhaus
d'albert tiefland/pepa

20 march 1942/wiesbaden
concert with arias from ariadne auf naxos and il re pastore
conductor carl schuricht

3 april 1942/berlin deutsches opernhaus
wagner parsifal/blumenmädchen
further performances on 4, 5 and 6 april 1942

9 april 1942/berlin deutsches opernhaus
mozart le nozze di figaro/susanna
further performance on 14 may 1942

16 april 1942/berlin deutsches opernhaus
wagner siegfried/waldvogel

17 april 1942/berlin deutsches opernhaus
lortzing zar und zimmermann/marie
further performance on 11 may 1942

9 may 1942/berlin beethovensaal der philharmonie
liederabend
pianist michael raucheisen

12 may 1942/berlin deutsches opernhaus
mozart la finta giardiniera/serpetta
further performance on 20 may 1942

24

18 may 1942/berlin deutsches opernhaus
strauss der zigeunerbaron/arsena

19 may 1942/berlin
mozart mass in c minor/soprano soloist

24 may 1942/berlin deutsches opernhaus
puccini la boheme/musetta

26 may 1942/berlin deutsches opernhaus
lortzing der wildschütz/gretchen

27 june 1942/berlin haus des rundfunks
*recording for reichsrundfunk of duets by weber and loewe with lea piltti
pianist michael raucheisen

8 july 1942/berlin charlottenburg
chemin-petit der gefangene vogel
conductor hans chemin-petit

28 august 1942/baden-baden
liederabend

15 september 1942/harzburg

september 1942/posen
concert for reichssender
conductor hans pfitzner

20 september 1942/vienna staatsoper
mozart die entführung aus dem serail/blondchen
conductor karl böhm

7 october 1942/vienna staatsoper
strauss ariadne auf naxos/zerbinetta
conductor rudolf moralt
other principals included rünger/ schulz/ svanholm/ poell

25 october 1942/berlin beethovensaal der philharmonie
liederabend
pianist michael raucheisen

28 october 1942/berlin deutsches opernhaus
flotow alessandro stradella/leonore
further performance on 29 january 1943

11 november 1942/vienna musikverein
liederabend
pianist maximilian kojetinsky

16 november 1942/vienna staatsoper
mozart die entführung aus dem serail/blondchen
conductor karl böhm
other principals included cebotari/ dermota/ sallaba/ alsen/ jürgens

29 november 1942/berlin schillertheater
liederabend
pianist michael raucheisen
recital repeated on 6 december 1942

26 december 1942/berlin beethovensaal der philharmonie
liederabend
pianist michael raucheisen

31 december 1942/berlin deutsches opernhaus
strauss die fledermaus/adele
further performance on 1 january 1943

6 january 1943/berlin deutsches opernhaus
weber der freischütz/ännchen

14 february 1943/berlin
liederabend
pianist michael raucheisen

21 february 1943/berlin deutsches opernhaus
lortzing der waffenschmied/marie
further performances on 1 and 2 march 1943 and 5 april 1943

22 february 1943/elblag
concert with arias from ariadne auf naxos and frühlingsstimmen

28 february 1943/berlin
concert with works by pfitzner

9 march 1943/berlin haus des rundfunks
recording for reichsrundfunk of lieder by loewe
pianist michael raucheisen

27 march 1943/berlin
höffer der reiche tag
conductor paul höffer

4 april 1943/berlin
liederabend

11 april 1943/berlin
liederabend
pianist michael raucheisen

15 april 1943/vienna musikverein
liederabend
pianist viktor graef

23 april 1943/berlin
bach matthäus-passion/soprano soloist
conductor schneider

27 march 1944/berlin europahaus
participation in an operatic concert

15 april 1944/vienna staatsoper
mozart die entführung aus dem serail/konstanze
conductor rudolf moralt
other principals included noni/ dermota/ sallaba/ alsen
further performance on 10 june 1944

21 april 1944/vienna staatsoper
puccini la boheme/musetta
conductor rudolf moralt
other principals included cebotari/ dermota/ ahlersmeyer

30 april 1944/vienna haus des rundfunks
recording for reichsrundfunk of works by handel and pfitzner
conductor hans weisbach

2 may 1944/vienna staatsoper
rossini il barbiere di siviglia/rosina
conductor rudolf moralt
other principals included dermota/ oeggl/ jerger/ rus

4 may 1944/vienna musikverein
vienna philharmonic orchestra concert
pfitzner songs with orchestra
conductor joseph keilberth

21 may 1944/vienna staatsoper
weber der freischütz/ännchen
conductor leopold reichwein
other principals included h.konetzni/ sattler/ rus/ krenn
further performance on 2 june 1944

25 may 1944/graz
liederabend

27 may 1944/vienna musikverein
participation in an operatic concert

28 may 1944/vienna staatsoper
puccini la boheme/musetta
conductor leopold reichwein
other principals included böttcher/ mazaroff/ poell

29 may 1944/neunkirchen
liederabend

9 june 1944/zwickau
liederabend
lieder by schumann and pfitzner

21 june 1944/vienna staatsoper
mozart die entführung aus dem serail/konstanze
conductor leopold reichwein
other principals included loose/ roswaenge/ sallaba/ koreh

28
4-5 july 1944/leipzig
brahms ein deutsches requiem/soprano soloist

20-21 august 1944/cracow
liederabend

31 august 1944/vienna musikverein
recording for reichsrundfunk
wagner götterdämmerung/wellgunde

5-6 september 1944/vienna musikverein
recording for reichsrundfunk
*mozart die entführung aus dem serail/konstanze
conductor rudolf moralt
other principals included loose/ dermota/ klein/ alsen

20 september 1944/berlin haus des rundfunks
*recordings of songs for reichsrundfunk
pianist michael raucheisen
further recording sessions took place on 21 and 30 september 1944 and 7 october 1944

12 october 1944/berlin
graun montezuma
further performances on 13 and 14 october 1944

23 october 1944/berlin
participation in concert of music for portugal

16 november 1944/berlin
participation in concert of music for latin america

20 november 1944/berlin
participation in operatic concert

25-26 november 1944/potsdam
brahms ein deutsches requiem/soprano soloist
conductor landgrebe

2 december 1944/vienna
participation in choral concert with a mass by bruckner

12 december 1944/vienna musikverein
liederabend
pianist viktor graef

15 december 1944/berlin haus des rundfunks
participation in operatic concert for reichsrundfunk

18-19 december 1944/berlin haus des rundfunks
reichsrundfunk recording
*weber abu hassan/fatima
conductor leopold ludwig
other principals included witte/bohnen

2 january 1945/berlin haus des rundfunks
*recordings of songs for reichsrundfunk
pianist michael raucheisen

24 january 1945/vienna musikverein
liederabend

28 june 1945/sankt johann
participation in choral concert
conductor joseph messner

16 september 1945/graz stadttheater
mozart die entführung ausdem serail/konstanze
conductor rudolf moralt
other principals included patzak/weber

24 september 1945/graz
liederabend
pianist kornauth
recital was repeated on 11 october 1945

12 october 1945/leoben
participation in concert

28 november 1945/salzburg mozarteum
participation in a johann strauss concert

9 december 1945/vienna musikverein
verdi messa da requiem/soprano soloist
conductor anton lippe
other soloists were schürhoff/patzak/weber

12 december 1945/vienna musikverein
liederabend
pianist viktor graef

12 december 1945/vienna staatsoper in der volkdoper
leoncavallo i pagliacci/nedda
conductor wilhelm loibner
other principals included baxevanos/ oeggl/ poell/ jaresch
further performances on 14 december 1945 and 29 january 1946

23 january 1946/vienna staatsoper in der volksoper
puccini la boheme/mimi
conductor heinrich schmidt
other principals included seefried/ dermota/ poell/ braun
further performances on 7, 14 and 28 february 1946, 6, 15 and 20 march 1946 and 24 april 1946

26 january 1946/vienna
participation in a concert

12 february 1946/vienna staatsoper in baden
rossini il barbiere di siviglia/rosina

3 march 1946/vienna staatsoper in der volksoper
rossini il barbiere di siviglia/rosina

26 april 1946/vienna staatsoper im theater an der wien
verdi rigoletto/gilda
conductor rudolf moralt
other principals included sydney/ dermota/ oeggl/ vogel
further performances on 2, 6, 23 and 24 may 1946

23 september 1946/vienna staatsoper im theater an der wien
verdi rigoletto/gilda
further performances on 5, 14 and 27 november 1946

29 september 1946/vienna staatsoper in der volksoper
rossini il barbiere di siviglia/rosina
further performances on 6 and 21 november 1946 and 31 december 1946

20 october 1946/vienna staatsoper im theater an der wien
mozart die entführung aus dem serail/konstanze
conductor rudolf moralt
other principals included loose/ dermota/ klein/ weber/ jürgens
further performances on 22 october 1946, 3 and 18 november 1946 and
1 and 5 december 1946

23-24 november 1946/vienna musikverein
vienna symphony orchestra concert
beethoven symphony no 9 "choral"
conductor rudolf moralt
other soloists were höngen/ dermota/ alsen

25 november 1946/vienna staatsoper in der volksoper
puccini la boheme/mimi

26 december 1946/vienna musikverein
liederabend
pianist otto schulhof

1 january 1947/vienna staatsoper im theater an der wien
mozart die entführung aus dem serail/konstanze
further performances on 7 january 1947 and 25 may 1947

5 january 1947/vienna musikverein
liederabend richard strauss
pianist pilss

10 january 1947/vienna staatsoper im theater an der wien
verdi rigoletto/gilda
further performances on 4 february 1947, 4 and 6 march 1947 and 18 june 1947

19 january 1947/vienna musikverein
participation in concert of schubert choral works
conductor hans swarowsky

19 january 1947/vienna staatsoper im theater an der wien
mozart don giovanni/elvira
conductor felix prohaska
other principals included h.braun/ seefried/ dermota/ schöffler/ hann
further performances on 22 january 1947 and 7 and 13 february 1947

27 january 1947/vienna staatsoper in der volksoper
mozart le nozze di figaro/susanna
conductor rudolf moralt

2 february 1947/vienna musikverein
liederabend
pianist viktor graef

18 february 1947/schönbrunn schlosstheater
johann strauss concert with the vienna philharmonic
strauss frühlingsstimmen
conductor josef krips

27 february 1947/vienna staatsoper im theater an der wien
verdi la traviata/violetta
conductor josef krips
other principals included dermota/ taddei
further performances on 12, 24 and 31 march 1947, 2, 8, 15 and 30 april 1947
and 24 june 1947

19-20 march 1947/vienna musikverein
brahms ein deutsches requiem/soprano soloist
conductor ferdinand grossmann
other soloist was hotter

10 april 1947/vienna staatsoper im theater an der wien
mozart don giovanni/elvira
conductor otto klemperer
other principals included welitsch/ seefried/ dermota/ kunz/ schöffler
further performance on 12 and 21 april 1947 and 25 june 1947

20 april 1947/vienna musikverein
vienna symphony orchestra concert
conductor rudolf moralt
berg 3 fragments from wozzeck

22 april 1947/vienna musikverein
participation in operatic benefit concert
other participants included rethy/ nikolaidi/ dermota

27 april 1947/vienna musikverein
concert with bach cantatas
conductor felix prohaska

2 may 1947/vienna musikverein
bach mass in b minor/soprano soloist
other soloists included höngen

8 may 1947/vienna staatsoper in der volksoper
rossini il barbiere di siviglia/rosina
further performances on 8, 18 and 29 may 1947

13 may 1947/vienna staatsoper im theater an der wien
strauss ariadne auf naxos/zerbinetta
conductor josef krips
other principals included reining/ seefried/ lorenz/ kunz/ poell

18 may 1947/vienna musikverein
participation in concert of choral works by haydn
conductor heinrich schmidt

7-8 june 1947/vienna musikverein
vienna symphony orchestra concert
haydn die schöpfung/soprano soloist
conductor clemens krauss
other soloists included patzak/ hann

14-15 june 1947/vienna musikverein
vienna philharmonic concert
beethoven symphony no 9 "choral"/soprano soloist
conductor clemens krauss
other soloists included anday/ patzak/ frantz

29 june 1947/baden kurpark
vienna philharmonic concert
beethoven symphony no 9 "choral"/soprano soloist
conductor josef krips
other soloists included schürhoff/ meyer-welfing/ alsen

6 july 1947/graz
haydn die schöpfung/soprano soloist
conductor anton lippe
other soloists included dermota/ alsen

13 july 1947/graz
liederabend
pianist kornauth

34

28 july 1947/salzburg festspielhaus
mozart le nozze di figaro/susanna
conductor josef krips
other principals included cebotari/ güden/ kunz/ höfermayer

20-21 august 1947/lucerne jesuitenkirche
*brahms ein deutsches requiem/soprano soloist
conductor wilhelm furtwängler
other soloist was hotter

24-25 august 1947/lucerne
concert conducted by paul sacher
mozart exsultate jubilate

2 september 1947/vienna staatsoper in der volksoper
rossini il barbiere di siviglia/rosina

5 september 1947/vienna staatsoper im theater an der wien
verdi rigoletto/gilda

9 september 1947/vienna staatsoper im theater an der wien
mozart die entführung aus dem serail/konstanze

16 september 1947/london royal opera house
guest performance by vienna staatsoper
mozart don giovanni/elvira
conductor josef krips
other principals included cebotari/ güden/ dermota/ kunz/ schöffler

17 september 1947/london royal opera house
guest performance by vienna staatsoper
*beethoven fidelio/marzelline
conductor clemens krauss
other principals included h.konetzni/ patzak/ schöffler/ weber
further performances on 19 and 24 september 1947

20 september 1947/london royal opera house
guest performance by vienna staatsoper
mozart don giovanni/elvira
conductor josef krips
other principals included welitsch/ loose/ dermota/ hann/ schöffler

21 september 1947/london royal opera house
guest performance by vienna staatsoper: concert of works by mozart and johann strauss
mozart martern aller arten/entführung
conductor josef krips
other participants included h.konetzni/ tauber/ dermota/ clemens krauss

27 september 1947/london royal opera house
guest performance by vienna staatsoper
*mozart don giovanni/elvira
conductor josef krips
other principals included cebotari/ güden/ tauber/ kunz/ schöffler
richard tauber's final appearance before his death

29 september 1947/london royal opera house
guest performance by vienna staatsoper
mozart don giovanni/elvira
conductor josef krips
other principals included cebotari/ güden/ dermota/ kunz/ hotter
further performance on 3 october 1947

9 october 1947/vienna musikverein
honegger jeanne d'arc au bucher/soprano soloist
conductor paul sacher

11 october 1947/vienna staatsoper in der volksoper
puccini la boheme/mimi
principals also included welitsch
further performances on 13 october 1947 and 28 december 1947

15 october 1947/vienna staatsoper im theater an der wien
verdi la traviata/violetta
further performances on 25 october 1947, 7 november 1947 and 10 december 1947

20 october 1947/schönbrunn schlosstheater
mozart le nozze di figaro/susanna

1 november 1947/vienna staatsoper im theater an der wien
mozart don giovanni/elvira
further performances on 25 december 1947 and 1 january 1948

5-6 november 1947/vienna musikverein
handel messiah/soprano soloist
conductor anton lippe
other soloists included höngen/ dermota/ schöffler

8 november 1947/vienna staatsoper in der volksoper
weber der freischütz/ännchen

24 november 1947/vienna staatsoper im theater an der wien
mozart die entführung aus dem serail/konstanze
further performances on 21 and 23 december 1947 and 9 january 1948

3-4 december 1947/vienna musikverein
vienna symphony orchestra concert
brahms ein deutsches requiem/soprano soloist
conductor wilhelm furtwängler
other soloist was schöffler

17 december 1947/berchtesgaden
liederabend
pianist kornauth

20-21 december 1947/vienna musikverein
vienna philharmonic concert
beethoven symphony no 9 "choral"/soprano soloist
conductor herbert von karajan
other soloists included höngen/patzak/hotter

4 january 1948/vienna staatsoper im theater an der wien
beethoven fidelio/marzelline

7 january 1948/vienna musikverein
liederabend
pianist karl hudez

14 january 1948/vienna staatsoper im theater an der wien
mozart die zauberflöte/pamina
conductor josef krips

3 february 1948/london royal opera house
mozart die zauberflöte/pamina
conductor karl rankl
further performances on 13 february 1948, 1 and 22 march 1948 and 7 and 27 may 1948

17 february 1948/london royal opera house
strauss der rosenkavalier/sophie
conductor karl rankl
further performance on 19 may 1948

20 february 1948/london royal opera house
participation in memorial concert for richard tauber

13 march 1948/bern
liederabend
pianist volkmar andreae

15 march 1948/chaux-de-fonds
liederabend
pianist volkmar andreae

17 march 1948/zürich
liederabend
pianist volkmar andreae

6 april 1948/london royal opera house
verdi la traviata/violetta
conductor reginald goodall
further performances on 9, 15, 20, 24 and 28 april 1948, 4 and 24 may 1948 and 1 june 1948

2 may 1948/london wigmore hall
liederabend
pianist gerald moore

10 may 1948/stockholm konserthuset
concert with operatic arias
conductor herbert sandberg

13 june 1948/vienna staatsoper im theater an der wien
verdi rigoletto/gilda

15 june 1948/vienna staatsoper im theater an der wien
verdi la traviata/violetta
further performance on 16 june 1948

17 june 1948/vienna staatsoper im theater an der wien
mozart die zauberflöte/pamina

19 june 1948/vienna staatsoper in der volksoper
mozart le nozze di figaro/susanna

21 june 1948/vienna staatsoper im theater an der wien
mozart die entführung aus dem serail/konstanze

25 june 1948/glyndebourne opera house
charity concert shared with the pianist isador goodman
liederabend
pianist ivor newton
schubert ave maria/ das lied im grünen/ gretchen am spinnrade/ du bist die ruh/ die vögel/ liebhaber in allen gestalten/ die forelle/ seligkeit
mozart das veilchen/ dove sono/ martern aller arten
come again/ drink to me only/ where the bee sucks/ when daisies pide

27 june 1948/london bbc studios
liederabend franz schubert
pianist frederick stone
schubert du bist die ruh/ gretchen am spinnrade/ der musensohn/ das lied im grünen/ im abendrot/ die vögel/ vedi quanto adoro

6 july 1948/london bbc studios
liederabend hugo wolf
pianist frederick stone
selection from the goethe- and mörike-lieder

11 july 1948/london royal opera house
philharmonia orchestra concert of works by bach and mozart
conductor richard austin

28 july 1948/salzburg felsenreitschule
gluck orfeo ed euridice/blessed spirit
conductor herbert von karajan
principals included höngen/ cebotari/ jurinac
further performances on 2, 7, 10, 13 and 16 august 1948

11 august 1948/salzburg festspielhaus
mozart le nozze di figaro/contessa
conductor herbert von karajan
other principals included seefried/ jurinac/ taddei/ höfermayer
further performances on 14, 17, 21 and 27 august 1948

22 august 1948/salzburg festspielhaus
vienna philharmonic concert
brahms ein deutsches requiem/soprano soloist
conductor herbert von karajan
other soloist was schöffler

28-29 august 1948/lucerne kunsthaus
beethoven symphony no 9 "choral"
conductor wilhelm furtwängler
other soloists included cavelti/ haefliger/ schöffler

1 september 1948/vienna staatsoper im theater an der wien
verdi rigoletto/gilda

4 september 1948/vienna staatsoper im theater an der wien
mozart don giovanni/elvira
further performance on 4 november 1948

5 september 1948/vienna staatsoper in der volksoper
weber der freischütz/agathe
conductor felix prohaska
further performance on 2 november 1948

8 september 1948/vienna staatsoper im theater an der wien
beethoven fidelio/marzelline

14 september 1948/vienna staatsoper im theater an der wien
verdi la traviata/violetta

16 september 1948/vienna staatsoper im theater an der wien
strauss der rosenkavalier/sophie
conductor rudolf moralt

25 september 1948/perugia
mozart mass in c minor/soprano soloist

30 september 1948/london royal opera house
mozart die zauberflöte/pamina

1 october 1948/london royal opera house
strauss der rosenkavalier/sophie

7 october 1948/london royal albert hall
johann strauss concert by the vienna philharmonic
strauss frühlingsstimmen
conductor josef krips

40

12 october 1948/london royal opera house
verdi la traviata/violetta
further performances on 20 and 26 october 1948, 12 and 19 november 1948 and 7 and 18 december 1948

15 october 1948/london royal opera house
puccini la boheme/mimi
conductor karl rankl
other principals included welitsch/schock
further performances on 18 and 30 october 1948, 3, 10 and 20 december 1948 and 1 and 24 january 1949

31 october 1948/brighton dome
concert of works by mozart and strauss
conductor herbert menges

23 november 1948/london royal opera house
wagner die meistersinger von nürnberg/eva
conductor karl rankl

9 december 1948/london royal opera house
beethoven fidelio/marzelline
further performances on 17 december 1948 and 7 january 1949

13 december 1948/london westminster central hall
philharmonia orchestra concert with works by mozart
conductor mosco carner

28 december 1948/milan teatro alla scala
guest performance by vienna staatsoper
*mozart le nozze di figaro/contessa
conductor herbert von karajan
other principals included seefried/jurinac/taddei/höfermayer
further performance on 31 december 1948

11 january 1949/london royal opera house
verdi la traviata/violetta

13 january 1949/london royal opera house
mozart die zauberflöte/pamina

16 january 1949/london royal albert hall
philharmonia orchestra concert in memory of richard tauber with works by mozart
conductor walter goehr

22 january 1949/london royal opera house
mozart le nozze di figaro/susanna
conductor karl rankl
further performances on 26 and 28 january 1949

23 january 1949/bournemouth winter gardens
bournemouth symphony orchestra concert
conductor rudolf schwarz

19 february 1949/vienna musikverein
vienna philharmonic concert
beethoven symphony no 9 "choral"/soprano soloist
conductor wilhelm furtwängler
other soloists included höngen/patzak/schöffler
concert repeated on 20 and 21 february 1949

20 february 1949/vienna staatsoper im theater an der wien
verdi rigoletto/gilda
conductor wilhelm loibner
further performances on 2 march 1949 and 9 april 1949

24 february 1949/vienna staatsoper im theater an der wien
verdi la traviata/violetta
further performances on 28 february 1949 and 3 and 6 april 1949

6 march 1949/vienna staatsoper im theater an der wien
puccini turandot/liu
conductor karl böhm
other principals included cebotari/friedrich/weber
further performance on 16 march 1949

10 march 1949/zürich tonhalle
liederabend
pianist volkmar andreae

11 march 1949/chaux-de-fonds
liederabend
pianist volkmar andreae

12 march 1949/lucerne
liederabend
pianist volkmar andreae

17 march 1949/vienna staatsoper im theater an der wien
mozart die zauberflöte/pamina

23 march 1949/paris théatre des champs-élysées
guest performance by vienna staatsoper
mozart le nozze di figaro/susanna
conductor karl böhm
other principals included reining/ jurinac/ hotter
further performances on 26, 28 and 29 march 1948

25 march 1949/london royal albert hall
philharmonia orchestra concert
brahms ein deutsches requiem/soprano soloist
conductor richard austin
other soloist was hotter

27 march 1949/london royal opera house
liederabend
pianist gerald moore

2 april 1949/vienna musikverein
liederabend
pianist erik werba

14-15 april 1949/vienna musikverein
vienna symphony orchestra concert
bach matthäus-passion/soprano soloist
conductor hans knappertsbusch
other soloists included anday/ patzak/ braun/ edelmann

19 april 1949/birmingham hippodrome theatre
guest performance by royal opera house
mozart le nozze di figaro/susanna

21 april 1949/birmingham hippodrome theatre
guest performance by royal opera house
wagner die meistersinger von nürnberg/eva
conductor reginald goodall

23 april 1949/birmingham hippodrome theatre
guest performance by royal opera house
puccini la boheme/mimi

24 april 1949/cambridge
liederabend
pianist peter gellhorn

26 april 1949/london royal opera house
mozart le nozze di figaro/susanna
further performance on 20 may 1949

28 april 1949/london royal opera house
verdi la traviata/violetta
further performances on 10 and 26 may 1949

29 april 1949/london royal opera house
beethoven fidelio/marzelline
further performance on 27 may 1949

4 may 1949/london royal opera house
verdi rigoletto/gilda

7 may 1949/london royal opera house
puccini la boheme/mimi
further performances on 18 and 23 may 1949

15 june 1949/bad salzschlirf
participation in concert

20 june 1949/brussels théatre de la monnaie
guest performance by vienna staatsoper
strauss der rosenkavalier/sophie
conductor karl böhm
other principals included reining/jurinac/weber
further performance on 24 june 1949

22 june 1949/brussels théatre de la monnaie
guest performance by vienna staatsoper
mozart don giovanni/elvira
conductor josef krips
other principals included welitsch/ seefried/ dermota/ kunz/ schöffler
further performance on 28 june 1949

2 july 1949/amsterdam stadsschouwburg
guest performance by vienna staatsoper
strauss der rosenkavalier/sophie
conductor karl böhm
other principals included reining/ jurinac/ weber

3 july 1949/amsterdam stadsschouwburg
guest performance by vienna staatsoper
mozart don giovanni/elvira
conductor josef krips
other principals included welitsch/ seefried/ dermota/ kunz/ schöffler

30 july-29 october 1949/australia
the tour comprised both lieder recitals accompanied by margaret schofield and orchestral concerts (some conducted by otto klemperer with works by bach, handel and mahler) in adelaide, brisbane, canberra, hobart, melbourne, newcastle, perth, sydney, towoomba and wollongong

13 november 1949/london bbc studios
liederabend hugo wolf

15 november 1949/london royal opera house
strauss der rosenkavalier/sophie
further performance on 10 december 1949

17 november 1949/london royal opera house
puccini la boheme/mimi
further performance on 14 december 1949

20 november 1949/ashington methodist central hall
liederabend
pianist gladys prendlock

21 november 1949/london royal opera house
mozart le nozze di figaro/susanna

24 november 1949/london royal opera house
mozart die zauberflöte/pamina
further performances on 5 january 1950 and 10 february 1950

25 november 1949/london royal albert hall
philharmonia orchestra concert
beethoven symphony no 9 "choral"/soprano soloist
conductor herbert von karajan
other soloists included watson/ w.ludwig/ christoff

29 november 1949/amsterdam concertgebouw
liederabend
pianist jean antonietti
bach bist du bei mir/ o jesulein süss/ mein gläubiges herze
mozart als luise die briefe/ alleluia
schubert gretchen am spinnrade/ das lied im grünen/ der jüngling
an der quelle/ vedi quanto adoro
wolf schlafendes jesuskind/ mühvoll komm ich und beladen/
in der frühe/ was soll der zorn/ nachtzauber/ storchenbotschaft
strauss die nacht/ morgen/ ständchen/ hat gesagt bleibt's nicht dabei

2 december 1949/belfast
liederabend
gerald moore

6 december 1949/london royal albert hall
philharmonia orchestra concert
sauguet la voyante
conductor george weldon

11 december 1949/portsmouth guildhall
participation in orchestral concert
conductor herbert menges

18 december 1949/london wigmore hall
liederabend hugo wolf
pianist gerald moore

28 december 1949/basel stadttheater
verdi la traviata/violetta
conductor alexander krannhals
further performances on 29 december 1949 and 24 march 1950

3 january 1950/london royal opera house
beethoven fidelio/marzelline

10 january 1950/london royal opera house
mozart le nozze di figaro/susanna
further performances on 14 february 1950 and 29 may 1950

17 january 1950/london royal opera house
puccini madama butterfly/title role
conductor warwick braithwaite
other principals included neate/williams
further performances on 25, 28 and 30 january 1950 and 16 and 22 february 1950

19 january 1950/london royal opera house
verdi la traviata/violetta
conductor reginald goodall
other principals included schock/walters

1 february 1950/london royal opera house
puccini la boheme/mimi
further performance on 11 may 1950

19 february 1950/uppingham
liederabend

20 february 1950/london royal albert hall
philharmonia orchestra concert
mozart exsultate jubilate
conductor rafael kubelik

25 february 1950/cambridge
liederabend
pianist gerald moore

3 march 1950/florence
participation in orchestral concert
conductor paul kletzki

6 march 1950/rome
liederabend
pianist giorgio favaretto

22 march 1950/zürich tonhalle
liederabend
pianist volkmar andreae

26 march 1950/bern
liederabend
pianist volkmar andreae

30 march 1950/lucerne
bach matthäus-passion/soprano soloist
further performance on 2 april 1950

31 march 1950/basel stadttheater
liederabend
pianist volkmar andreae

3 april 1950/hilversum
radio filharmonisch orkest concert
mozart exsultate jubilate
strauss songs with orchestra
conductor paul van kempen

13 april 1950/vienna musikverein
liederabend hugo wolf
pianist hermann von nordberg

18 april 1950/edinburgh kings theatre
guest performance by royal opera house
mozart die zauberflöte/pamina

20 april 1950/edinburgh kings theatre
guest performance by royal opera house
verdi la traviata/violetta

24 april 1950/edinburgh kings theatre
guest performance by royal opera house
mozart le nozze di figaro/susanna

26 april 1950/london royal opera house
mozart die zauberflöte/pamina
further performance on 22 may 1950

30 april 1950/frankfurt-am-main
beethoven symphony no 9 "choral"/soprano soloist
concert repeated on 1 may 1950

9 may 1950/london royal opera house
strauss der rosenkavalier/sophie

18 may 1950/london royal opera house
massenet manon/title role
conductor warwick braithwaite
other principals included midgely/ g.evans/ walters
further performances on 24, 27 and 31 may 1950

19 may 1950/worthing pavilion theatre
liederabend
pianist gerald moore

20 may 1950/london wigmore hall
liederabend
pianist gerald moore

25 may 1950/london kingsway hall
participation in philharmonia concert society chamber concert
medtner songs

3 june 1950/florence
liederabend
pianist giorgio favaretto

9-10 june/basel stadttheater
haydn die schöpfung/soprano soloist

12 june 1950/vienna musikverein
vienna symphony orchestra concert for bach bi-centenary celebrations
bach cantata no 51 "jauchzet gott in allen landen"/soprano soloist
conductor paul hindemith

13 june 1950/klosterneuburg
beethoven mass in c/soprano soloist

15 june 1950/vienna musikverein
vienna symphony orchestra concert for bach bi-centenary celebrations
*bach mass in b minor/soprano soloist
conductor herbert von karajan
other soloists included ferrier/ w.ludwig/ schöffler/ poell

29-30 june 1950/milan teatro alla scala
vienna symphony orchestra and vienna singverein
beethoven missa solemnis/soprano soloist
conductor herbert von karajan
other soloists included höngen/ w.ludwig/ christoff

2-3 july 1950/milan teatro alla scala
vienna symphony orchestra and vienna singverein
bach mass in b minor/soprano soloist
conductor herbert von karajan
other soloists included ferrier/ w.ludwig/ christoff
performance repeated again on 5 july 1950

7 july 1950/bad salzschlirf
liederabend
pianist stieler

27 july 1950/salzburg festspielhaus
*mozart don giovanni/elvira
conductor wilhelm furtwängler
other soloists included welitsch/ seefried/ dermota/ kunz/ gobbi
further performances on 31 july 1950 and 4 and 18 august 1950

5 august 1950/salzburg festspielhaus
*beethoven fidelio/marzelline
conductor wilhelm furtwängler
other soloists included flagstad/ patzak/ dermota/ greindl/ schöffler/ braun
further performances on 11, 14, 17 and 22 august 1950

26-27 august 1950/lucerne kunsthaus
*berlioz la damnation de faust/marguérite
conductor wilhelm furtwängler
other soloists included vroons/ hotter/ pernerstorfer

31 august 1950/edinburgh usher hall
participation in concert by london harpsichord ensemble
arias by rameau and bach

4 september 1950/edinburgh freemasons hall
participation in concert of chamber music by bach
bach cantata no 211 "schweigt stille plaudert nicht"/soprano soloist

5 september 1950/edinburgh freemasons hall
liederabend hugo wolf
pianist gerald moore

50

12 september 1950/london royal albert hall
london philharmonic orchestra concert at henry wood proms
schubert-liszt der hirt auf dem felsen
conductor basil cameron

8 october 1950/brighton dome
liederabend
pianist gerald moore

20 october 1950/london royal opera house
verdi la traviata/violetta
further performance on 7 november 1950

26 october 1950/london royal opera house
puccini la boheme/mimi
further performances on 13 and 29 november 1950

28 october 1950/london royal opera house
massenet manon/title role
conductor warwick braithwaite
other principals included midgley/ g.evans/ walters
further performance on 15 november 1950

1 november 1950/london royal opera house
mozart die zauberflöte/pamina
further performances on 9 and 25 november 1950

4 november 1950/london royal opera house
strauss der rosenkavalier/sophie
conductor karl rankl
other principals included fisher/ shacklock/ glynne/ clifford
further performance on 23 november 1950

6 november 1950/london kingsway hall
participation in philharmonia concert society programme of chamber music by nicolas medtner
medtner songs on texts of goethe, pushkin, chamisso and eichendorff
pianist ernest lush

11 november 1950/london royal opera house
mozart le nozze di figaro/susanna
conductor karl rankl
other principals included fisher/ leigh/ g.evans/ walters
further performance on 27 november 1950

20 november 1950/london kingsway hall
participation in philharmonia orchestra concert of works by bach
bach cantata no 51 "jauchzet gott in allen landen"
conductor edwin fischer

21 november 1950/london royal opera house
beethoven fidelio/marzelline

30 november 1950/olten
participation in winterthur orchestra concert with works by bach and strauss

2-3 december 1950/basel stadttheater
mozart mass in c minor/soprano soloist
conductor hans münch
other soloists included patzak

6 december 1950/turin
liederabend
pianist giorgio favaretto

15 december 1950/rome rai auditorium
liederabend
pianist giorgio favaretto

27 december 1950/milan teatro alla scala
wagner tannhäuser/elisabeth
conductor herbert von karajan
other principals included cavelti/ beirer/ braun/ frick
further performances on 30 december 1950 and 6, 9 and 14 january 1951

15 january 1951/milan teatro alla scala
mozart don giovanni/elvira
conductor herbert von karajan
other principals included de los angeles/ noni/ prandelli/ petri/ taddei
further performances on 18, 21, 23 and 28 january 1951

3 february 1951/naples teatro san carlo
mozart le nozze di figaro/contessa
conductor karl böhm
other principals included loose/ zareska/ stabile/ badioli
further performance on 5 february 1951

7 february 1951/london royal opera house
mozart die zauberflöte/pamina
further performance on 19 february 1951

9 february 1951/london royal opera house
strauss der rosenkavalier/sophie
further performance on 22 february 1951

12 february 1951/london kingsway hall
liederabend
pianist gerald moore

14 february 1951/birmingham town hall
liederabend
pianist gerald moore

18 february 1951/southsea king's theatre
participation in orchestral concert
conductor herbert menges

25 february 1951/cambridge guildhall
liederabend
pianist gerald moore

26 february 1951/london kingsway hall
liederabend brahms
pianist joerg demus

13 march 1951/vienna musikverein
operatic concert with vienna symphony orchestra
conductor maximilian kojetinsky
recital repeated on 15 march 1951

17 march 1951/vienna musikverein
participation in vienna philharmonic concert
conductor max schönherr

18 march 1951/graz
liederabend

21-22 march 1951/vienna musikverein
vienna symphony orchestra and vienna singverein
bach mass in b minor/soprano soloist
conductor herbert von karajan
other soloists included höngen/dermota/petri

4 april 1951/london royal opera house
verdi la traviata/violetta
further performance on 19 april 1951

9 april 1951/london royal albert hall
philharmonia orchestra concert
strauss closing scenes from daphne and capriccio *first british performances*
mahler symphony no 4/soprano soloist
conductor paul kletzki

11 april 1951/bbc studios
recordings for bbc of works by mozart

14 april 1951/amsterdam concertgebouw
liederabend
pianist jean antonietti
> *purcell the blessed virgin's expostulation/ gluck einem bach der fliesset*
> *mozart sehnsucht nach dem frühlinge/ schubert der musensohn/ suleika 1/ ave maria*
> *schumann aufträge/ mondnacht/ der nussbaum*
> *wolf lebewohl/ an den schlaf/ die spröde/ die bekehrte/ wiegenlied im sommer/*
> *mausfallensprüchlein/ strauss freundliche vision/ schlechtes wetter/ morgen*

16 april 1951/hilversum
radio filharmonisch orkest concert
strauss 4 letzte lieder
conductor paul van kempen

18 april 1951/den haag diligentia
liederabend
pianist jean antonietti

19 april 1951/hilversum
radio filharmonisch orkest concert
mozart exsultate jubilate
puccini arias from la boheme and madama butterfly
conductor paul van kempen

27-28 april 1951/basel stadttheater
berlioz la damnation de faust/soprano soloist

2 may 1951/stuttgart
duet recital with walter ludwig
pianist hubert giesen

4 may 1951/london royal festival hall
bbc symphony orchestra concert for inauguration of royal festival hall
beethoven symphony no 9 "choral"
conductor sir malcolm sargent
other soloists included ripley/ herbert/ walker
performance repeated on 8 may 1951

9 may 1951/vienna musikverein
vienna symphony orchestra concert
strauss 4 letzte lieder
mahler symphony no 4
conductor paul kletzki

11 may 1951/london bbc studios
concert with the london baroque ensemble
mozart 4 notturni for 2 sopranos and baritone
conductor karl haas
other soloists included shacklock/ g.evans

12 may 1951/edinburgh freemasons' hall
liederabend
pianist gerald moore

15 may 1951/london royal opera house
puccini la boheme/mimi
conductor peter gellhorn
other principals included bowman/ midgely/ walters/ nowakovski/ g.evans

16 may 1951/london royal opera house
***beethoven fidelio**/marzelline
conductor karl rankl
other principals included flagstad/ patzak/ williams/ stephenson/ glynne
further performance on 21 may 1951

19 may 1951/worthing
liederabend

20 may 1951/oxford town hall
liederabend

26 may 1951/london royal festival hall
hallé orchestra concert
verdi messa da requiem/soprano soloist
conductor sir john barbirolli
other soloists included ripley/ lewis/ t.williams

31 may 1951/bern
la traviata/violetta
further performance on 1 june 1951

10 june 1951/london royal festival hall
london symphony orchestra concert
beethoven missa solemnis/soprano soloist
conductor sir malcolm sargent

13 june 1951/london royal festival hall
london philharmonic orchestra concert
beethoven symphony no 9 "choral"/soprano soloist
conductor victor de sabata

14 june 1951/york minster
london philharmonic orchestra concert
beethoven symphony no 9 "choral"/soprano soloist
conductor victor de sabata

16 june 1951/york minster
london philharmonic orchestra concert
verdi messa da requiem/soprano soloist
conductor victor de sabata

29 july 1951/bayreuth festspielhaus
concert to re-inaugurate bayreuth festival
*beethoven symphony no 9 "choral"/soprano soloist
conductor wilhelm furtwängler
other soloists included höngen/ hopf/ edelmann

31 july 1951/bayreuth festspielhaus
*wagner das rheingold/woglinde
conductor hans knappertsbusch
principals included h.ludwig/ windgassem/ fritz/ kuen/ s.björling/ faulhaber/ pflanzl

3 august 1951/bayreuth markgräfliches opernhaus
liederabend
pianist maximilian kojetinsky
recital repeated on 14 august 1951

4 august 1951/bayreuth festspielhaus
*wagner götterdämmerung/woglinde
conductor hans knappertsbusch
principals included varnay/ mödl/ höngen/ aldenhoff/ weber/ uhde/ pflanzl

5 august 1951/bayreuth festspielhaus
*wagner die meistersinger von nürnberg/eva
conductor herbert von karajan
other principals included malaniuk/ hopf/ stolze/ edelmann/ dalberg/ kunz
further performances on 8, 16, 19 and 21 august 1951

11 august 1951/bayreuth festspielhaus
*wagner das rheingold/woglinde
conductor herbert von karajan
principals included malaniuk/ windgassem/ fritz/ kuen/ s.björling/ faulhaber/ pflanzl

15 august 1951/bayreuth festspielhaus
*wagner götterdämmerung/woglinde
conductor herbert von karajan
principals included varnay/ mödl/ töpper/ aldenhoff/ weber/ uhde/ pflanzl

24 august 1951/bayreuth fesrspielhaus
die meistersinger von nürnberg/eva
conductor hans knappertsbusch
other principals included malaniuk/ hopf/ stolze/ edelmann/ dalberg/ kunz
further performance on 26 august 1951

1-2 september 1951/lucerne kunsrhaus
vienna symphony orchestra and vienna singverein
bach mass in b minor/soprano soloist
conductor herbert von karajan
other soloists included simionato/ cavelti/ haefliger/ braun

8 september 1951/venice teatro la fenice
guest performance by teatro alla scala milano
verdi messa da requiem/soprano soloist
conductor victor de sabata
other soloists included stignani/ tagliavini/ siepi

11 september 1951/venice teatro la fenice
*stravinsky the rake's progress/anne truelove *world premiere performance*
conductor igor stravinsky
other principals included tourel/ rounseville/ o.kraus/ arié
further performances on 13 and 14 september 1951

19 september 1951/oslo
liederabend
pianist robert levin
recital repeated on 27 september 1951

22 september 1951/copenhagen royal theatre
mozart le nozze di figaro/contessa

25 september 1951/stockholm
mozart le nozze di figaro/contessa

28 september 1951/copenhagen
liederabend
pianist robert levin

4-5 october 1951/munich aula der universität
concert with bavarian radio symphony orchestra
*bach cantata no 51 "jauchzet gott in allen landen"
conductor eugen jochum

8 october 1951/bonn
concert with works by mozart and strauss
conductor volkmann

18 october-13 november 1951/south africa
the tour comprised both lieder recitals and concerts in johannesburg, durban, pretoria, cape town, stallenbusch, paarl, port elizabeth and worcester

17-19 november 1951/vienna musikverein
vienna symphony orchestra and vienna singverein
brahms ein deutsches requiem/soprano soloist
conductor herbert von karajan
other soloist was s.björling

20 november 1951/vienna musikverein
liederabend
pianist maximilian kojetinsky

8 december 1951/milan teatro alla scala
stravinsky the rake's progress/anne truelove
conductor ferdinand leitner
other principals included elmo/picchi/o.kraus/modesti
further performances on 10, 22 and 30 december 1951

12 december 1951/den haag
liederabend
recital repeated on 16 december 1951

14 december 1951/arnhem
liederabend

12 january 1952/florence teatro della pergola
liederabend
pianist giorgio favaretto

26 january 1952/milan teatro alla scala
*strauss der rosenkavalier/marschallin
conductor herbert von karajan
other principals included jurinac/ della casa/ edelmann/ kunz
further performances on 31 january 1952 and 3, 6, 13 and 17 february 1952

9 february 1952/parma
liederabend
pianist giorigio favaretto

11 february 1952/bolzano conservatorio
liederabend
pianist giorgio favaretto
recital repeated on 20 february 1952

16 february 1952/rome rai auditorium
*liederabend franz schubert
pianist giorgio favaretto

18 february 1952/trieste
liederabend

23 february 1952/monte-carlo
puccini la boheme/mimi
conductor argeo quadri
further performance on 24 february 1952

29 february 1952/rome
liederabend

2 march 1952/florence teatro communale
concert by maggio musicale orchestra
beethoven symphony no 9 "choral"/soprano soloist
conductor hans knappertsbusch

3 march 1952/milan conservatorio
liederabend

5 march 1952/geneva victoria hall
concert with suisse romande orchestra in arias by bach and stravinsky
conductor ernest ansermet

9 march 1952/cambridge guildhall
liederabend
pianist gerald moore

11 march 1952/liverpool philharmonic hall
concert with liverpool philharmonic orchestra
conductor hugo rignold

12 march 1952/bolton town hall
liederabend
pianist gerald moore

14 march 1952/london royal festival hall
philharmonia orchestra concert with works by bach
conductor walter goehr

17 march 1952/chelsea town hall
liederabend
pianist gerald moore

18 march 1952/woking christchurch hall
liederabend
pianist gerald moore

19 march 1952/southall kings hall
liederabend
pianist gerald moore

21 march 1952/london royal festival hall
philharmonia orchestra concert
mozart exsultate jubilate
stravinsky 2 arias from the rake's progress
conductor harry blech

23 march 1952/brighton dome
liederabend
pianist gerald moore

29-30 march 1952/basel münster
bach johannes-passion/soprano soloist
conductor hans münch
other soloists included pitzinger/ w.ludwig/ rehfuss

2 april 1952/basel
liederabend
pianist willi haeusslin

4 april 1952/zürich tonhalle
liederabend
pianist willi haeusslin

15 april 1952/stockholm
puccini la boheme/mimi
conductor nils grevillius
further performance on 17 april 1952

21 april 1952/stockholm
liederabend
pianist kjall olsson
recital repeated on 25 april 1952

22 april 1952/copenhagen
liederabend
pianist kjall olsson
recital repeated on 24 april 1952

29 april 1952/oslo
liederabend
pianist kjall olsson

2 may 1952/hastings pavilion
participation in orchestral concert
conductor peter gellhorn

8 may 1952/london kingsway hall
liederabend
pianist gerald moore
> *schubert an die musik/ im abendrot/ an die laute/ der musensohn*
> *rossini 8 serate musicali*
> *wolf schlafendes jesuskind/ lebewohl/ nixe binsenfuss/ nimmersatte liebe/*
> *elfenlied/ wer rief dich denn?/ wir haben beide lange zeit geschwiegen/*
> *nein junger herr/ die zigeunerin*
> *strauss die nacht/ schlechtes wetter/ hat gesagt bleibts nicht dabei*

12 may 1952/edinburgh freemasons' hall
liederabend
pianist gerald moore

30 may 1952/turin rai auditorium
*mozart betulia liberata/amital
conductor mario rossi
other principals included pirazzini/ valletti/ christoff

5 june 1952/amsterdam concertgebouw
concertgebouw orchestra concert
*mahler symphony no 4/soprano soloist
conductor bruno walter
concert repeated on 8 june 1952

6 june 1952/scheveningen kurzaal
concertgebouw orchestra concert
mahler symphony no 4/soprano soloist
conductor bruno walter

9 june 1952/hilversum
*liederabend
pianist jean anronietti
    haydn she never told her love/ schubert an die musik/ auf dem wasser zu singen/
    der vollmond strahlt/ schumann marienwürmchen

10 june 1952/scheveningen kurzaal
liederabend
pianist jean antonietti
    schubert an die musik/ der musensohn/ auf dem wasser zu singen/
    der vollmond strahlt/ ungeduld
    bach bist du bei mir/ patron das macht der wind/ gluck einem bach der fliesset
    mozart abendempfindung/ der zauberer/ beethoven wonne der wehmut
    schumann aufträge/ der nussbaum/ marienwürmchen
    brahms der tod das ist die kühle nacht/ da unten im tale/ wie komm ich denn
    zur tür herein?/ wolf lebewohl/ in dem schatten meiner locken/ o wär dein haus
    durchsichtig/ wer rief dich denn?/ nein junger herr/ die zigeunerin
    strauss die nacht/ hat gesagt bleibt's nicht dabei/ schlechtes wetter

11 june 1952/scheveningen kurzaal
stravinsky programme with residentie orchestra
stravinsky 2 arias from the rake's progress
conductor igor markevitch

20 june 1952/london royal opera house
puccini la boheme/mimi
conductor franco capuana
other principals included sladen/ johnston/ walters/ glynne
further performances on 23 and 25 june 1952

29 june 1952/london royal festival hall
london philharmonic orchestra concert
verdi messa da requiem/soprano soloist
conductor victor de sabata

3 july 1952/london royal festival hall
concert by london mozart players
mozart die schuldigkeit des ersten gebotes/soprano soloist
conductor harry blech
other soloists included vyvyan/ leigh/ r.nilsson/ worthley
concert repeated on 4 july 1952 in bbc studios

26 july 1952/salzburg festspielhaus
mozart le nozze di figaro/contessa
conductor rudolf moralt
other principals included seefried/ güden/ kunz/ london
further performances on 2, 8, 23 and 29 august 1952

20-21 august 1952/salzburg festspielhaus
vienna philharmonic orchestra concert
verdi messa da requiem/soprano soloist
conductor victor de sabata
other soloists included barbieri/ dermota/ greindl

30-31 august 1952/lucerne kunsthaus
handel messiah/soprano soloist
conductor roberto denzler
other soloists included haefliger/ schey

13 october-5 november 1952/south america
tour included lieder recitals in recife, brasilia, sao paulo, puerto rico and mexico city

1 december 1952/turin rai auditorium
martini-rossi concert of operatic arias
*mozart arias from die zauberflöte, idomeneo and don giovanni
conductor mario rossi
other soloists included jurinac/ petri

4 december 1952/vienna musikverein
liederabend
pianist viktor graef

6 december 1952/hamburg ndr studios
*arias by handel, korngold, mozart, puccini and strauss
conductor wilhelm schüchter

19 december 1952/turin rai auditoriun
beethoven symphony no 9 "choral"/soprano soloist
conductor wilhelm furtwängler
other soloists included klose/ dermota/ edelmann

22 december 1952/amsterdam
concertgebouw
liederabend
pianist jean antonietti

23 december 1952/den haag
liederabend
pianist jean antonietti

10 january 1953/milan teatro alla scala
wagner lohengrin/elsa
conductor herbert von karajan
other principals included mödl/ windgassen/ metternich/ edelmann/ neidlinger
further performances on 13, 17, 20 and 25 january 1953 and 1 february 1953

28 january 1953/milan teatro alla scala
mozart don giovanni/elvira
conductor herbert von karajan
other principals included martinis/ noni/ simoneau/ petri/ panerai/ bruscantini
further performances on 31 january 1953 and 5, 8 and 11 february 1953

14 february 1953/milan teatro alla scala
orff trionfi/soprano soloist
comprising staged versions of carmina burana, catulli carmina and trionfo d'afrodite
conductor herbert von karajan
other principals included pirino/ gedda/ ego/ panerai
further performances on 16, 18 and 24 february 1953

17 february 1953/turin
liederabend
pianist giorgio favaretto

20 february 1953/turin rai studios
tippett a child of our time
conductor herbert von karajan
other soloists were cavelti/ gedda/ petri

27 february 1953/rome teatro argentina
liederabend
pianist giorgio favaretto

5-6 march 1953/munich herkulessaal
bavarian radio orchestra concert
orff trionfi/soprano soloist
conductor eugen jochum
other principals included holm/ gedda/ kuen/ braun

10 march 1953/london royal festival hall
duet recital with dietrich fischer-dieskau
wolf italienisches liederbuch
pianist hermann reutter

17 march 1953/bbc studios
liederabend
pianist ernest lush

31 march 1953/paris salle gaveau
liederabend
pianist jaqueline bonneau

2-3 april 1953/zürich tonhalle
beethoven missa solemnis/soprano soloist
conductor erich schmid

5 april 1953/glyndebourne opera house
royal philharmonic orchestra concert
mozart exsultate jubilate
bach cantata no 145
conductor john pritchard
other soloists included pears/hemsley

12 april 1953/london royal festival hall
liederabend
pianist ernest lush
> *bach bist du bei mir*
> *gluck einem bach der fliesset*
> *beethoven wonne der wehmut*
> *mozart abendempfindung/ der zauberer*
> *schubert nähe des geliebten/ die junge nonne/ an sylvia/ ganymed/*
> *liebe schwärmt auf allen wegen/ ungeduld*
> *martini plaisir d'amour*
> *bizet pastorella*
> *dvorak songs my mother taught me*
> *brahms da unten im tale/ och moder ich will en ding han*
> *wolf morgenstimmung/ als ich auf dem euphrat schiffte/ elfenlied/ in dem*
> *schatten meiner locken/ bedeckt mich mit blumen/ kennst du das land?/*
> *nachtzauber/ die zigeunerin*

22 april 1953/den haag diligentia
liederabend
pianist jean antonietti
> *bach mein gläubiges herze/ bist du bei mir/ mozart alleluja*
> *schubert nähe des geliebten/ am see/ die junge nonne/ an sylvia/*
> *liebe schwärmt auf allen wegen/ gretchen am spinnrade*
> *brahms da unten im tale/ wiegenlied/ sandmännchen/ och moder ich will en ding han/*
> *wolf morgenstimmung/ wandl' ich in dem morgentau/ wie glänzt der helle mond/*
> *nachtzauber/ auf ein altes bild/ nixe binsenfuss/ storchenbotschaft*

24 april 1953/hilversum
***wolf italienisches liederbuch**
pianist felix de nobel

24 april 1953/hilversum
concert with omroeporkest
***strauss 4 letzte lieder**
conductor othmar nussio

26 april 1953/cambridge guildhall
liederabend
pianist ernest lush

27 april 1953/paris théatre des champs-élysées
concert with orchestre national
***schmitt psaume 67**/soprano soloist
conductor igor markevitch

30 april 1953/paris théatre des champs-élysées
concert with orchestre national
***verdi messa da requiem**/soprano soloist
conductor igor markevitch
other soloists included barbieri/ berdini/ rohr

17 may 1953/milan teatro alla scala
debussy pelleas et mélisande/mélisande
conductor victor de sabata
other principals included gayaud/ jansen/ roux/ clavensy
further performances on 19, 29 and 31 may 1953

22 may 1953/basel
beck der tod zu basel
conductor paul sacher

28 may 1953/zürich tonhalle
liederabend
pianist willi haeusslin

3 june 1953/london bbc television studios
participation in a tv concert celebrating coronation of queen elizabeth II
conductor eric robertson
other soloists included markova/ cohen/ noble

5-7 june 1953/vienna musikverein
vienna symphony orchestra concert performances
*beethoven fidelio/marzelline
conductor herbert von karajan
other principals included mödl/ windgassen/ schock/ edelmann/ braun/ metternich

8 june 1953/vienna musikverein
liederabend
pianist viktor graef

10 june 1953/riehen landgasthof
concert of bach cantatas
conductor hans münch

12 june 1953/oslo
liederabend
pianist robert levin

13 june 1953/sparsborg
liederabend
pianist robert levin

16 june 1953/copenhagen tivoli hall
concert of lieder and arias
concert repeated on 18 june 1953

17 june 1953/gothenburg
liederabend
pianist robert levin

20 june 1953/london
liederabend
pianist ernest lush

3 july 1953/london royal opera house
performances for the coronation season
wagner die meistersinger von nürnberg/eva
conductor clemens krauss
other principals included hopf/ dickie/ schöffler/ kusche
further performances on 6, 8 and 10 july 1953

13 july 1953/den haag diligentia
liederabend hugo wolf
pianist jean antonietti
> *mörike-lieder: im frühling/ in der frühe/ nixe binsenfuss/ lebewohl/ storchenbotschaft*
> *spanisches liederbuch: ach des knaben augen/ herr was trägt der boden hier/ wenn du*
> *zu den blumen gehst/ in dem schatten meiner locken/ mögen alle bösen zungen*
> *goethe-lieder: die spröde/ die bekehrte/ kennst du das land?/ blumengruss/*
> *gleich und gleich/ phänomen/ frühling übers jahr*
> *italienisches liederbuch: was soll der zorn/ nun lass uns frieden schliessen/ du denkst*
> *mit einem fädchen/ o wär dein haus durchsichtig/ wer rief dich denn?/ wir haben*
> *beide lange zeit geschwiegen/ nein junger herr*

14 july 1953/amsterdam concertgebouw
liederabend hugo wolf
pianist jean antonietti
> *programme as for 13 july 1953*

27 july 1953/salzburg felsenreitschule
*mozart don giovanni/elvira
conductor wilhelm furtwängler
other principals included grümmer/ berger/ dermota/ siepi/ edelmann/ berry
further performances on 3, 8, 18 and 28 august 1953

7 august 1953/salzburg festspielhaus
*mozart le nozze di figaro/contessa
conductor wilhelm furtwängler
other principals included seefried/ güden/ kunz/ schöffler
further performances on 11, 14 and 29 august 1953

12 august 1953/salzburg mozarteum
*liederabend hugo wolf
pianist wilhelm furtwängler
> *mörike-lieder: im frühling/ elfenlied/ lebewohl/ schlafendes jesuskind*
> *goethe-lieder: phänomen/ die spröde/ die bekehrte/ anakreons grab/*
> *blumengruss/ epiphanias*
> *italienisches liederbuch: wie lange schon/ was soll der zorn/ nein junger herr/*
> *mein liebster hat zu tische mich geladen*
> *spanisches liederbuch: bedeckt mich mit blumen/ herr was trägt der boden hier/*
> *in dem schatten meiner locken/ mögen alle bösen zungen*
> *wie glänzt der helle mond*
> *wiegenlied im sommer*
> *eichendorff-lieder: nachtzauber/ die zigeunerin*

19 august 1953/munich bayerische staatsoper
guest performance by teatro alla scala
mozart don giovanni/elvira
conductor herbert von karajan
other principals included martinia/ noni/ simoneau/ petri/ bruscantini/ panerai
further performance on 21 august 1953

22 august 1953/munich
liederabend hugo wolf

30 august 1953/lucerne kunsthaus
verdi messa da requiem/soprano soloist
conductor antonino votto
other soloists included dominguez/ di stefano/ siepi

6 september 1953/bournemouth winter gardens
bournemouth symphony orchestra concert
bach cantata no 51 "jauchzet gott in allen landen"
strauss 4 letzte lieder
conductor charles groves

9 september 1953/london royal albert hall
london philharmonic orchestra concert at henry wood proms
mozart exsultate jubilate/soprano soloist
conductor sir adrian boult

12 september 1953/london bbc studios
liederabend
programme included rossini serate musicali

22 september 1953/ascona
liederabend
pianist giorgio favaretto

27 september 1953/dorchester plaza cinema
liederabend
pianist gerald moore

29 september 1953/canterbury cathedral
liederabend
pianist gerald moore

3 october 1953/belfast queen's university
liederabend
pianist gerald moore

6 october 1953/carlisle central hall
liederabend
pianist gerald moore

8 october 1953/leeds town hall
delius a mass of life/soprano soloist
conductor sir malcolm sargent

11 october 1953/skipton town hall
liederabend
pianist gerald moore

13 october 1953/bridge of allan museum hall
liederabend
pianist gerald moore

16 october 1953/edinburgh usher hall
scottish national orchestra concert
conductor karl rankl

17 october 1953/glasgow saint andrew's hall
scottish national orchestra concert
conductor karl rankl

25 october 1953/new york town hall
liederabend *north american début*
pianist arpad sandor

28 october 1953/basel
vienna symphony orchestra and vienna singverein
beethoven fidelio/leonore *concert performance*
conductor herbert von karajan
other principals included felbernayer/ fehenberger/ majkut/ schlott/ metternich/ uhde

29 october 1953/geneva victoria hall
programme as for 28 october 1953

30 october 1953/zürich tonhalle
programme as for 28 october 1953

3 november 1953/munich herkulessaal
liederabend
pianist hermann reutter

6-8 november 1953/vienna musikverein
vienna symphony orchestra and vienna singverein
bach matthäus-passion/soprano soloist
conductor herbert von karajan
other soloists included höffgen/ haefliger/ edelmann/ rehfuss

9 november 1953/vienna musikverein
liederabend
pianist viktor graef

12 november 1953/düsseldorf robert-schumann-saal
liederabend
pianist eugen szenkar
recital repeated on 13 november 1953

15 november 1953/berlin titania palast
liederabend
pianist michael raucheisen

18 november 1953/copenhagen tivoli hall
liederabend
pianist kjall olsson
recital repeated on 25 november 1953

20 november 1953/stockholm
liederabend
pianist robert levin
recital repeated on 28 november 1953

21 november 1953/oslo
participation in orchestral concert
concert repeated on 26 november 1953

23 november 1953/sparsborg
liederabend
pianist kjall olsson

2 december 1953/paris théatre des champs-élysées
liederabend
pianist jaqueline bonneau

12 december 1953/rome teatro dell' opera
mozart don giovanni/elvira
conductor herbert von karajan
other principals included martinis/ noni/ gedda/ petri/ bruscantini
further performances on 15, 20 and 22 december 1953

19 december 1953/rome rai auditorium
***mozart die zauberflöte**/pamina *concert performance*
conductor herbert von karajan
other principals included streich/ noni/ gedda/ taddei/ petri

21 december 1953/rome rai auditorium
***bach magnificat**/soprano soloist
sutermeister messa da requiem/soprano soloist
conductor herbert von karajan
other soloists included orell/ dominguez/ gedda/ petri/ tadeo

14 january 1954/langenthal hotel bär
liederabend
pianist madeleine lipatti

15 january 1954/basel casino
liederabend
pianist madeleine lipatti

20 january 1954/milan teatro lirico
liederabend
pianist giorgio favaretto

26 january 1954/rome santa cecilia
liederabend
pianist giorgio favaretto

4 february 1954/milan teatro alla scala
***mozart le nozze di figaro**/contessa
conductor herbert von karajan
other principals included seefried/ jurinac/ panerai/ petri
further performances on 6, 9, 14 and 20 february 1954

6 february 1954/milan rai auditorium
***humperdinck hänsel und gretel**/gretel *concert performance*
conductor herbert von karajan
other principals included jurinac/ streich/ panerai/ palombini

12 february 1954/milan teatro alla scala
gounod faust/marguérite
conductor artur rodzinski
other principals included poggi/ christoff/ mascherini
further performances on 16, 18, 24 and 28 february 1954

21 february 1954/rome rai auditorium
***liederabend johannes brahms**
pianist edwin fischer

22 february 1954/rome teatro manzoni
liederabend
pianist giorgio favaretto
recital repeated on 26 february 1954

3 march 1954/palermo teatro massimo
liederabend
pianist giorgio favaretto

7 march 1954/london royal festival hall
joint recital with dietrich fischer-dieskau
schumann frauenliebe und –leben
pianist gerald moore
fischer-dieskau performed schumann dichterliebe

9 march 1954/anvers
liederabend
pianist felix de nobel

10 march 1954/brussels
liederabend
pianist felix de nobel

19 march 1954/toulouse
participation in concert with works by mozart
conductor pedro de freitas-branco

25 march 1954/monte-carlo opéra
liederabend
pianist marcelle gastaldo

28 march 1954/monte-carlo opéra
strauss der rosenkavalier/marschallin
conductor rudolf moralt
other principals included della casa/ stich-randall/ böhme/ kunz
further performance on 30 march 1954

9 april 1954/basel
strauss 4 letzte lieder

25 april 1954/cambridge guildhall
liederabend
pianist gerald moore

30 april 1954/london royal festival hall
liederabend
pianist edwin fischer
> *beethoven wonne der wehmut/ der wachtelschlag/ adelaide/ mit einem gemalten band*
> *schubert an die musik/ nähe des geliebten/ im frühling/ an sylvia/ nachtviolen/*
> *gretchen am spinnrade*
> *brahms von ewiger liebe/ wie melodien zieht es mir/ liebestreu/ am sonntagmorgen/*
> *immer leiser wird mein schlummer/ der jäger/ in stiller nacht/ therese/ des liebsten*
> *schwur/ meine liebe ist grün*

8 may 1954/lisbon
liederabend
pianist alfredo rossi

15 may 1954/braga teatro circo
liederabend
pianist alfredo rossi

26 may 1954/london royal festival hall
dvorak commemoration concert by bbc symphony orchestra
*dvorak where art thou, father?/the spectre's bride
*dvorak te deum
conductor sir malcolm sargent
other soloist was boyce

5 june 1954/bergen
liederabend
pianist robert levin

7 june 1954/bergen
concert with oslo philharmonic orchestra
conductor odd grüner-hegge

23 july 1954/aix-en-provence
*liederabend
pianist hans rosbaud
> *bach bist du bei mir/ gluck einem bach der fliesset*
> *beethoven wonne der wehmut/ mozart abendempfindung/ warnung*
> *pergolesi se tu m'ami/ handel caro selve/ martini plaisir d'amour*
> *schubert an sylvia/ die liebe hat gelogen/ der einsame/ die vögel/ ungeduld*
> *schumann der nussbaum/ aufträge/ brahms da unten im tale/ von ewiger liebe*
> *wolf kennst du das land?/ wir habe beide lange zeit geschwiegen/*
> *in dem schatten meiner locken/ sohn der jungfrau/ liebesqual/ nein junger herr/*
> *nachtzauber/ die zigeunerin*

3 august 1954/salzburg felsenreitschule
*mozart don giovanni/elvira
conductor wilhelm furtwängler
other principals included grümmer/ berger/ dermota/ siepi/ edelmann/ ernster/ berry
further performances on 6, 10, 13 and 18 august 1954

14 august 1954/salzburg mozarteum
liederabend hugo wolf
pianist gerald moore

21-22 august 1954/lucerne kunsthaus
philharmonia orchestra concert
*beethoven symphony no 9 "choral"/soprano soloist
conductor wilhelm furtwängler
other soloists included cavelti/ haefliger/ edelmann

26 august 1954/oostende kurzaal
liederabend
pianist felix de nobel

31 august 1954/edinburgh freemasons hall
liederabend
pianist gerald moore

2 september 1954/edinburgh freemasons hall
duet recital with hans hotter
pianist gerald moore

4 september 1954/edinburgh usher hall
hallé orchestra concert in memory of kathleen ferrier
verdi messa da requiem/soprano soloist
conductor sir john barbirolli
other soloists were shacklock/lewis/hotter

5 september 1954/london bbc studios
liederabend
pianist gerald moore

14 september 1954/manchester
liederabend
pianist gerald moore

2 october 1954/amsterdam
concert with utrecht stedelijk orkest
haydn die schöpfung/soprano soloist
conductor willem wiesehahn
other soloists included patzak/schey

16 october 1954/lebanon pennsylvania melton auditorium
liederabend
pianist arpad sandor

19 october 1954/oberlin music conservatory
liederabend
pianist arpad sandor

20 october 1954/wesleyville ohio university
liederabend
pianist arpad sandor

22 october 1954/atlanta music club
liederabend
pianist arpad sandor

24 october 1954/boston
liederabend
pianist arpad sandor

25 october 1954/baltimore lyric theatre
liederabend
pianist arpad sandor

28-29 october 1954/chicago orchestra hall
chicago symphony orchestra concert
strauss closing scene from capriccio and 4 letzte lieder
conductor fritz reiner

1 november 1954/milwaukee
liederabend
pianist arpad sandor

2 november 1954/saint paul
liederabend
pianist arpad sandor

4 november 1954/toronto
liederabend
pianist arpad sandor

6 november 1954/new york hunter college
liederabend
pianist arpad sandor

8 november 1954/seattle
liederabend
pianist arpad sandor

10 november 1954/los angeles
liederabend
pianist arpad sandor

12 november 1954/santa barbara
liederabend
pianist arpad sandor

13 november 1954/beverly hills
liederabend
pianist arpad sandor

16 november 1954/houston
mozart concert with houston symphony orchestra
conductor ferenc fricsay

18 november 1954/dallas
liederabend
pianist arpad sandor

21 november 1954/chicago
liederabend
pianist arpad sandor

23 november 1954/saint louis
liederabend
pianist arpad sandor

25 november 1954/montreal
liederabend
pianist arpad sandor

28 november 1954/new york
liederabend hugo wolf
pianist arpad sandor

29 november 1954/brunswick
liederabend
pianist arpad sandor

30 november 1954/holyoke
liederabend
pianist arpad sandor

2-3 december 1954/havana
liederabend
pianist arpad sandor

5 december 1954/san juan
liederabend
pianist arpad sandor

8 december 1954/danbury
liederabend
pianist arpad sandor

19 december 1954/rome rai auditorium
*debussy pelléas et mélisande/mélisande *concert performance*
conductor herbert von karajan
other principals included haefliger/roux/petri

4 january 1955/amsterdam concertgebouw
liederabend
pianist felix de nobel
>*schubert an die musik/ im frühling/ auf dem wasser zu singen/ der vollmond strahlt/*
>*der einsame/ liebe schwärmt auf allen wegen/ ungeduld*
>*schumann mein schöner stern/ marienwürmchen*
>*brahms immer leiser wird mein schlummer/ von ewiger liebe*
>*wolf der genesene an die hoffnung/ nachtzauber/ philine/ zum neuen jahr/ bedeckt mich*
>*mit blumen/ elfenlied/ mögen alle bösen zungen*
>*strauss wiegenliued/ die nacht/ schlechtes wetter/ hat's gesagt bleibts nicht dabei*

5 january 1955/den haag diligentia
liederabend
pianist felix de nobel
>*programme as for 4 january 1955*

8 january 1955/brussels
liederabend
pianist madeleine lipatti

10 january 1955/anvers
liederabend
pianist madeleine lipatti

18 january 1955/paris palais de chaillot
concert with works by mozart and strauss
conductor georges sébastian

20 january 1955/bordeaux
liederabend
pianist madeleine lipatti

23 january 1955/albi
liederabend
pianist madeleine lipatti

25 january 1955/avignon
liederabend
pianist madeleine lipatti

26 january 1955/marseille
concert with works by mozart and strauss
conductor audoli

28 january 1955/ales
liederabend
pianist madeleine lipatti

30 january 1955/lyon
concert with works by bach and mozart
conductor jean martinon

2 february 1955/zürich tonhalle
liederabend
pianist madeleine lipatti

4 february 1955/aarau
liederabend
pianist madeleine lipatti

12-13 february 1955/milan rai auditorium
wagner die meistersinger von nürnberg/eva *concert performance*
conductor hans rosbaud
other principals malaniuk/ hopf/ unger/ edelmann/ weber/ kunz
acts 1 and 2 performed on 12 february, act 3 on 13 february

17 february 1955/bologna
liederabend
pianist giorgio favaretto
recital repeated on 27 february 1955

5 march 1955/monte-carlo salle gaveau
liederabend
pianist otto ackermann

6 march 1955/monte-carlo opéra
mozart le nozze di figaro/contessa
conductor otto ackermann
further performance on 8 march 1955

10 march 1955/geneva victoria hall
liederabend
pianist madeleine lipatti

13 march 1955/london royal festival hall
liederabend
pianist gerald moore

15 march 1955/bradford
liederabend
pianist ernest lush

16-17 march 1955/manchester free trade hall
hallé orchestra concert
strauss 4 letzte lieder
conductor sir john barbirolli

21 march 1955/edinburgh freemasons' hall
liederabend
pianist gerald moore

28 march 1955/london middle temple hall
liederabend
pianist ernest lush

2-3 april 1955/paris théatre du chatelet
colonne orchestra concert with works by bach and mozart
conductor eugene bigot

7 may 1955/rome conservatorio
liederabend
pianist giorgio favaretto

11 may 1955/birmingham town hall
liederabend hugo wolf

15 may 1955/london royal festival hall
duet recital with irmgard seefried
pianist gerald moore
> *monteverdi ardo e scoprir/ io son pur vezzosetta pastorella/ tornate o cari baci/ bel pastoe carissimi e pur vuole il cielo e amore/ lungi omai/ il mio core/ a pie d'un verde dvorak 13 moravian duets*

21 may 1955/nantes
liederabend
pianist jaqueline bonneau

2 june 1955/oslo
concert with works by mozart and puccini
conductor dean dixon
other soloist was björling

4 june 1955/bergen
liederabend
pianist robert levin

6 june 1955/oslo
liederabend
pianist robert levin

8 june 1955/copenhagen
liederabend
pianist kjall olsson

9 june 1955/stockholm
liederabend
pianist robert levin

11 june 1955/helsinki/finnish radio
*songs by sibelius
pianist cyril szalkiewicz

14 june 1955/helsinki
*sibelius luonnotar
conductor tauno hannikainen

17 june 1955/lisbon
liederabend
pianist madeleine lipatti
recital repeated on 22 june 1955

19 june 1955/tangier
liederabend
pianist herbert von karajan

24 june 1955/granada
liederabend
pianist madeleine lipatti

27 june 1955/granada
beethoven symphony no 9 "choral"
conductor franco caracciolo

12 july 1955/amsterdam
liederabend
pianist felix de nobel

13 july 1955/scheveningen kurzaal
liederabend
pianist felix de nobel

29-30 july 1955/ravinia
chicago symphony orchestra concert
conductor enrique jorda

2 august 1955/stratford ontario
liederabend
pianist paul ulanowsky
recital repeated on 5 august 1955

3 august 1955/stratford ontario
hart house orchestra concert
*bach cantata no 202
*mozart exsultate jubilate
conductor boyd neel

9 august 1955/hollywood bowl
strauss 4 letzte lieder
conductor iszler solomon

13 august 1955/menton
liederabend
pianist jaqueline bonneau

14 august 1955/menton
concert with works by bach and mozart
conductor karl ristenpart

16 august 1955/lucerne kunsthaus
liederabend
pianist gerald moore

18 august 1955/oostende kurzaal
liederabend
felix de nobel

21 august 1955/deauville
concert with works by mozart

9 september 1955/besancon
liederabend
pianist jaqueline bonneau

20 september 1955/san francisco war memorial opera house
***strauss der rosenkavalier/**marschallin
conductor erich leinsdorf
other principals included bible/ warenskjold/ edelmann/ herbert
further performance on 24 september 1955

30 september 1955/san francisco war memorial opera house
mozart don giovanni/elvira
conductor erich leinsdorf
other principals included carteri/ albanese/ peerce/ siepi/ alvary
further performance on 6 october 1955

2 october 1955/beverly hills high school
liederabend
pianist paul ulanowsky

4 october 1955/carmel california sunset school auditorium
liederabend
pianist paul ulanowsky

9 october 1955/vancouver
participation in orchestral concert

13-14 ocrober 1955/chicago
*chicago symphony orchestra concert
with works by mozart and strauss*
conductor fritz reiner

16 october 1955/boston
liederabend

17 october 1955/charlotteville
liederabend

19 october 1955/middletown
liederabend

22 october 1955/new york
hunter college
liederabend

24 october 1955/milwaukee
liederabend

25 october 1955/salt lake city
liederabend

28 october 1955/los angeles
strauss der rosenkavalier/
marschallin

30 october 1955/san francisco
liederabend
recital repeated on 3 november 1955

31 october 1955/santa barbara
liederabend

1 november 1955/eugene
liederabend

5 november 1955/los angeles
mozart don giovanni/elvira

7-8 november 1955/seattle
strauss 4 letzte lieder
conductor milton katims

10 november 1955/denver
liederabend

13 november 1955/chicago
liederabend

15 november 1955/ithaca
*rochester philharmonic concert
with works by mozart and strauss*

17 november 1955/rochester
*rochester philharmonic concert
with works by mozart and strauss*

19 november 1955/brookville
liederabend

21 november 1955/springfield
liederabend

22 november 1955/englewood
liederabend

24 november 1955/toronto
liederabend

26 november 1955/new york
town hall
liederabend

29-30 november 1955/chicago
chicago symphony orchestra concert

1 december 1955/cleveland music hall
liederabend

10 december 1955/milan teatro alla scala
mozart die zauberflöte/pamina
conductor herbert von karajan
other principals included sciutti/ köth/ gedda/ zaccaria/ taddei
further performances on 13, 18, 20 and 22 december 1955

14 january 1953/rome
liederabend
pianist giorgio favaretto

15 january 1955/siena
liederabend
pianist giorgio favaretto

27 january 1956/milan piccolo scala
*mozart cosi fan tutte/fiordiligi
conductor guido cantelli
other principals included merriman/ sciutti/ alva/ panerai/ calabrese
further performances on 29 and 31 january 1956 and 3, 9, 19, 22 and 26 february 1956

8 february 1956/milan teatro alla scala
mozart don giovanni/elvira
conductor otto ackermann
other principals included stella/ carteri/ monti/ aiepi/ tajo/ stefanoni
further performances on 11, 13 and 15 february 1956

27 february 1956/milan piccolo scala
concert with works by mozart
other participants included tonini/ favaretto

29 february 1956/milan piccolo scala
liederabend
pianist giorgio favaretto

4 march 1956/london royal festival hall
liederabend
pianist gerald moore

84

9 march 1956/madrid
participation in orchestral concert
conductor nicolai malko

12 march 1956/madrid
liederabend
pianist madeleine lipatti

14 march 1956/san sebastian
liederabend
pianist madeleine lipatti

16 march 1956/bilbao
liederabend
pianist madeleine lipatti

18 march 1956/barcelona
liederabend
pianist madeleine lipatti

22 march 1956/monte-carlo
liederabend
pianist otto ackermann

25 march 1956/monte-carlo
mozart don giovanni/elvira
conductor otto ackermann
further principals included jurinac/ mazzoleni/ dermota/ roux/ capecchi/ bruscantini
further performance on 27 march 1956

25 may 1956/basel
beck der tod zu basel/soprano soloist
conductor paul sacher
performance repeated on 27 may 1956

29 may 1956/bern stadttheater
mozart idomeneo/ilia *concert performance*
conductor balmer
other principals included zadek/ haefliger/ kmentt

6 june 1956/paris théatre des champs-élysées
liederabend
pianist jaqueline bonneau

20 june 1956/london royal festival hall
philharmonia orchestra concert
*strauss 4 letzte lieder
conductor herbert von karajan

1 july 1956/london royal festival hall
philharmonia orchestra concert
verdi messa da requiem/soprano soloist
conductor guido cantelli
other soloists included stignani/ tagliavini/ modesti
concert repeated on 6 july 1956

21 july 1956/salzburg festspielhaus
mozart le nozze di figaro/contessa
conductor karl böhm
other principals included seefried/ ludwig/ fischer-dieskau/ kunz
further performances on 28 july 1956 and 3, 10, 21 and 30 august 1956

7 august 1956/salzburg mozarteum
*liederabend
pianist gerald moore
> *bach bist du bei mir/ pergolesi se tu m'ami/ handel caro selve/*
> *gluck einem bach der fliesset/ beethoven wonne der wehmut*
> *schubert an sylvia/ der vollmond strahlt/ die vögel/ der einsame/ vedi quanto adoro*
> *wolf kennst du das land?/ philine/ nachtzauber/ die zigeunerin*
> *strauss ruhe meine seele/ wiegenlied/ schlechtes wetter/ hat gesagt bleibt's nicht dabei*
> *mozart warnung/ schumann der nussbaum/ schubert ungeduld*

28 august 1956/lucerne kunsthaus
duet recital with dietrich fischer-dieskau
wolf italienisches liederbuch
pianist gerald moore

4 september 1956/lucerne kunsthaus
philharmonia orchestra concert
strauss 4 letzte lieder
conductor george szell

8 september 1956/stuttgart sdr studios
operatic concert with anton dermota
conductor wilhelm schüchter

21 september 1956/san francisco war memorial opera house
verdi falstaff/alice ford
conductor william steinberg
other principals included dominguez/ campora/ warren/ guarrera
further performance on 27 september 1956

2 october 1956/san francisco war memorial opera house
mozart cosi fan tutte/fiordiligi
conductor hans schwieger
other principals included rankin/ munsel/ lewis/ guarrera/ alvary
further performances on 6 and 14 october 1956

8 october 1956/salt lake city
liederabend
pianist george reeves

9 october 1956/denver
liederabend
pianist george reeves

11 october 1956/salem
liederabend
pianist george reeves

15 october 1956/tempe
liederabend
pianist george reeves

17 october 1956/claremont
liederabend
pianist george reeves

19 october 1956/burlingame
liederabend
pianist george reeves

21 october 1956/chicago
liederabend
pianist george reeves

23 october 1956/los angeles
verdi falstaff/alice ford

25 october 1956/san diego
mozart cosi fan tutte/
fiordiligi

27 october 1956/berkeley
liederabend
pianist george reeves
recital repeated on 30 october 1956

2 november 1956/los angeles
mozart cosi fan tutte/
fiordiligi

4 november 1956/san francisco
liederabend
pianist george reeves

11 november 1956/beverly hills
liederabend
pianist george reeves

13 november 1956/buffalo
liederabend
pianist george reeves

14 november 1956/ann arbor
liederabend
pianist george reeves

16 november 1956/ithaca
liederabend
pianist george reeves

18 november 1956/boston
liederabend
pianist george reeves

20 november 1956/toronto
concert with works by strauss
conductor walter susskind

25 november 1956/new york carnegie hall
***liederabend**
pianist george reeves
    mozart abendempfindung/ als luise die briefe/ dans un bois solitaire/ un moto di gioia/
    come scoglio
    schubert an sylvia/ der einsame/ der vollmond strahlt/ die vögel/ gretchen am spinnrade/
    seligkeit
    schumann der nussbaum/ gluck einem bach der fliesset
    strauss ruhe meine seele/ schlechtes wetter/ hat gesagt bleibt's nicht dabei/ wiegenlied
    brahms vergebliches ständchen
    wolf was trägt der boden hier/ bedeckt mich mit blumen/ in dem schatten meiner locken/
    zum neuen jahr/ philine/ kennst du das land?/ wir haben beide lange zeit geschwiegen/
    was soll der zorn?/ wiegenlied im sommer/ elfenlied/ nachtzauber/ die zigeunerin/
    ich hab' in penna
    handel care selve/ traditional gsätzli

26 november 1956/great neck
liederabend
pianist george reeves

29-30 november 1956/chicago
concert with works by weber and wolf
conductor fritz reiner

1 december 1956/cleveland
liederabend
pianist george reeves

5 december 1956/new york
**concert with works by mozart and strauss*
conductor fernando previtali

8-10 december 1956/berlin hochschule für musik
berlin philharmonic orchestra concert
*strauss es gibt ein reich/ariadne auf naxos
conductor herbert von karajan

20 january 1957/zürich tonhalle
liederabend
pianist madeleine lipatti

22 january 1957/nancy
liederabend
pianist jaqueline bonneau

26-27 january 1957/paris théatre des champs-élysées
concert with works by mozart and strauss
conductor pierre dervuax

29 january 1957/nice
liederabend
pianist jaqueline bonneau

30 january 1957/cannes
concert with works by mozart and wagner

4 february 1957/paris théatre des champs-élysées
liederabend
pianist jaqueline bonneau

6-7 february 1957/amsterdam concertgebouw
concertgebouw orchestra concert
*bach cantata no 202 "weichet nur betrübte schatten"
*mozart ch'io mi scordi di te, concert aria
conductor otto klemperer

9 february 1957/amsterdam
liederabend
pianist felix de nobel

11 february 1957/hilversum
*liederabend
pianist felix de nobel

12 february 1957/munich herkulessaal
liederabend
pianist madeleine lipatti

14 february 1957/mainz
liederabend
pianist madeleine lipatti

16 february 1957/hamburg
liederabend
pianist madeleine lipatti

24 february 1957/london royal festival hall
liederabend hugo wolf
pianist wolfgang sawallisch

> *goethe-lieder: die spröde/ die bekehrte/ epiphanias/ philine/ kennst du das land?*
> *mörike-lieder: zum neuen jahr/ auf eine christblume/ erstes liebeslied eines mädchens/ elfenlied/ storchenbotschaft*
> *italienisches liederbuch: o wär dein haus durchsichtig/ wer rief dich denn?/ ich esse nun mein brot/ du sagst mir dass ich keine fürstin sei/ wir haben beide lange zeit geschwiegen/ wir lange schon/ du denkst mit einem fädchen/ nein junger herr/ schweig einmal still/ ich hab' in penna*
> *spanisches liederbuch: herr was trägt der boden hier?/ alle gingen herz zur ruh'/ geh geliebter geh jetzt!*
> *eichendorff-lieder: nachtzauber/ die zigeunerin*
> *mausfallensprüchlein/ in der frühe/ in dem schatten meiner locken*

11 march 1957/milan teatro alla scala
verdi falstaff/ alice ford
conductor herbert von karajan
other principals included moffo/ barbieri/ alva/ gobbi/ panerai
further performances on 14, 16, 19 and 23 march 1957

20 march 1957/milan
liederabend
pianist giorgio favaretto

28 march 1957/siena
liederabend
pianist giorgio favaretto

1 april 1957/turin conservatorio
liederabend
pianist giorgio favaretto

4 april 1957/milan piccolo scala
liederabend
pianist giorgio favaretto

5 april 1957/brescia teatro grande
liederabend
pianist giorgio favaretto

24 april 1957/copenhagen tivoli hall
liederabend
pianist kjall olsson

25 april 1957/stockholm
liederabend
pianist kjall olsson

27 april 1957/oslo
liederabend
pianist kjall olsson

29 april 1957/skien
liederabend
pianist kjall olsson

3 may 1957/copenhagen
participation in orchestral concert

6 may 1957/aalborg
liederabend
pianist kjall olsson

17 may 1957/amsterdam concertgebouw
concertgebouw orchestra concert
*beethoven missa solemnis/soprano soloist
conductor otto klemperer
other soloists included merriman/ simandy/ rehfuss
concert repeated on 19 and 21 may 1957

4 june 1957/london royal festival hall
philharmonia orchestra concert with bach cantatas
conductor thurston dart

19 june 1957/vienna musikverein
liederabend
pianist gerald moore

25 june 1957/london royal festival hall
philharmonia orchestra concert
*berlioz la damnation de faust/marguérite
conductor massimo freccia
other soloists included lloyd/ roux/ brannigan

30 july 1957/salzburg festspielhaus
*mozart le nozze di figaro/contessa
conductor karl böhm
other principals included seefried/ ludwig/ kunz/ fischer-dieskau
further performances on 3, 8, 13 and 24 august 1957

10 august 1957/salzburg festspielhaus
*verdi falstaff/alice ford
conductor herbert von karajan
other principals included moffo/ simionato/ alva/ gobbi/ panerai
further performances on 14, 21 and 27 august 1957

19 august 1957/salzburg mozarteum
*liederabend hugo wolf
pianist gerald moore
> *mörike-lieder: der genesene an die hoffnung/ elfenlied/ storchenbotschaft*
> *italienisches liederbuch: wer rief dich denn?/ nun lass uns frieden schliessen/*
> *ich esse nun mein brot/ nein junger herr/ o wär' dein haus durchsichtig/ du sagst mir*
> *dass ich keine fürstin sei/ schweig einmal still/ verschling der abgrund/ ich hab' in penna*
> *spanisches liederbuch: klinge mein pandero/ sie blasen zum abmarsch/ mögen alle bösen*
> *zungen/ in dem schatten meiner locken/ geh' geliebter geh' jetzt*
> *eichendorff-lieder: nachtzauber/ die zigeunerin*

15 september 1957/vienna staatsoper
verdi falstaff/alice ford
conductor herbert von karajan
other principals included moffo/ simionato/ alva/ gobbi/ panerai
further performances on 17, 20 and 23 september 1957

1 october 1957/san francisco war memorial opera house
strauss der rosenkavalier/marschallin
conductor erich leinsdorf
other principals included bible/ streich/ edelmann/ herbert
further performances on 3 and 13 october 1957

15-16 october 1957/washington
participation in concert with works by handel and mozart

22 october 1957/san francisco war memorial opera house
cosi fan tutte/fiordiligi
conductor erich leinsdorf
other principals included merriman/ streich/ lewis/ blankenburg/ alvary
further performance on 24 october 1957

27 october 1957/los angeles
strauss der rosenkavalier/marschallin

29 october 1957/stockton california
liederabend
pianist george reeves

30 october 1957/santa rosa california
liederabend
pianist george reeves

4 november 1957/portland
concert with works by mozart and strauss
conductor theordore bloomfield

6 november 1957/los angeles
cosi fan tutte/fiordiligi

9 november 1957/san antonio
concert with works by mozart and strauss

10 november 1957/san francisco
liederabend

12 november 1957/los angeles
liederabend

14 november 1957/toronto
liederabend

18-19 november 1957/new york town hall
concert with works by hugo wolf
conductor thomas scherman

20 november 1957/baltimore
concert with works by mozart and strauss
conductor massimo freccia

22-23 november 1957/madison
liederabend

25 november 1957/chicago
liederabend

29 november 1957/brooklyn
liederabend

1 december 1957/south bend
participation in concert

3 december 1957/montreal
liederabend

5-6 december 1957/new york town hall
new york philharmonic concert with works by mozart and strauss
conductor fernando previtali
concert repeated on 8 december 1957

10 december 1957/kansas city
concert with works by mozart and strauss
conductor hans schwieger

13 december 1957/pittsburgh
concert with works by mozart and strauss
conductor william steinberg
concert repeated on 15 december 1957

19 december 1957/rotterdam
participation in concert

22 december 1957/amsterdam
***liederabend**
pianist felix de nobel

6 january 1958/berlin
***liederabend**
pianist michael raucheisen

16 january 1958/london royal festival hall
goldsbrough orchestra concert
***haydn scena di berenice**
***mozart 2 arias/le nozze di figaro**
conductor charles mackerras

19 january 1958/sankt gallen
liederabend
pianist willi haeusslin

20 january 1959/vienna musikverein
liederabend

23 january 1958/vienna redoutensaal
mozart cosi fan tutte/fiordiligi
conductor rudolf kempe
other principals included loose/ ludwig/ dermota/ kunz/ schöffler

25 january 1958/vienna staatsoper
le nozze di figaro/contessa
conductor herbert von karajan
other principals included seefried/ ludwig/ wächter/ kunz
further performance on 27 january 1958

28 january 1958/vienna staatsoper
mozart don giovanni/elvira
conductor rudolf moralt
other principals included stich-randall/ streich/ dermota/ wächter/ berry

31 january 1958/aachen
liederabend
pianist wolfgang sawallisch

2 february 1958/düsseldorf
liederabend
pianist michael raucheisen

4 february 1958/hamburg
liederabend
pianist michael raucheisen

7 february 1958/berlin
liederabend
pianist michael raucheisen
recital repeated on 1 march 1958

10 february 1958/basel
liederabend
pianist michael raucheisen
recital repeated on 4 march 1958

12 february 1958/frankfurt-am-main
liederabend
pianist michael raucheisen
recital repeated on 3 march 1958

15-16 february 1958/lyon
participation in concert

27 february 1958/london royal festival hall
philharmonia orchestra concert
mozart ch'io mi scordi di te
mozart 2 arias/cosi fan tutte
conductor wolfgang sawallisch

8-9 march 1958/paris théatre des champs-élysées
strauss closing scene/capriccio
conductor jean fournet

11 march 1958/london royal festival hall
liederabend
pianist jörg demus
schwarzkopf replaced dietrich fischer-dieskau for this recital

16 march 1958/paris théatre des champs-élysées
liederabend
pianist jaqueline bonneau

10 april 1958/brescia
liederabend
pianist giorgio favaretto

12 april 1958/florence
liederabend
pianist giorgio favaretto

15 april 1958/naples rai auditorium
*concert with arias by bach and mozart
conductor ugo rapalo

18 april 1958/rome
liederabend
pianist giorgio favaretto

22-23 april 1958/barcelona
liederabend
pianist jaqueline bonneau

25 april 1958/madrid
concert with works by mozart and strauss
conductor jean fournet

27-28 april 1958/lisbon
participation in orchestral concert

30 april 1958/oporto
participation in concert

5 may 1958/brussels théatre de la monnaie
guest performance by vienna staatsoper
mozart le nozze di figaro/contessa
further performance on 9 may 1958

7 may 1958/ghent
participation in concert with felix de nobel

13 may 1958/london royal festival hall
liederabend
pianist gerald moore
> *scarlatti togliatemi la vita ancor/ campra air de la folie/ caldara selve amiche/*
> *pergolesi siciliana/ purcell what can we poor females do?*
> *schubert suleika I/ suleika II/ wanderers nachtlied/ der jüngling an der quelle*
> *schumann schöne fremde/ die stille/ abendlied/ widmung*
> *wolf herr was trägt der boden hier?/ mühvoll komm ich und beladen/*
> *verschwiegene liebe/ der schäfer/ wie lange schon/ ich hab' in penna/ mausfallensprüchlein*
> *strauss waldseligkeit/ ich schwebe/ meinem kinde/ junghexenlied/ einkehr*
> *schubert seligkeit/ gluck einem bach der fliesset/ bohm was i' hab'*

3 june 1958/bath assembly rooms
liederabend
pianist gerald moore

8 june 1958/vienna staatsoper
verdi falstaff/alice ford
conductor herbert von karajan
other principals included moffo/ simionato/ zampieri/ gobbi/ panerai
further performance on 10 june 1958

16 june 1958/vienna redoutensaal
mozart cosi fan tutte/fiordiligi
conductor karl böhm
other principals included ludwig/ streich/ dermota/ schöffler/ borriello

23 june 1958/scheveningen kurzaal
liederabend
pianist felix de nobel
> *scarlatti togliatemi la vita ancor/ campra air de la folie/ caldara selve amiche/*
> *handel lascia ch'io piango/ pergolesi siciliana/ gluck arietta*
> *schubert an die musik/ der einsame/ wanderers nachtlied/ suleika II/*
> *der jüngling an der quelle/ die vögel/ wiegenlied*
> *schumann widmung/ die stille/ schöne fremde/ abendlied/ frühlingsnacht*
> *strauss waldseligkeit/ ich schwebe/ die nacht/ meinem kinde/ hat's gesagt*
> *bleibt's nicht dabei/ zueignung*

24 june 1958/amsterdam concertgebouw
netherlands chamber orchestra concert
*haydn scena di berenice
bach cantata no 199 "mein herze schwimmt in blut"
conductor szymon goldberg

25 june 1958/scheveningen kurzaal
programme as for 24 june 1958

1-2 july 1958/new york
participation in stadium concert

5 july 1958/ravinnia
participation in concert

8 july 1958/ravinnia
liederabend

11 july 1958/bridgeport
liederabend

12 july 1958/bridgeport
participation in concert

15 july 1958/san diego
liederabend

17 july 1958/los angeles
concert of viennese music in
hollywood bowl
conductor william steinberg

19 july 1958/los angeles
hollywood bowl concert
conductor felix slatkin

27 july 1958/salzburg mozarteum
*liederabend hugo wolf
pianist gerald moore
> *mörike-lieder: im frühling/ auf eine christblume/ lied vom winde*
> *goethe-lieder: ganymed/ blumengruss/ anakreons grab/ phänomen/ frühling übers jahr/ der schäfer*
> *spanisches liederbuch: mühvoll komm ich und beladem/ bedeckt mich mit blumen/ wer tat deinem füsslein weh?/ wehe der die mir verstrickte/ in dem schatten meiner locken*
> *keller-lieder: tretet ein hoher krieger/ singt mein schatz wie ein fink/ du milchjunger knabe/ wandl' ich in dem morgentau/ das köhlerweib ist trunken/ wie glänzt der helle mond*
> *philine/ kennst du das land?/ nun lass uns frieden schliessen/ mausfallensprüchlein*

4 august 1958/salzburg festspielhaus
*mozart le nozze di figaro/contessa
conductor karl böhm
other principals included seefried/ ludwig/ fischer-dieskau/ kunz
further performances on 14, 19, 23 and 30 august 1958

11 august 1958/salzburg residenzhof
*mozart cosi fan tutte/fiordiligi
conductor karl böhm
other principals included ludwig/ sciutti/ alva/ panerai/ calabrese
further performances on 17, 24 and 31 august 1958

28 august 1958/lucerne kunsthaus
liederabend
pianist gerald moore

8 september 1958/ascona
liederabend

10 september 1958/vienna staatsoper
mozart don giovanni/elvira
conductor karl böhm
other principals included jurinac/ seefried/ kmentt/ wächter/ kunz

12 september 1958/vienna redoutensaal
mozart cosi fan tutte/fiordiligi
conductor karl böhm

14 september 1958/vienna staatsoper
verdi falstaff/alice ford
conductor herbert von karajan
other principals included beltrami/ simionato/ alva/ gobbi/ wächter
further performance on 17 september 1958

30 september 1958/san francisco war memorial opera house
smetana the bartered bride/marie
conductor leopold ludwig
other principals included lewis/tozzi
further performances on 4 and 12 october 1958

18 october 1958/san antonio
participation in concert

21 october 1958/san francisco war memorial opera house
mozart le nozze di figaro/contessa
conductor kurt herbert adler
other principals included ratti/ward/panerai/modesti
further performance on 23 october 1958

27 october 1958/seattle
liederabend
pianist george reeves

28 october 1958/new york carnegie hall
liederabend
pianist george reeves

30 october 1958/san diego
mozart le nozze di figaro/contessa

2 november 1958/san francisco
liederabend

5 november 1958/los angeles
smetana the bartered bride/marie

9 november 1958/los angeles
mozart le nozze di figaro/contessa

13-15 november 1958/cleveland
cleveland orchestra concert with works by mozart and strauss
conductor george szell

16 november 1958/cleveland
liederabend

18 november 1958/new york carnegie hall
handel giulio cesare/cleopatra
concert performance
conductor gamson
other principals included forrester/ siepi

19 november 1958/boston
liederabend

21 november 1958/austin
liederabend

24 november 1958/atlanta
liederabend

28 november 1958/toronto
liederabend

30 november 1958/new york
liederabend
pianist george reeves
*recital included premiere performance
of strauss 3 liebeslieder (rosenlieder)*

2 december 1958/evansville
liederabend

4 december 1958/michigan
liederabend

10 december 1958/pennsylvania
liederabend

11 december 1958/indiana
liederabend

29 december 1958/milan teatro alla scala
*handel eracle/iole
conductor lovro von matacic
*other principals included barbieri/ corelli/ bastianini/ hines/ ferrin
further performances on 1, 5 and 7 january 1959*

13 january 1959/hamburg musikhalle
liederabend
pianist karl engel

18 january 1959/london royal festival hall
royal philharmonic orchestra concert
conductor harry newstone
pianist gerald moore
    *handel arias from psalm CXII, solomon, giulio cesare, belsazar, eracle,
alcina and judas maccabaeus
strauss 3 rosenlieder/ ruhe meine seele/ hat gesagt bleibt's nicht dabei/
schlechtes wetter
wolf tretet ein hoher krieger/ singt mein schatz wie ein fink/ du milchjunger knabe/
wandl' ich in dem morgentau/ das köhlerweib ist trunken/ wie glänzt der helle mond/
die zigeunerin
schubert seligkeit*

100

january 1959/london bbc studios
*strauss 3 liebeslieder (rosenlieder)
pianist gerald moore

17 february 1959/wuppertal
liederabend
pianist hermann reutter
recital repeated on 3 april 1959

22-23 february 1959/frankfurt-am-main
participation in orchestral concert
conductor georg solti

26 february 1959/munich
liederabend
pianist hermann reutter

28 february 1959/wiesbaden
liederabend
pianist hermann reutter

3-4 march 1959/paris théatre des champs-élysées
orchestre national concert
*handel v'adoro pupille/giulio cesare
*mozart 3 arias from cosi fan tutte
conductor manuel rosenthal

5 march 1959/cannes
participation in concert

10 march 1959/innsbruck
liederabend
pianist kurt rapf

6 april 1959/stuttgart sdr television studios
*mozart porgi amor/le nozze di figaro
conductor carl schuricht

27 april 1959/london royal festival hall
philharmonia orchestra concert
mozart 3 arias from cosi fan tutte
strauss closing scene/capriccio
conductor heinz wallberg

29 april 1959/copenhagen
liederabend

3 may 1959/odense
liederabend

5 may 1959/stockholm
liederabend
recital repeated on 8 may 1959

7 may 1959/stockholm
concert with works by handel and mozart

11 may 1959/oslo
liederabend

12 may 1959/skien
liederabend

14 may 1959/oslo
concert with works by handel and mozart

27 may 1959/vienna staatsoper
mozart le nozze di figaro/contessa
conductor herbert von karajan
other principals included seefried/ ludwig/ wächter/ kunz

30 may 1959/vienna staatsoper
mozart don giovanni/elvira
conductor heinrich hollreiser
other principals included zadek/ güden/ dermota/ london/ kunz

4 june 1959/vienna staatsoper
mozart le nozze di figaro/contessa
conductor karl böhm
other principals included seefried/ ludwig/ wächter/ kunz
further performance on 13 june 1959

17 june 1959/vienna redoutensaal
mozart cosi fan tutte/fiordiligi
conductor karl böhm
other principals included ludwig/ loose/ simoneau/ schöffler/ kunz
further performance on 21 june 1959

10 september 1959/lucerne kunsthaus
philharmonia orchestra concert
handel messiah/soprano soloist
conductor sir thomas beecham
other soloists included ludwig/ gedda/ bell

28 september 1959/london royal festival hall
philharmonia orchestra concert
mozart le nozze di figaro/contessa *concert performance*
conductor carlo maria giulini
other principals included moffo/ cossotto/ taddei/ wächter

18 october 1959/london royal festival hall
philharmonia orchestra concert
*mozart don giovanni/elvira *concert performance*
conductor colin davis
other principals included sutherland/ sciutti/ alva/ wächter/ taddei
further performance on 20 october 1959

23 october 1959/worcester massachusetts
detroit symphony orchestra concert with works by handel and strauss
conductor paul paray

24 october 1959/new york
concert for united nations
beethoven symphony no 9 "choral"/soprano soloist
conductor eleazar de carvalho
other soloists included forrester/ peerce/ borg

28 october 1959/new york carnegie hall
liederabend
pianist george reeves

9 november 1959/chicago lyric opera
mozart cosi fan tutte/fiordiligi
conductor josef krips
other principals included ludwig/ stahlman/ simoneau/ berry/ corena

11 november 1959/chicago lyric opera
mozart cosi fan tutte/fiordiligi
conductor lovro von matacic
other principals included ludwig/ stahlman/ simoneau/ berry/ corena
further performance on 14 november 1959

4 december 1959/london royal opera house
*strauss der rosenkavalier/marschallin
conductor georg solti
other principals included steffek/ jurinac/ böhme/ lewis
further performances on 7, 10, 14 and 17 december 1959

29 december 1959/vienna staatsoper
wagner die meistersinger von nürnberg/eva
conductor heinrich hollreiser
other principals included feiersinger/ klein/ schöffler/ hotter

1 january 1960/vienna staatsoper
strauss der rosenkavalier/marschallin
conductor heinrich hollreiser
other principals included rothenberger/ jurinac/ edelmann/ wiener
further performance on 4 january 1960

6 january 1960/vienna staatsoper
mozart le nozze di figaro/contessa
conductor herbert von karajan
other principals included seefried/ jurinac/ wächter/ kunz

9 january 1960/vienna staatsoper
mozart don giovanni/elvira
conductor heinrich hollreiser
other principals included stich-randall/ seefried/ kmentt/ wächter/ edelmann

10 january 1960/beromünster
mozart arias from cosi fan tutte
conductor jean-marie auberson

13 january 1960/havana
liederabend
recital repeated on 15 january 1960

18 january 1960/camaguey
liederabend

20 january 1960/san juan
liederabend

25 january 1960/mexico city
liederabend
recital repeated on 27 january 1960

28 january 1960/monterey
liederabend

31 january 1960/nassau
liederabend
pianist john wustman

8 february 1960/montreal
recording for canadian television

11 february 1960/bloomington
liederabend
pianist george reeves

15 february 1960/princeton
liederabend
pianist george reeves

18 february 1960/detroit
**detroit symphony orchestra concert
with works by handel and strauss*
conductor paul paray

21 february 1960/boston
liederabend

23-24 february 1960/washington
*washington national symphony concert
with works by mozart and strauss*
conductor howard mitchell

26 february 1960/new york
liederabend

1 march 1960/ithaca
liederabend

6 march 1960/reno
liederabend

8 march 1960/lincoln
liederabend

13 march 1960/new york
liederabend hugo wolf
pianist george reeves

16-18 march 1960/san francisco
*san francisco symphony orchestra
concert with works by mozart and strauss*
conductor enrique jorda

20 march 1960/berkeley
liederabend

23 march 1960/middleton
liederabend

27 march 1960/washington
liederabend

29 march 1960/akron
cleveland orchestra concert
strauss 4 letzte lieder
conductor george szell

7 april 1960/zürich tonhalle
liederabend
pianist gerald moore

10 april 1960/london royal festival hall
liederabend hugo wolf
pianist gerald moore
    mörike-lieder: der genesene an die hoffnung/ in der frühe
    goethe-lieder: epiphanias/ sankt nepomuks vorabend/ philine/ kennst du das land?
    keller-lieder: wandl' ich in dem morgentau/ das köhlerweib ist trunken
    reinick: wiegenlied im sommer
    eichendorff-lieder: nachtzauber/ die zigeunerin
    spanisches liederbuch: herr was trägt der boden hier?/ bedeckt mich mit blumen/
    mögen alle bösen zungen/ in dem schatten meiner locken/ geh' geliebter geh' jetzt
    italienisches liederbuch: was soll der zorn?/ o wär' dein haus durchsichtig/ gesegnet
    sei das grün/ wir haben beide lange zeit geschwiegen/ du denkst mit einem fädchen/
    verschling' der abgrund/ ich hab' in penna
    anakreons grab/ wer rief dich denn?/ mausfallensprüchlein/ nun lass uns frieden
    schliessen

22 april 1960/düsseldorf
liederabend
pianist heinrich schmidt

26 april 1960/kassel stadthalle
liederabend
pianist heinrich schmidt

28 april 1960/london royal festival hall
philharmonia orchestra concert
strauss 4 letzte lieder
conductor carlo maria giulini

1 may 1960/wiesbaden hessisches staatsthater
guest performance by vienna staatsoper
mozart le nozze di figaro/contessa
conductor herbert von karajan
other principals included seefried/ ludwig/ wächter/ kunz

3 may 1960/wiesbaden hessisches staatstheater
guest performance by vienna staatsoper
mozart cosi fan tutte/fiordiligi
conductor karl böhm
other principals included ludwig/ streich/ dermota/ berry/ schöffler
further performance on 8 may 1960

15 may 1960/vienna staatsoper
*strauss capriccio/madeleine
conductor karl böhm
other principals included goltz/ köth/ dermota/ uhde/ berry/ schöffler
further performances on 20 and 23 may 1960 and 9 june 1960

18 may 1960/vienna musikverein
liederabend
pianist heinrich schmidt

27 may 1960/vienna staatsoper
strauss der rosenkavalier/marschallin
conductor andré cluytens

29 may 1960/vienna musikverein
vienna philharmonic orchestra concert
*mahler 3 lieder
*mahler symphony no 4
conductor bruno walter

30 may 1960/vienna musikverein
philharmonia orchestra concert
strauss 4 letzte lieder
conductor carlo maria giulini

3 june 1960/vienna staatsoper
strauss der rosenkavalier/marschallin
conductor heinrich hollreiser

6 june 1960/vienna redoutensaal
mozart cosi fan tutte/fiordiligi
conductor lovro von matacic

13 june 1960/paris théatre des champs-élysées
liederabend
pianist jaqueline bonneau

15 june 1960/strassburg palais des fetes
*liederabend
pianist jaqueline bonneau
> *schubert an die musik/ auf dem wasser zu singen/ fischerweise/ der vollmond strahlt/ liebe*
> *schwärmt auf allen wegen/ der einsame/ seligkeit/ du bist die ruh'*
> *wolf herr was trägt der boden hier?/ sankt nepomuks vorabend/ nun lass uns frieden*
> *schliessen/ in dem schatten meiner locken/ wiegenlied im sommer/ geh' geliebter geh' jetzt*
> *strauss freundliche vision/ ruhe meine seele/ zueignung*
> *wolf schlechtes wetter/ mausfallensprüchlein*

17 june 1960/luxembourg
liederabend
pianist jaqueline bonneau

22 june 1960/amsterdam concertgebouw
concertgebouw orchestra concert
*vivaldi gloria
*verdi 4 pezzi sacri
conductor carlo maria giulini
other soloist was boese

23 june 1960/utrecht stadsschouwburg
details as for 22 june 1960

24 june 1960/scheveningen kurzaal
details as for 22 june 1960

27 june 1960/granada patio de los arrayanes
liederabend
pianist gerald moore

2 july 1960/scheveningen kurzaal
netherlands chamber orchestra concert
mozart ch'io mi scordi di te, concert aria
mozart 2 arias from cosi fan tutte
conductor carlo maria giulini

3 july 1960/rotterdam schouwburg
details as for 2 july 1960

5 july 1960/amsterdam concertgebouw
details as for 2 july 1960

27 july 1960/salzburg landestheater
*mozart cosi fan tutte/fiordiligi
conductor karl böhm
other principals included ludwig/ sciutti/ kmentt/ prey/ dönch
further performances on 7, 21 and 27 august 1960

3 august 1960/salzburg kleines festspielhaus
*mozart don giovanni/elvira
conductor herbert von karajan
other principals included l.price/ sciutti/ valletti/ wächter/ panerai
further performances on 10, 17, 25 and 29 august 1960

6 august 1960/salzburg grosses festspielhaus
*strauss der rosenkavalier/marschallin
conductor herbert von karajan
other principals included jurinac/ rothenberger/ edelmann/ poell

13 august 1960/salzburg mozarteum
*liederabend
pianist gerald moore

27-30 august 1960/salzburg grosses festspielhaus
sessions for paul czinner's film of the opera
*strauss der rosenkavalier/marschallin
conductor herbert von karajan
other principals included jurinac/ rothenberger/ edelmann/ kunz

2 september 1960/vienna staatsoper
strauss capriccio/madeleine
conductor karl böhm

4 september 1960/vienna staatsoper
mozart don giovanni/elvira
conductor karl böhm
other principals included l.price/ seefried/ dermota/ wächter/ kunz

10 september 1960/vienna staatsoper
strauss der rosenkavalier/marschallin
conductor karl böhm

29 september 1960/san francisco war memorial opera house
strauss der rosenkavalier/marschallin
conductor silvio varviso
other principals included töpper/ stahlman/ böhme/ wentworth
further performances on 7 and 16 october 1960

15 october 1960/san francisco war memorial opera house
mozart cosi fan tutte/fiordiligi
conductor kurt herbert adler
other principals included hilgenberg/ costa/ lewis/ guarrera/ schöffler
further performance on 18 october 1960

26 october 1960/chicago lyric opera
mozart le nozze di figaro/contessa
conductor josef krips
other principals included streich/ ludwig/ wächter/ berry
further performances on 29 and 31 october 1960

3 november 1960/san diego
strauss der rosenkavalier/marschallin

5 november 1960/los angeles
strauss der rosenkavalier/marschallin

9 november 1960/los angeles
mozart cosi fan tutte/fiordiligi

13 november 1960/san francisco
liederabend
pianist john wustman

15 november 1960/san josé
liederabend
pianist john wustman

20 november 1960/dallas civic opera
mozart don giovanni/elvira
conductor nicola rescigno
other principals included sutherland/ ratti/ alva/ wächter/ taddei/ zaccaria
further performance on 23 november 1963

27 november 1960/new york carnegie hall
liederabend

2 december 1960/new york town hall
*handel eracle/iole *concert performance*
conductor nicola rescigno
other principals included ludwig/ berry/ ludgin/ verreau

4 december 1960/washington
liederabend

6 december 1960/atlanta
liederabend

8 december 1960/delaware
liederabend

13 december 1960/new orleans
participation in concert

20 december 1960/vienna staatsoper
strauss der rosenkavalier/marschallin
conductor karl böhm
further performance on 3 january 1961

30 december 1960/vienna redoutensaal
mozart cosi fan tutte/fiordiligi
conductor heinrich hollreiser
further performance on 7 january 1961

5 january 1961/vienna staatsoper
strauss capriccio/madeleine
conductor hans swarovsky
other principals included goltz/ dermota/ nöcker/ imdahl/ wiener
further performance on 12 january 1961

10 january 1961/vienna musikverein
liederabend
pianist heinrich schmidt

24 january 1961/stuttgart
liederabend
pianist hermann reutter

26 january 1961/frankfurt-am-main
liederabend
pianist hermann reutter

28 january 1961/hamburg musikhalle
liederabend
pianist hermann reutter

6 february 1961/london royal festival hall
mozart le nozze di figaro/contessa *concert performance*
conductor carlo maria giulini
other principals included söderström/ berganza/ blanc/ corena

11-12 february 1961/paris théatre des champs-élysées
conservatoire orchestra concert with works by mozart and wagner
conductor georges pretre

20 february 1961/london royal festival hall
mozart don giovanni/elvira *concert performance*
conductor carlo maria giulini
other principals included grümmer/freni/haefliger/wächter/taddei/frick

22 february 1961/marseille
liederabend

25 february 1961/monte-carlo
concert with works by mozart and wagner
conductor louis frémaux

27 february 1961/paris théatre des champs-élysées
liederabend
pianist jaqueline bonneau

3 march 1961/london royal festival hall
brahms ein deutsches requiem/soprano soloist
conductor otto klemperer
other soloist was fischer-dieskau

5 march 1961/zürich tonhalle
strauss 4 letzte lieder
conductor roberto denzler

8 march 1961/highland park
liederabend
pianist john wustman

10 march 1961/naperville
liederabend
pianist john wustman

14 march 1961/birmingham
participation in concert
conductor arthur winograd

16 march 1961/delaware
liederabend
pianist john wustman

21-22 march 1961/toronto
concert with works by handel and strauss
conductor walter susskind

26 march 1961/los angeles
liederabend
pianist john wustman

28 march 1961/san diego
liederabend

4 april 1961/quebec
liederabend

6 april 1961/gettysburg
liederabend

11 april 1961/toledo
participation in concert

14 april 1961/chicago
liederabend

16 april 1961/miami
liederabend

18 april 1961/winston-salem
liederabend

24 april 1961/london royal festival hall
philharmonia orchestra concert
mahler 3 lieder
mahler symphony no 4
conductor otto klemperer

1 may 1961/wiesbaden hessisches staatstheater
strauss der rosenkavalier/marschallin
conductor heinz wallberg
other principals included ludwig/ lipp/ edelmann
further performance on 3 may 1961

18 may 1961/milan teatro alla scala
strauss der rosenkavalier/marschallin
conductor karl böhm
other principals included ludwig/ rothenberger/ edelmann/ kunz
further performances on 20, 22, 29 and 30 may 1961

26 may 1961/london royal festival hall
liederabend
pianist gerald moore

    schubert das lied im grünen/ abendröte/ der jüngling an der quelle/ der schmetterling/
    du bist die ruh'
    brahms liebestreu/ immer leiser wird mein schlummer/ von ewiger liebe
    liszt kennst du das land?/ es muss ein wunderbares sein/ die drei zigeuner
    strauss sonett/ von händlern wird die kunst bedroht/ o schröpferschwarm/ ruhe
    meine seele/ für 15 pfennige/ meinem kinde/ schlechtes wetter/ zueignung
    group of folksongs
    wolf in dem schatten meiner locken/ du denkst mit einem fädchen/ du sagst mir dass
    ich keine fürstin sei

10 june 1961/vienna staatsoper
mozart don giovanni/elvira
conductor karl böhm
other principals included l.price/ güden/ dermota/ wächter/ kunz/ kreppel

16 june 1961/vienna musikverein
liederabend
pianist joerg demus

19 june 1961/vienna staatsoper
strauss capriccio/madeleine
conductor karl böhm
other principals included goltz/ dermota/ schmitt-walter/ berry/ wiener

21 june 1961/vienna redoutensaal
mozart cosi fan tutte/fiordiligi
conductor karl böhm
other principals included ludwig/ streich/ kmentt/ kunz/ schöffler
further performance on 25 june 1961

23 june 1961/vienna staatsoper
strauss der rosenkavalier/marschallin
conductor karl böhm
other principals included ludwig/ güden/ böhme/ kunz

3 july 1961/amsterdam stadschouwburg
***mozart le nozze di figaro**/contessa
conductor carlo maria giulini
other principals included sciutti/ malagu/ prey/ taddei
further performance on 9 july 1961

6 july 1961/rotterdam
details as for 3 july 1961

13 july 1961/den haag
details as for 3 july 1961

22 july 1961/munich
participation in concert

28 july 1961/salzburg grosses festspielhaus
strauss der rosenkavalier/marschallin
conductor karl böhm
other principals included ludwig/ rothenberger/ edelmann/ wiener
further performances on 3, 12, 18, 25 and 30 august 1961

1 august 1961/salzburg kleines festspielhaus
mozart cosi fan tutte/fiordiligi
conductor karl böhm
other principals included ludwig/ sciutti/ kmentt/ prey/ dönch
further performances on 8, 14 and 27 august 1961

5 august 1961/salzburg mozarteum
liederabend hugo wolf
pianist gerald moore

7 september 1961/vienna staatsoper
strauss der rosenkavalier/marschallin
conductor karl böhm
other principals included jurinac/ güden/ czerwenka/ poell
further performance on 23 september 1961

12 september 1961/bucarest
liederabend

20 september 1961/vienna redoutensaal
mozart cosi fan tutte/fiordiligi
further performance on 28 september 1961

26 september 1961/vienna staatsoper
mozart le nozze di figaro/contessa
conductor herbert von karajan
other principals included seefried/ simionato/ wächter/ kunz

29 september 1961/amsterdam
liederabend

6 october 1961/stuttgart
strauss closing scene/capriccio
conductor ferdinand leitner

9 october 1961/turin rai television studio
television recording

10 october 1961/naples rai auditorium
*mozart ch'io mi scordi di te, concert aria
*mozart 2 arias from cosi fan tutte
conductor carlo franci

17 october 1961/london royal festival hall
liederabend
pianist geoffrey parsons
> *schubert an die musik/ das lied im grünen/ du bist die ruh'/ gretchen am spinnrade*
> *brahms in stiller nacht/ liebestreu/ von ewiger liebe/ vergebliches ständchen*
> *strauss ruhe meine seele/ schlechtes wetter/ meinem kinde/ für 15 pfennige*
> *wolf mignon I-III/ philine/ kennst du das land?/ herr was trägt der boden hier?/*
> *bedeckt mich mit blumen/ in dem schatten meiner locken/ wer rief dich denn?/*
> *o wär' dein haus durchsichtig/ nachtzauber/ die zigeunerin*

24 october 1961/london bbc television studios
*strauss kann mich auch an ein mädel erinnern.....to end of act I/
der rosenkavalier/ marschallin
conductor charles mackerras
other principal was töpper

25 october 1961/london bbc television studios
*liederabend
pianist gerald moore
recording was shown on 30 december 1961
> *anon drink to me only/ mozart die kleine spinnerin/ gluck einem bach der fliesset/*
> *schubert an die musik/ seligkeit/ wolf philine/ o wär' dein haus durchsichtig/*
> *strauss hat gesagt bleibt's nicht dabei*

1 november 1961/chicago lyric opera
mozart cosi fan tutte/ fiordiligi
conductor peter maag
other principals included ludwig/ stahlman/ simoneau/ berry/ cesari
further performance on 3 november 1961

8 november 1961/chicago lyric opera
mozart don giovanni/ elvira
conductor peter maag
other principals included stich-randall/ seefried/ simoneau/ wächter/ berry/ wildermann
further performance on 11 november 1961

15 november 1961/watertown
liederabend

19 november 1961/new york
television recording for the ed sullivan show

22 november 1961/new york orchard park
liederabend
pianist john wustman

25 november 1961/new york hunter college
liederabend
pianist john wustman

12 december 1961/wiesbaden
liederabend
pianist hermann reutter

15 december 1961/vienna redoutensaal
mozart cosi fan tutte/fiordiligi
conductor wilhelm loibner
other principals included sjöstedt/ martino/ kmentt/ kunz/ welter

20 december 1961/vienna staatsoper
strauss capriccio/madeleine
conductor hans swarovsky
other principals included goltz/ wehofschitz/ krukowski/ berry/ schöffler

21 december 1961/london bbc television studios
***scenes from don giovanni, la boheme and die lustige witwe**
conductor charles mackerras

25 december 1961/vienna staatsoper
strauss der rosenkavalier/marschallin
conductor karl böhm

2 january 1962/vienna musikverein
liederabend

26 january 1962/paris théatre de l'opéra
strauss der rosenkavalier/marschallin
conductor louis fourestier
other principals included sarroca/ berton/ langdon/ mars
further performances on 29 january 1962 and 5 and 12 february 1962

2 february 1962/paris théatre de l'opéra
strauss capriccio/madeleine
conductor georges pretre
other principals included berton/ roux/ sénéchal
further performance on 9 february 1962

20 february 1962/munich herkulessaal
liederabend
pianist hermann reutter

28 february 1962/hamburg musikhalle
liederabend
pianist hermann reutter

2 march 1962/hannover musikstudio im funkhaus
*liederabend
pianist hermann reutter
schubert an die musik/ der einsame/ seligkeit/ gretchen am spinnrade
brahms da unten im tale/ liebestreu/ vergebliches ständchen
strauss ruhe meine seele/ wiegenlied/ meinem kinde/ schlechtes wetter/ hat gesagt bleibt's
nicht dabei/ zueignung
wolf mignon I-III/ philine/ kennst du das land?/ herr was trägt der boden hier?/
bedeckt mich mit blumen/ in dem schatten meiner locken/ wer rief dich denn?/
wiegenlied im sommer/ die zigeunerin/ nachtzauber

13 april 1962/chicago
participation in concert
conductor franz allers

16 april 1962/norfolk virginia
liederabend
pianist john wustman

18 april 1962/cambridge mass
liederabend
pianist john wustman

9 may 1962/copenhagen
liederabend
pianist kjall olsson

11 may 1962/oslo
liederabend

14 may 1962/stockholm
liederabend

16 may 1962/copenhagen
participation in concert

30 may 1962/paris théatre des
champs-élysées
liederabend
pianist jaqueline bonneau

4 june 1962/vienna redoutensaal
mozart cosi fan tutte/fiordiligi
conductor heinz wallberg
further performances on 14 and 24 june 1962

7 june 1962/vienna staatsoper
strauss der rosenkavalier/marschallin
conductor herbert von karajan
other principals included seefried/ güden/ edelmann/ kunz

12 june 1962/vienna staatsoper
mozart le nozze di figaro/contessa
conductor hans swarovsky
other principals included sciutti/ jurinac/ wächter/ berry

15 june 1962/vienna musikverein
liederabend
pianist joerg demus

17 june 1962/zürich
liederabend
pianist joerg demus

19 june 1962/vienna staatsoper
strauss capriccio/madeleine
conductor georges pretre
other principals included goltz/ dermota/ uhde/ berry/ kusche

22 june 1962/vienna staatsoper
mozart don giovanni/elvira
conductor joseph keilberth
other principals included scheyrer/ sciutti/ gedda/ jedlicka/ berry

29 june 1962/amsterdam concertgebouw
*liederabend
pianist felix de nobel
    schumann liederkreis op 39
    wolf morgentau/ das vöglein/ die spinnerin/ wiegenlied im sommer/ wiegenlied im
    winter/ mausfallensprüchlein/ mignon I-III/ philine/ kennst du das land?/
    wer rief dich denn?/ nun lass uns frieden schliessen/ die zigeunerin

18 july 1962/london goldsmith's hall
liederabend
pianist gerald moore
> *schubert an die musik/ der einsame/ der vollmond strahlt/ an sylvia/ du bist die ruh'/*
> *auf dem wasser zu singen*
> *strauss ruhe meine seele/ meinem kinde/ schlechtes wetter/ zueignung*
> *walton a song for the lord mayor's table, song cycle (premiere performance)*
> *wolf mein liebster hat zu tische mich geladem/ wie lange schon war immer mein verlangen/*
> *nun lass uns frieden schliessen/ kennst du das land?/ die zigeunerin*
> *purcell what can we poor females do?/ arne where the bee sucks/ anon drink to me only*

8 august 1962/salzburg kleines festspielhaus
*mozart cosi fan tutte/fiordiligi
conductor karl böhm
other principals included ludwig/ sciutti/ knentt/ prey/ dönch
further performances on 15, 21 and 26 august 1962

11 august 1962/salzburg mozarteum
berlin philharmonic orchestra concert
strauss 4 letzte lieder
conductor istvan kertesz

17 august 1962/salzburg mozarteum
liederabend
pianist gerald moore

29 august 1962/deauville
participation in concert

31 august 1962/biarritz
liederabend

2 september 1962/saint-juan-de-luz
participation in concert

19 september 1962/london royal festival hall
mozart cosi fan tutte/fiordiligi *concert performance*
conductor karl böhm
other principals included ludwig/ steffek/ kraus/ taddei/ berry

27 september 1962/san francisco war memorial opera house
strauss der rosenkavalier/marschallin
conductor janos ferencsik
other principals included meyer/ lipp/ langdon/ tipton
further performance on 12 october 1962

5 october 1962/berkeley california
liederabend
recital repeated on 8 october 1962

16 october 1962/san francisco war memorial opera house
mozart don giovanni/elvira
conductor leopold ludwig
other principals included de los angeles/ meneguzzer/ lewis/ tozzi/ evans/ langdon
further performances on 20 and 28 october 1962

1 november 1962/san diego
mozart don giovanni/elvira

7 november 1962/los angeles
strauss der rosenkavalier/marschallin

9 november 1962/los angeles
mozart don giovanni/elvira

11 november 1962/san francisco
liederabend
pianist john wustman

13 november 1962/des moines
liederabend

15 november 1962/durham
liederabend

19 november 1962/baton rouge
liederabend

26-27 november 1962/nashville
participation in concert

30 november 1962/new york carnegie hall
liederabend

18 december 1962/brussels théatre de la monnaie
strauss der rosenkavalier/marschallin
conductor andré vandernoot
other principals included sarfaty/ arnaud/ berry
further performances on 21, 24, 27 and 31 december 1962

13 january 1963/basel
liederabend
pianist hermann reutter

15 january 1963/zürich
liederabend
pianist hermann reutter

27 january 1963/london royal festival hall
philharmonia orchestra concert
strauss 4 letzte lieder
conductor lorin maazel

6 february 1963/paris opéra-comique
mozart cosi fan tutte/fiordiligi
conductor serge baudo
other principals included berbié/ harbell/ lecocq/ linsolas/ hurteau
further performances on 9, 19 and 25 february 1963

11 february 1963/paris théatre de l'opéra
strauss der rosenkavalier/marschallin
conductor louis fourestier
other principals included meyer
further performances on 15 and 17 february 1963

4 march 1963/london royal festival hall
philharmonia orchestra concert of viennese operetta
conductor willi boskovsky

6-7 march 1963/stuttgart sdr studios
participation in radio concert

8 march 1963/stuttgart	11 march 1963/zürich
liederabend	**liederabend**

28 march 1963/milan teatro alla scala
mozart don giovanni/elvira
conductor hermann scherchen
other principals included l.price/ freni/ alva/ ghiaurov/ ganzarolli
further performances on 30 march 1963 and 2, 4 and 9 april 1963

7 april 1963/london royal festival hall
liederabend
pianist gerald moore
> *mozart die ihr des unermesslichen weltalls/ abendenpfindung/ warnung*
> *schubert der einsame/ auf dem wasser zu singen/ die forelle/ an sylvia/ der vollmond strahlt/ vedi quanto adoro*
> *britten six hölderlin fragments*
> *wolf lebewohl/ im frühling/ nimmersatte liebe/ selbstgeständnis/ storchenbotschaft/ du denkst mit einem fädchen/ nein junger herr!/ o wär dein haus durchsichtig*
> *schubert seligkeit*

21 april 1963/frankfurt-am-main	26 april 1963/munich
liederabend	*participation in concert*
pianist hermann reutter	conductor meinhard von zallinger

122

29 april 1963/heidelberg stadthalle
liederabend
pianist hermann reutter

2 may 1963/hamburg staatsoper
strauss der rosenkavalier/marschallin
conductor leopold ludwig
other principals included ludwig/ rothenberger/ berry/ kusche

5 may 1963/hamburg staatsoper
mozart cosi fan tutte/fiordiligi
conductor janos kulka
other principals included ludwig/ duske/ alva/ blankenburg/ blankenheim

13 may 1963/paris théatre des champs-élysées
liederabend
pianist jacqueline bonneau

16 may 1963/vienna staatsoper
strauss capriccio/madeleine
conductor robert heger
other principals included malaniuk/ dermota/ uhde/ berry/ schöffler

18 may 1963/vienna staatsoper
strauss der rosenkavalier/marschallin

23 may 1963/vienna staatsoper
mozart le nozze di figaro/contessa
conductor heinz wallberg
other principals included rothenberger/ jurinac/ engen/ taddei

29 may 1963/vienna staatsoper
wagner tannhäuser/elisabeth
conductor herbert von karajan
other principals included janowitz/ ludwig/ windgassen/ kmentt/ wächter/ kreppel

2 june 1963/deauville
liederabend

23 june 1963/london royal festival hall
verdi messa da requiem/soprano soloist
conductor carlo maria giulini
other soloists included ludwig/ gedda/ ghiaurov

29 june 1963/ravinia
concert of viennese oporetta
conductor willi boskovsky

2 july 1963/chicago
chicago symphony orchestra concert
conductor walter hendl

3 july 1963/montreal
**tv concert of viennese opoeretta*
conductor willi boskovsky
recorded for later transmission

4 july 1963/montreal
liederabend

9 july 1963/los angeles
*hollywood bowl concert of
viennese opoeretta*
conductor willi boskovsky

11 july 1963/new york lewisohn stadium
concert of viennese operetta
conductor willi boskovsky

14 july 1963/ann arbor
concert of viennese operetta
conductor willi boskovsky

31 july 1963/salzburg grosses festspielhaus
*strauss der rosenkavalier/marschallin
conductor herbert von karajan
*other principals included rothenberger/jurinac/edelmann/dönch
further performances on 10 and 29 august 1963*

8 august 1963/salzburg kleines festspielhaus
mozart cosi fan tutte/fiordiligi
conductor karl böhm
*other principals included ludwig/sciutti/kmentt/prey/dönch
further performances on 14, 20 and 25 august 1963*

15 august 1963/lucerne
liederabend
pianist gerald moore

17 august 1963/salzburg mozarteum
*liederabend hugo wolf
pianist gerald moore

6 september 1963/lucerne
liederabend
pianist gerald moore

8 september 1963/besancon
liederabend
pianist gerald moore

11 september 1963/luxembourg
participation in concert
conductor louis de froment

4 october 1963/new canaan
liederabend
pianist john wustman

6 october 1963/beverly hills
liederabend
pianist john wustman

19 october 1963/san francisco war memorial opera house
mozart cosi fan tutte/fiordiligi
conductor janos ferencsik
other principals included vanni/ grist/ valletti/ prey/ wolansky
further performance on 29 october 1963

25 october 1963/san francisco war memorial opera house
strauss capriccio/madeleine
conductor georges pretre
other principals included cervena/ valletti/ prey/ stewart/ wolansky
further performance on 31 october 1963

6 november 1963/los angeles
strauss capriccio/madeleine

8 november 1963/los angeles
mozart cosi fan tutte/fiordiligi

13 november 1963/houston
liederabend
pianist john wustman

15 november 1963/wisconsin
liederabend
pianist john wustman

16 november 1963/madison
liederabend
pianist john wustman

19 november 1963/wheaton
liederabend
pianist john wustman

22 november 1963/evanston
liederabend
pianist john wustman

26 november 1963/milwaukee
participation in concert

27 november 1963/hamilton
participation in concert

30 november 1963/new york
hunter college
liederabend
pianist john wustman

3-4 december 1963/louisville
participation in concert

16 december 1963/paris théatre
des champs-élysées
liederabend

26 december 1963/vienna
staatsoper
strauss der rosenkavalier/
marschallin

30 december 1963/vienna
staatsoper
mozart le nozze di figaro/
contessa

16 january 1964/london royal festival hall
philharmonia orchestra concert for richard strauss centenary
strauss closing scene/capriccio
conductor karl böhm

19 january 1964/barcelona teatro del liceo
mozart cosi fan tutte/fiordiligi
conductor eykmann
other principals included canne-meyer/ blankenship/ mertz/ talasko
further performances on 21 and 26 january 1964

31 january 1964/innsbruck
liederabend
pianist georg fischer

7 february 1964/london royal festival hall
liederabend
pianist geoffrey parsons
schubert das lied im grünen/ wehmut/ der vollmond strahlt/ an sylvia/ der einsame/ ganymed
mahler des antonius von padua fischpredigt/ ich atmet' einen linden duft/ rheinlegendchen/
lob des hohen verstandes
wolf herr was trägt der boden hier?/ köpfchen köpfchen nicht gewimmert/ sagt seid ihr's
feiner herr/ trau nicht der liebe/ in dem schatten meiner locken/ geh' geliebter geh' jetzt
strauss meinem kinde/ heinliche aufforderung/ ruhe meine seele
schubert seligkeit/ wolf wer rief dich denn?/ nun lass uns frieden schliessen/ nein junger herr/
strauss zueignung

10 february 1964/london bbc studios
*liederabend
pianist geoffrey parsons

12 february 1964/vienna staatsoper
strauss der rosenkavalier/marschallin
conductor heinz wallberg
other principals included jurinac/ streich/ edelmann/ kunz

25 february 1964/geneva grand théatre
strauss der rosenkavalier/marschallin
conductor christian vochting
further performances on 27 and 29 february 1964

6 march 1964/marseille
strauss der rosenkavalier/marschallin
conductor george sébastian
other principals included sarfaty/ berton/ greindl
further performance on 8 march 1964

18 march 1964/paris théatre
des champs-élysées
liederabend

21 march 1964/geneva victoria hall
liederabend

29 march 1964/london royal
festival hall
*philharmonia orchestra concert of
viennese operetta*
conductor lovro von matacic

9 april 1964/london royal festival hall
philharmonia orchestra concert
mozart ch'io mi scordi di te
mozart laudate dominum
mozart nehmt meinen dank
conductor carlo maria giulini

18 april 1964/salzburg
liederabend
pianist georg fischer

20 april 1964/salzburg
participation in concert

30 april 1964/paris théatre
des champs-élysées
liederabend

5-6 may 1964/berlin philharmonie
*berlin philharmonic orchestra concert
for richard strauss centenary*
strauss 4 letzte lieder
conductor herbert von karajan

14 may 1964/auckland
liederabend
recital repeated on 16 may 1964

19 may 1964/wellington
liederabend
recital repeated on 23 may 1964

21 may 1964/christchurch
liederabend
recital repeated on 26 may 1964

5 june 1964/vienna staatsoper
strauss capriccio/madeleine
conductor georges pretre
other principals included ludwig/ wunderlich/ kmentt/ schöffler/ prey

9 june 1964/vienna staatsoper
mozart le nozze di figaro/contessa
conductor josef krips
other principals included rothenberger/ miljakovic/ prey/ kunz

13 june 1964/vienna staatsoper
strauss der rosenkavalier/marschallin
conductor heinz wallberg

19 june 1964/amsterdam concertgebouw
concertgebouw orchestra concert for the richard strauss centenary
*strauss 4 letzte lieder
conductor george szell

20 june 1964/scheveningen kurzaal
details as for 19 june 1964

23 june 1964/amsterdam concertgebouw
liederabend
pianist geoffrey parsons
    schubert das lied im grünen/ an den mond/ schäfers klagelied/ dass sie hier gewesen/ die forelle
    mahler des antonius zu padua fischpredigt/ ich atmet' einen linden duft/ rheinlegendchen/
    lob des hohen verstandes
    duparc chanson triste/ debussy beau soir/ mandoline/ fauré clair de lune/ notre amour
    strauss sonett/ meinem kinde/ heimliche aufforderung
    wolf elfenlied/ schubert seligkeit/ wolf köpfchen köpfchen nicht gewimmert

1 august 1964/salzburg grosses festspielhaus
*strauss der rosenkavalier/marschallin
conductor herbert von karajan
other principals included jurinac/ rothenberger/ edelmann/ ferenz
further performances on 13 and 29 august 1964

10 august 1964/salzburg kleines festspielhaus
mozart cosi fan tutte/fiordiligi
conductor karl böhm
other principals included ludwig/ sciutti/ kmentt/ prey/ dönch
further performances on 16, 22 and 26 august 1964

15 august 1964/salzburg grosses festspielhaus
berlin philharmonic orchestra concert for the richard strauss centenary
*strauss 4 letzte lieder
conductor herbert von karajan

19 august 1964/salzburg mozarteum
liederabend hugo wolf
pianist gerald moore

22 september 1964/san francisco war memorial opera house
strauss der rosenkavalier/marschallin
conductor ferdinand leitner
other principals included seefried/ grist/ edelmann/ ludgin
further performances on 24 and 27 september 1964

13 october 1964/new york metropolitan opera house
strauss der rosenkavalier/marschallin
conductor thomas schippers
other principals included della casa/ rothenberger/ konya/ edelmann/ mittelmann
further performances on 24 and 29 october 1964 and 2, 12 and 17 november 1964

19 october 1964/jacksonville   5 november 1964/atlanta
participation in concert   **liederabend**

22 november 1964/new york carnegie hall
duet recital with dietrich fischer-dieskau
wolf italienisches liederbuch
pianist gerald moore

26 november 1964/los angeles
strauss der rosenkavalier/marschallin
conductor ferdinand leitner

29 november 1964/new york metropolitan opera house
gala performance also involving renata tebaldi and joan sutherland
strauss der rosenkavalier act 1/marschallin
conductor thomas schippers
other principals included della casa/ morell/ edelmann

4 december 1964/monclair
liederabend
pianist gerald moore

8 december 1964/new york metropolitan opera house
*strauss der rosenkavalier/marschallin
conductor thomas schippers
other principals included della casa/ raskin/ morell/ edelmann/ dönch
further performance on 19 december 1964

15 december 1964/baltimore
liederabend
pianist john wustman

10 january 1965/vienna staatsoper
strauss capriccio/madeleine
conductor robert heger
other principals included ludwig/ kmentt/ kerns/ ostenburg/ schöffler

13 january 1965/vienna staatsoper
strauss der rosenkavalier/marschallin
conductor heinz wallberg
other principals included ast/ lipp/ edelmann/ kohn
further performances on 21 and 30 january 1965 and 3 february 1965

16 january 1965/vienna staatsoper
mozart le nozze di figaro/contessa
conductor heinz wallberg
other principals included holm/ janowitz/ kerns/ kunz
further performances on 24 and 27 january 1965

12 february 1965/lyon
strauss der rosenkavalier/marschallin
conductor richard kraus
further performance on 14 february 1965

21 february 1965/brussels théatre de la monnaie
strauss der rosenkavalier/marschallin
conductor richard kraus
other principals included sarfaty/ arnaud/ devos/ greindl/ ferenz
further performances on 24 and 27 february 1965

4 march 1965/london royal festival hall
liederabend
pianist gerald moore
    schubert nacht und träume/ suleika I-II/ fischerweise
    strauss 3 ophelia-lieder/ wer lieben will/ ach was kummer/ morgen/ ständchen
    wolf wenn du zu den blumen gehst/ sagt seid ihr es feiner herr?/ trau nicht der liebe/
    unfall/ die zigeunerin
    wolf-ferrari songs from the italian songbook
    wolf wie lange schon/ in dem schatten meiner locken/ mein liebster ist so klein
    strauss hat gesagt bleibt's nicht dabei

14 march 1965/monte-carlo
mozart le nozze di figaro/contessa
conductor eduard van remoortel
other principals included sciutti/ miljakovic/ kerns/ kunz
further performance on 16 march 1965

20 march 1965/bordeaux
participation in concert
conductor george sébastian

22 march 1965/nantes
liederabend
pianist geoffrey parsons

24 march 1965/paris théatre
des champs-élysées
liederabend
pianist geoffrey parsons

6-7 april 1965/washington
washington national symphony concert
conductor howard mitchell

9 april 1965/new york carnegie hall
liederabend
pianist geoffrey parsons

20 may 1965/london royal festival hall
liederabend
pianist gerald moore
    schubert das lied im grünen/ wohin?/ der einsame
    schumann aus den östlichen rosem/ leis' rudern hier/ wenn durch die piazetta/ der nussbaum
    mahler des antonius von padua fischpredigt/ lob des hohen verstandes
    marx japanisches regenlied/ venezianisches wiegenlied
    wolf italienisches liederbuch: wer rief dich denn?/ verschling' der abgrund/ nun lass uns
    frieden schliessen/ du denkst mit einem fädchen/ wie lange schon war immer mein verlangen/
    man sagt mir dass ich keine fürstin sei/ mein liebster singt/ ich esse nun mein brot/ mein
    liebster ist so klein/ wohl kenn' ich euren stand/ man sagt mir/ o wär dein haus durchsichtig
    wie ein glas/ nein junger herr!/ gesegnet sei das grün/ ihr jungen leute/ wie soll ich fröhlich sein?/
    ich hab' in penna/ schweig' einmal still
    schubert seligkeit/ an sylvia
    debussy mandoline/ swiss trad. gschätzli

26 may 1965/copenhagen
liederabend
pianist robert levin

28 may 1965/bergen
liederabend
pianist robert levin

31 may 1965/stockholm
liederabend
pianist robert levin

9 june 1965/madrid
strauss der rosenkavalier/marschallin
conductor richard kraus

17 june 1965/paris
participation in concert
conductor willi boskovsky

19 june 1965/vichy
liederabend

13 july 1965/ravinia
participation in concert
conductor willi boskovsky
concert repeated on 17 july 1965

15 july 1965/ravinia
participation in concert
conductor seiji ozawa

21 july 1965/new york
lewissohn stadsium
participation in concert
conductor joseph rosenstock

24 july 1965/new york
lewissohn stadium
participation in concert
conductor willi boskovsky

29 july 1965/los angeles
hollywood bowl concert
conductor sixten ehrling

31 july 1965/los angeles
hollywood bowl concert
conductor willi boskovsky

11 august 1965/menton
liederabend
pianist nadia gedda-nova

14 august 1965/santander
liederabend
pianist nadia gedda-nova

17 august 1965/santander
participation in concert
conductor andré vandernoot

17 november 1965/brussels
liederabend
pianist geoffrey parsons

22 november 1965/paris
salle pleyel
liederabend
pianist geoffrey parsons

6 december 1965/bern
liederabend
pianist geoffrey parsons

9 december 1965/geneva
liederabend
pianist geoffrey parsons

12 december 1965/zürich
liederabend
pianist geoffrey parsons

17 december 1965/lyon opéra de lyon
mozart cosi fan tutte/fiordiligi
conductor reinhard peters
other principals included sarfaty/miljakovic/sénéchal/blankenburg/roux
further performance on 19 december 1965

8 january 1966/new york
carnegie hall
liederabend
pianist geoffrey parsons

12 january 1966/ripon
liederabend
pianist john wustman

29 january 1966/new york metropolitan opera house
mozart don giovanni/elvira
conductor joseph rosenstock
other principals included stich-randall/elias/peerce/siepi/evans

4 march 1966/westbury long island
televised recital
*liederabend
pianist gerald moore
> *mozart voi che sapete*
> *schubert an die musik/ der einsame/ an sylvia*
> *brahms da unten im tale/ sandmännchen/ vergebliches ständchen*
> *wolf kennst du das land/ in dem schatten meiner locken/ mausfallensptüchlein/ die zigeunerin*
> *strauss schlechtes wetter/ hat gesagt bleibt's nicht dabei*
> *och modr ich will en ding han/ o du liebs ängeli/ gsätzli*

11 march 1966/new orleans
liederabend
pianist martin isepp

15 march 1966/newhaven
liederabend
pianist john wustman

18 march 1966/new york
hunter college
liederabend
pianist martin isepp

19 march 1966/washington
liederabend
pianist john wustman

22 march 1966/new orleans
participation in concert

30 march 1966/hartford
participation in concert

6 may 1966/london royal festival hall
liederabend
pianist gerald moore
> *wolf peregrina I-II/ erstes liebeslied eines mädchens/ gesang weylas/ um mitternacht/*
> *herr was trägt der boden hier?/ in dem schatten meiner locken/ mögen alle bösen*
> *zungen/ tretet ein hoher krieger/ du milchjunger knabe/ wie glänzt der helle mond/*
> *die zigeunerin*
> *strauss zueignung/ muttertändelei/ waldseligkeit/ meinem kinde/ ständchen/ morgen*
> *brahms da unten im tale/ jungfräulein soll ich mit euch gehen/ in stiller nacht/*
> *dort in den weiden/ schöne augen schöne strahlen*
> *schubert seligkeit/ wolf wie lange schon/ wer rief dich denn?/ mausfallensprüchlein*

10 may 1966/drottningholm
mozart cosi fan tutte/fiordiligi
conductor ferenc koltay
other principals included ludwig/ sciutti/ kmentt/ berry/ dönch
further performance on 13 may 1966

20 may 1966/versailles
liederabend
pianist geoffrey parsons

29 may 1966/london bbc studios
recording with yehudi menuhin

3 june 1966/paris théatre de l'opéra
strauss der rosenkavalier/marschallin
conductor george sébastian
other principals included sarroca/ michels/ vanzo/ böhme
further performances on 6 and 8 june 1966

17 june 1966/zürich
liederabend
pianist geoffrey parsons

19 june 1966/bath assembly rooms
liederabend
pianist geoffrey parsons
strauss zueignung/ waldseligkeit/ meinem kinde/ muttertändelei/ wer lieben will/
ach was kummer/ 3 ophelia-lieder/ ruhe meine seele/ morgen/ hat gesagt bleibt's nicht
dabei/ schlechtes wetter
wolf kennst du das land?/ anakreons grab/ als ich auf dem euphrat schiffte/ der schäfer/
unfall/ die zigeunerin/ wer rief dich denn?/ wie lange schon/ wohl kenn' ich euren stand/
ich hab' in penna/ verborgenheit/ mausfallensprüchlein/ in dem schatten meiner locken

22 june 1966/divonne
liederabend
pianist geoffrey parsons

30 june 1966/lyon
liederabend
pianist geoffrey parsons

7 july 1966/new york
participation in concert
conductor lukas foss

13 july 1966/new yotk
liederabend
pianist john wustman

16 july 1966/middlesboro
liederabend
pianist geoffrey parsons

23 july 1966/baalbek
liederabend

25 july 1966/istanbul
liederabend

30 july 1966/vichy
participation in concert
conductor louis de froment

3 august 1966/nice
participation in concert

7 august 1966/chichester festival theatre
liederabend
pianist martin isepp
> *schubert an die musik/ das lied im grünen/ an sylvia/ der vollmond strahlt/ der einsame/*
> *an mein klavier/ liebe schwärmt auf allen wegen*
> *schumann mein schöner stern/ leis' rudern her/ wenn durch die piazetta/ widmung*
> *strauss ruhe meine seele/ muttertändelei/ meinem kinde/ hat gesagt bleibt's nicht dabei/*
> *schlechtes wetter*
> *wolf kennst du das land?/ als ich auf dem euphrat schiffte/ in dem schatten meiner locken/*
> *mein liebster ist so klein/ die zigeunerin*
> *schubert seligkeit/ strauss zueignung*

14 august 1966/harrogate
liederabend
pianist martin isepp

24 august 1966/oostende
liederabend
pianist joerg demus

26 august 1966/ghent
liederabend

31 august 1966/edinburgh
liederabend

5 september 1966/stresa
liederabend
pianist joerg demus

7 september 1966/sankt gallen
liederabend
pianist martin isepp

1 october 1966/montreux
*bamberg symphony orchestra concert
with works by mozart and strauss
conductor antal dorati

5 october 1966/hamburg
liederabend
pianist martin isepp

18 october 1966/madrid
liederabend
pianist martin isepp

20 october 1966/las palmas
liederabend
pianist martin isepp

24 october 1966/paris théatre des champs-élysées
liederabend
pianist martin isepp

2 november 1966/stockholm
*strauss der rosenkavalier/marschallin
conductor silvio varviso
other principals included söderströn/ dobbs/ tyren/ sundquist
further performance on 5 november 1966

20 november 1966/brussels théatre de la monnaie
mozart cosi fan tutte/fiordiligi
conductor dimitri chorofas
further performances on 23 and 26 november 1966 and 1 december 1966

8 december 1966/barcelona teatro del liceo
strauss der rosenkavalier/marschallin
conductor richard kraus
other principals included naaf/ deutekom/ freedman/ engels
further performances on 10 and 12 december 1966

20 january 1967/zürich tonhalle
liederabend
pianist martin isepp
schwarzkopf replaced teresa berganza for this recital

27 january 1967/salzburg grosses festspielhaus
vienna philharmonic orchestra concert with works by mozart
conductor berislav klobucar

10 february 1967/rome santa cecilia
liederabend
pianist giorgio favaretto

20 february 1967/london royal festival hall
*recital in homage to gerald moore with victoria de los angeles and dietrich fischer-dieskau
pianist gerald moore
    mozart la partenza/ piu non si trovano/ caro bell' idol mio
    rossini la regata veneziana/ la pesca/ duetto buffo di due gatti
    schumann in der nacht/ unterm fenster/ ich denke dein/ liebhabers ständchen/ tanzlied/
    er und sie
    wolf kennst du das land?/ sonne der schlummerlosen/ wer rief dich denn?/ das
    verlassene mägdlein/ die zigeunerin
    haydn an den vetter/ daphnens einziger fehler/ mozart soave sia il vento

6 march 1967/chicago	8 march 1967/muskogee
liederabend	**liederabend**
pianist martin isepp	pianist martin isepp
11 march 1967/new orleans	14 march 1967/denton
liederabend	**liederabend**
pianist martin isepp	pianist martin isepp

18 march 1967/new york hunter college
liederabend
pianist martin isepp

4 april 1967/new york carnegie hall
*gluck orfeo ed euridice/euridice *concert performance*
conductor jonel perlea
other principals included popp/ fischer-dieskau
further performance on 7 april 1967

9 april 1967/miami
participation in concert
concert repeated on 11 april 1967

15 april 1967/los angeles
liederabend

20 april 1967/stockholm
liederabend

23 april 1967/oslo
liederabend

25 april 1967/copenhagen
liederabend

27 april 1967/bergen
participation in concert

2 may 1967/lancaster
liederabend
pianist geoffrey parsons

6 may 1967/london royal festival hall
liederabend
pianist geoffrey parsons
> *schumann maria-stuart-lieder/ lied der suleika/ die kartenlegerin*
> *mussorgsky sternlein/ die pilze*
> *tchaikovsky nur wer die sehnsucht kennt/ pimpinella*
> *rachmaninov to the children/ vor meinem fenster*
> *stravinsky pastorale*
> *strauss die heiligen drei könige/ all mein gedanken/ ruhe meine seele/ wiegenliedchen/ muttertändelei/ morgen*
> *wolf das verlassene mägdlein/ köpfchen köpfchen nicht gewimmert/ trau nicht der liebe/ wenn du zu den blumen gehst/ in dem schatten meiner locken/ wer tat deinem füsslein weh?*
> *strauss meinem kinde/ schubert seligkeit*

18 may 1967/paris théatre des champs-élysées
liederabend
pianist geoffrey parsons

22 may 1967/bordeaux
liederabend
pianist geoffrey parsons

26 may 1967/brescia
liederabend

7 june 1967/paris
participation in concert
conductor berislav klobucar

5 july 1967/cincinnati
strauss der rosenkavalier/marschallin
further performance on 9 july 1967

15 july-14 september 1967/australia, new zealand and hong kong
the tour comprised lieder recitals with geoffrey parsons in melbourne, adelaide, perth, newcastle, sydney, canberra, brisbane, auckland, christchurch, wellington and hong kong, an orchestral concert in sydney and a television appearance in melbourne

6 october 1967/ascona gemeindeschule
liederabend
pianist geoffrey parsons
>*mozart abendempfindung/ das veilchen/ warnung/ ich möchte wohl der kaiser sein*
>*schubert der einsame/ an sylvia/ der vollmond strahlt*
>*schumann wie mit innigstem behagen/ leis' rudern her/ wenn durch die piazetta/*
>*der nussbaum/ die kartenlegerin*
>*wolf kennst du das land?/ das verlassene mägdlein/ in dem schatten meiner locken/*
>*trau nicht der liebe/ wie lange schon/ die zigeunerin*
>*schubert seligkeit/ wolf-ferrari preghiera*

13 october 1967/london royal festival hall
washington national symphony orchestra concert
strauss songs with orchestra
conductor howard mitchell
>*ruhe meine seele/ die heiligen drei könige/ meinem kinde/ muttertändelei/ morgen*

15 october 1967/london royal opera house
gala performance for bbc television
*verdi willow song and ave maria/otello
conductor edward downes

17 october 1967/birmingham
liederabend
pianist geoffrey parsons

8 november 1967/turin conservatorio
liederabend
pianist geoffrey parsons

10 november 1967/rome
liederabend
pianist geoffrey parsons

15 november 1967/paris
liederabend
pianist geoffrey parsons

19-20 november 1967/brussels
participation in concert
conductor thomas schippers

24 november 1967/lyon opéra de lyon
strauss der rosenkavalier/marschallin
conductor hans gierster
further performance on 26 november 1967

1 december 1967/barcelona
participation in concert
conductor antoni ros-marba

8 december 1967/budapest
liederabend
pianist geoffrey parsons

19 december 1967/amsterdam concertgebouw
kunstmaand orchestra concert with arias by mozart, smetana and puccini
conductor anton kersjes

24 december 1967/brussels théatre de la monnaie
strauss der rosenkavalier/marschallin
conductor richard kraus
other principals included sarroca/ arnaud/ langdon
further performances on 27 and 31 december 1968

5 january 1968/pittsburgh
pittsburgh symphony orchestra concert with works by mahler
conductor william steinberg
concert repeated in pittsburgh on 7 january 1968 and in new york on 15 january 1968

10 january 1968/minneapolis
liederabend
pianist geoffrey parsons

21 january 1968/chicago
liederabend
pianist geoffrey parsons

25 january 1968/detroit
detroit symphony orchestra concert with works by verdi and strauss
conductor sixten ehrling
concert repeated on 27 january 1968

31 january 1968/saskatoon
liederabend

3 february 1968/calgary
liederabend

6 february 1968/edmonton
liederabend

10 february 1968/winnipeg
liederabend

12 february 1968/seattle
liederabend

18 february 1968/new york
liederabend

21 february 1968/baltimore
concert with works by mozart and strauss
conductor kurt herbert adler

22 february 1968/bainbridge
concert with works by mozart and strauss
conductor kurt herbert adler

24 february 1968/texas university
liederabend

26 february 1968/el paso
liederabend

29 february 1968/baton rouge
liederabend

7 march 1968/london royal festival hall
london symphony orchestra concert
mahler des knaben wunderhorn
conductor george szell
other soloist was fischer-dieskau/concert repeated on 10 march 1968

18 march 1968/cardiff
liederabend
pianist geoffrey parsons

20 march 1968/monmouth
liederabend
pianist geoffrey parsons

22 march 1968/london bbc television studios
***liederabend**
pianist gerald moore
> *schubert an die musik/ gluck einem bach der fliesset/ mozart warnung/ ich möchte wohl*
> *der kaiser sein/ schubert seligkeit/ an sylvia/ schumann der nussbaum*
> *brahms vergebliches ständchen/ da unten im tale/ mahler lob des hohen verstandes*
> *wolf das verlassene mägdlein/ in dem schatten meiner locken/ strauss morgen/*
> *hat gesagt bleibt's nicht dabei/ anon drink to me only*

26 march 1968/milan
liederabend
pianist geoffrey parsons

5 april-2 may 1968/japan
*this tour comprised lieder recitals with geoffrey parsons in tokyo, sapporo, yokohama,
osaka and fukuoka*

12 may 1968/stockholm
participation in concert
conductor stig westerberg

16 may 1968/copenhagen
participation in concert
pianist robert levin

21 may 1968/oslo
participation in concert

23 may 1968/tunis
liederabend
pianist robert levin

14 july 1968/washington
concert of viennese operetta
conductor willi boskovsky

16 july 1968/ravinnia
concert of viennese operetta
conductor willi boskovsky

19 july 1968/philadelphia
liederabend
pianist john wustman

21 july 1968/philadelphia
participation in concert

26 july 1968/cleveland
cleveland orchestra concert
strauss 4 letzte lieder
conductor george szell

28 july 1968/cleveland
cleveland orchestra concert
with works by mozart and mahler
conductor george szell

12 august 1968/rio de janeiro
liederabend
pianist geoffrey parsons

15 august 1968/buenos aires
liederabend
pianist geoffrey parsons
recital repeated on 18 and 21 august 1968

31 august 1968/lucques
liederabend
pianist viola tunnard

4 september 1968/saint-jean-de-luz
liederabend
pianist viola tunnard

13 september 1968/glasgow
liederabend
pianist geoffrey parsons

15 october 1968/liverpool
liederabend
pianist geoffrey parsons

17 october 1968/bournemouth
bournemouth symphony orchestra
**strauss 5 songs with orchestra
verdi willow song and
ave maria/otello**
conductor constantin silvestri

30 october 1968/lisbon
liederabend
pianist geoffrey parsons

6 november 1968/turin
liederabend
pianist geoffrey parsons

10 november 1968/perugia
liederabend
pianist geoffrey parsons

13 november 1968/paris
liederabend
pianist geoffrey parsons

19 november 1968/rome
liederabend
recital repeated on 22 november 1968

24 november 1968/wiesbaden
liederabend

2 december 1968/london royal festival hall
concert in memory of ernest newman
*liederabend
pianist geoffrey parsons
> wolf was für ein lied soll dir gesungen werden?/ im frühling/ phänomen/ wandl' ich in dem morgentau/ kennst du das land?
> schubert suleika I-II/ gretchen am spinnrade
> wolf wiegenlied im sommer/ anakreons grab/ die zigeunerin
> strauss 3 ophelia-lieder/ meinem kinde/ das rosenband/ ach was kummer
> wolf sagt seid ihr es feiner herr?/ in dem schatten meiner locken/ ach im maien war's/ o wär dein haus durchsichtig/ nein junger herr/ wir haben beide lange zeit geschwiegen/ wer rief dich denn?
> strauss muttertändelei/ schubert seligkeit

6 december 1968/hilversum
radio filharmonisch orkest concert
with works by mozart, strauss and verdi
conductor paul hupperts

17 december 1968/luxembourg
liederabend

2 february 1969/new york
liederabend
pianist geoffrey parsons

4 february 1969/waynesford
liederabend

7 february 1969/charlotte
liederabend

8 february 1969/new york
liederabend

10-11 february 1969/nashville
participation in concert

15 february 1969/urbana
participation in concert

17 february 1969/chicago
participation in concert

18 february 1969/cedar falls
liederabend
pianist geoffrey parsons
recital repeated on 21 february 1969

25 february 1969/springfield
liederabend

28 february 1969/naperville
liederabend

2 march 1969/chicago
liederabend

6 march 1969/appleton
liederabend

10 march 1969/stevens point
liederabend

14 march 1969/grand rapids
liederabend

17 march 1969/uplands
liederabend

21-22 march 1969/cincinnati
participation in concert

12 april 1969/budapest
liederabend
pianist geoffrey parsons
recital repeated on 14 april 1969

21 april 1969/rotterdam
liederabend
pianist geoffrey parsons

23 april 1969/amsterdam
liederabend
pianist geoffrey parsons

26 april 1969/utrecht geertekerk
***liederabend**
pianist geoffrey parsons

5 may 1969/brussels
liederabend

10 may 1969/luxembourg
liederabend

13 may 1969/paris
liederabend

23 may 1969/prague
liederabend

12-13 june 1969/gothenburg
participation in concert
conductor stig westerberg

19 june 1969/birmingham
liederabend

22 june 1969/york
liederabend

29 june 1969/nohant
***liederabend**
pianist aldo ciccolini
    *schubert der einsame/ der vollmond strahlt/ an sylvia/ schumann suleika/ der nussbaum
liszt die 3 zigeuner/ es muss ein wunderbares sein/ chopin 4 polish songs
wolf kennst du das land?/ wenn du zu den blumen gehst/ in dem schatten meiner locken/
die zigeunerin
strauss ruhe meine seele/ meinem kinde/ morgen/ hat gesagt bleibt's nicht dabei
mozart ich möchte wohl der kaiser sein/ strauss ach was kummer/ schubert seligkeit*

26 july 1969/los angeles
hollywood bowl concert
conductor anton paulik

29 july 1969/los angeles
hollywood bowl concert
conductor sixten ehrling

3 august 1969/ravinnia
participation in concert
conductor franz allers

10 august 1969/columbia
participation in concert
conductor franz allers

13 august 1969/washington
participation in concert
conductor franz allers

17 august 1969/stratford
liederabend
pianist john wustman

20 august 1969/ottawa
liederabend
pianist john wustman

23-24 august 1969/rochester
participation in concert
conductor sixten ehrling

26-28 august 1969/montreal
canadian television recordings

25 september 1969/london
royal festival hall
london symphony orchestra concert
*strauss 4 letzte lieder
conductor sir john barbirolli
concert repeated on 28 september 1969

29 september 1969/whitehaven
liederabend
pianist brian lamport

2 october 1969/birmingham
participation in concert
conductor louis frémaux

6 october 1969/frankfurt-am-main
liederabend
pianist geoffrey parsons

10 october 1969/marseille
liederabend
pianist geoffrey parsons

20 october 1969/london royal festival hall
liederabend
pianist geoffrey parsons
    haydn un tetto umil/ gluck einem bach der fliesset
    mozart der zauberer/ ich möchte wohl der kaiser sein
    schubert der musensohn/ der vollmond strahlt/ das lied im grünen
    schumann suleika/ der nussbaum/ die kartenlegerin
    wagner träume/ chopin maidem's wish/ handsome boy
    liszt es muss ein wunderbares sein/ die drei zigeuner
    strauss die nacht/ schlechtes wetter
    wolf wer rief dich denn?/ mein liebster ist so klein/ ihr jungen leute/ mein liebster singt/
    ich esse nun mein brot/ ich hab' in penna/ nun lass uns frieden schliessen
    strauss ach was kummer/ schubert seligkeit

16 november 1969/new york
liederabend

19 november 1969/minneapolis
liederabend

23 november 1969/philadelphia
liederabend

25 november 1969/akton
liederabend

30 november 1969/boston
liederabend

1 december 1969/fort lauderdale
liederabend

3 december 1969/tampa
liederabend

12 december 1969/rome
liederabend

16 december 1969/amsterdam concertgebouw
kunstmaand orchestra concert
strauss 4 letzte lieder
conductor anton kersjes

17 january-13 february 1970/japan
this tour consisted of lieder recitals with geoffrey parsons in tokyo, osaka, fukuoka, hiroshima, kobe, nagoya and sapporo

15 february 1970/toronto
television concert with
john newmark and martin rich
concert repeated on 22 february 1970

19 february 1970/pasadena
liederabend

26 february 1970/san antonio
participation in concert
concert repeated on 28 february 1970

3 march 1970/ashville
liederabend

8 march 1970/chicago
liederabend

14 march 1970/naples
liederabend

17 march 1970/fort myers
liederabend

21 march 1970/washington
liederabend

12 may 1970/paris théatre
des champs-élysées
liederabend
pianist geoffrey parsons

28 may 1970/zagreb
liederabend

1 june 1970/belgrade
liederabend

6 june 1970/strassburg
participation in concert with works by mozart

15 june 1970/lyon opéra
liederabend
pianist brian lamport

4 july 1970/tours grange de meslay
liederabend
pianist brian lamport

12 august 1970/gothenburg
participation in concert
conductor okko kamu

11 september 1970/stresa
liederabend
pianist geoffrey parsons

17 october 1969/london royal fesrival hall
liederabend
pianist geoffrey parsons
> schubert an sylvia/ suleika I-II/ hänflings liebeswerbung/ das lied im grünen
> brahms wie melodien zieht es mir/ immer leiser wird mein schlummer
> loewe kleiner haushalt/ liszt die drei zigeuner/ mahler um schlimme kinder artig zu machen
> grieg letzter frühling/ mit einer wasserlilie/ lauf der welt
> wolf ach im maien war's/ lebewohl/ wandl' ich in dem morgentau/ sagt seid ihr es
> strauss meinem kinde/ muttertändelei/ morgen/ zueignung
> brahms vergebliches ständchen/ wiegenlied/ wolf kennst du das land?/
> strauss ach was kummer

20 october 1970/dublin
liederabend
pianist geoffrey parsons

24 october 1970/elstree haberdashers school
liederabend
pianist geoffrey parsons
> mozart abendempfindung/ gluck einem bach der fliesset/ mozart das veilchen/ ich möchte
> wohl der kaiser sein
> schubert der einsame/ der vollmond strahlt/ an sylvia
> schumann suleika/ der nussbaum/ die kartenlegerin
> wolf kennst du das land?/ das verlassene mägdlein/ in dem schatten meiner locken/
> die zigeunerin
> mahler um schlimme kinder artig zu machen
> strauss meinem kinde/ muttertändelei/ morgen/ ach was kummer/ zueignung
> anon gsätzli

27 october 1970/birmingham
liederabend
pianist geoffrey parsons

3-29 november 1970/south africa
this tour consisted of lieder recitals with geoffrey parsons in pretoria, johannesburg, stellenbosch, bloemfontein, cape town and durham

9 december 1970/budapest
liederabend
pianist geoffrey parsons

14 december 1970/budapest
participation in concert
conductor janos ferencsik

11 january 1971/bologna
liederabend
pianist geoffrey parsons

15 january 1971/rome
liederabend
pianist geoffrey parsons

20 january 1971/turin
liederabend
pianist geoffrey parsons

26-27 january 1971/washington
washington national symphony orchestra
strauss 4 letzte lieder
conductor antal dorati

5-6 february 1971/louisville
louisville orchestra concert
*strauss 4 letzte lieder
conductor jorge mester

9 february 1971/saint cloud
liederabend
pianist john wustman

12 february 1971/toronto
participation in concert
conductor martin turnovsky

15 february 1971/urbana
liederabend

18-19 february 1971/indianapolis
participation in concert
conductor izler solomon

24 april-6 june 1971/new zealand, australia and hong kong
this tour consisted of an orchestral concert in wellington and lieder recitals with geoffrey parsons in wellington, auckland, canberra, adelaide, melbourne, sydney, brisbane and hong kong

30 june 1971/versailles
liederabend
pianist aldo ciccolini

16 july 1971/carcassonne
liederabend
pianist aldo ciccolini

19 july 1971/provence
liederabend
pianist aldo ciccolini

31 july 1971/barcelona
liederabend
pianist miguel zanetti

5 august 1971/cervo
liederabend

8 august 1971/monte-carlo
participation in concert

13 august 1971/dubrovnik
liederabend
pianist geoffrey parsons

20 august 1971/turku
liederabend
pianist robert levin

6 september 1971/saint-jean-de-luz
liederabend
pianist geoffrey parsons

21 september 1971/claydon
liederabend
pianist geoffrey parsons

25 september 1971/aldeburgh
liederabend
pianist geoffrey parsons

28 september 1971/windsor waterloo chamber
liederabend
pianist geoffrey parsons
> schubert ellens gesänge I-III/ brahms der jäger/ immer leiser wird mein schlummer/
> da unten im tale/ vergebliches ständchen
> liszt die drei zigeuner/ mahler ich atmet' einen linden duft/ loewe kleiner haushalt
> wolf kennst du das land?/ gesegnet sei das grün/ wie lange schon/ die zigeunerin
> strauss ruhe meine seele/ muttertändelei/ morgen/ ach was kummer/ zueignung

1 october 1971/brighton dome
liederabend
pianist geoffrey parsons
> schubert an sylvia/ suleika I-II/ das lied im grünen
> schumann die kartenlegerin/ der nussbaum/ brahms vergebliches ständchen/
> liszt die drei zigeuner/ mahler ich atmet' einen londen duft/ loewe kleiner haushalt
> wolf kennst du das land?/ das verlassene mägdlein/ die zigeunerin
> strauss meinem kinde/ muttertändelei/ morgen/ ach was kummer/ zueignung
> wolf wer rief dich denn?/ wie lange schon/ du denkst mit einem fädchen/ ich hab' in penna

6 october 1971/saint helens
liederabend

9 october 1971/york
liederabend

12 october 1971/swansea
liederabend

16 october 1971/london royal festival hall
liederabend
pianist geoffrey parsons
> schubert ellens gesänge I-III/ brahms der jäger/ immer leiser wird mein schlummer/ ständchen
> wolf goethe-lieder: mignon I-III/ philine/ kennst du das land?
> mahler das irdische leben/ ich stmet' einen linden duft/ rheinlegendchen/ loewe kleiner haushalt
> wolf italienisches liederbuch: was soll der zorn?/ ich esse nun mein brot/ wie lange schon/
> gesegnet sei das grün/ wer rief dich denn?/ ich hab' in penna
> strauss meinem kinde/ muttertändelei

21 october 1971/lancaster
liederabend

24 october 1971/glasgow
liederabend

27 october 1971/dublin
liederabend

31 october 1971/manchester free trade hall
*hallé orchestra concert in memory of
sir john barbirolli*
**strauss 5 songs with orchestra
verdi willow song and ave maria/otello**
conductor james loughran

4 november 1971/strassburg
liederabend

12 november 1971/paris opéra
liederabend
pianist geoffrey parsons

17 november 1971/madrid
liederabend
pianist nadia gedda-nova

23 november 1971/ivrea
liederabend
pianist geoffrey parsons

26 november 1971/rome
liederabend
pianist geoffrey parsons

17 december 1971/brussels théatre de la monnaie
**strauss 5 songs with orchestra
strauss der rosenkavalier act one/**marschallin
conductor george sébastian
*other principals included martin/ferro/mazura
further performances on 19, 22, 26, 28 and 31 december 1971*

24 january-20 february 1972/japan
this tour consisted of lieder recitals with geoffrey parsons in nagoya, tokyo, osaka, kyoto and yokohama

3 march 1972/vancouver
liederabend

7 march 1972/san francisco
liederabend

12 march 1972/new orleans
liederabend

15 march 1972/burlington
liederabend

19 march 1972/new york
liederabend

22 march 1972/dayton
concert with works by mozart and strauss

25 march 1972/indianapolis
participation in concert

28 april 1972/aldeburgh
liederabend
pianist geoffrey parsons

1 may 1972/portsmouth
liederabend
pianist geoffrey parsons

4 may 1972/paris
liederabend
pianist geoffrey parsons

8 may 1972/london camden town hall
liederabend
pianist geoffrey parsons
> *schubert ellens gesänge I-II/ an sylvia*
> *wolf spanisches liederbuch: mühvoll komm' ich und beladen/ trau nicht der liebe/ köpfchen*
> *köpfchen nicht gewimmert/ geh geliebter geh jetzt!*
> *liszt die drei zigeuner/ schumann die kartenlegerin/ loewe kleiner haushalt*
> *mahler ich atmet' einen linden duft/ rheinlegendchen*
> *strauss meinem kinde/ muttertändelei/ ach was kummer/ zueignung*
> *wolf italienisches liederbuch: wer rief dich denn?/ wie lange schon/ schweig' einmal still/*
> *wohl kenn' ich euren stand/ nein junger herr/ ich esse nun mein brot/ ich hab' in penna*

31 may 1972/vienna musikverein
liederabend
pianist geoffrey parsons

13 june 1972/geneva
liederabend
pianist brian lamport

15 june 1972/toulon
liederabend
pianist brian lamport

19-20 june 1972/paris
participation in concert
conductor lorin maazel

22 june 1972/versailles
liederabend
pianist aldo ciccolini

24 june 1972/sens
liederabend
pianist aldo ciccolini

1 october 1972/newcastle-upon-tyne
liederabend
pianist geoffrey parsons

5 october 1972/southport
liederabend
pianist geoffrey parsons

11 october 1972/breda
television concert with works by mozart,
mahler, strauss and wolf
conductor jean fournet

21 october 1972/london royal festival hall
liederabend
pianist geoffrey parsons
> *schubert wehmut/ die sterne/ die liebe hat gelogen/ erntelied*
> *strauss die georgine/ heimkehr/ wiegenliedchen/ hat gesagt bleibt's nicht dabei/*
> *mahler des antonius von padua fischpredigt/ rheinlegendchen/ um schlimme*
> *kinder artig zu machen*
> *wolf an eine äolsharfe/ auf einer wanderung/ das verlassene mägdlein/ begegnung/*
> *heimweh/ geh geliebter geh jetzt!/ trau nicht der liebe/ du sagst mir dass ich keine*
> *fürstin sei/ schweig einmal still/ nein junger herr/ das köhlerweib ist trunken/*
> *ich esse nun mein brot/ wie lange schon/ ich hab' in penna*
> *strauss ach was kummer/ zueignung/ anon gsätzli*

27 october 1972/birmingham town hall
liederabend
pianist geoffrey parsons

10 november 1972/columbus
liederabend

14 november 1972/tucson
liederabend

18 november 1972/pasadena
liederabend

22 november 1972/cupertino
liederabend

25 november 1972/london ontario
liederabend

28 november 1972/towson
liederabend

3 december 1972/new york
liederabend

6 december 1972/oakland
liederabend

9 december 1972/washington
liederabend

3 january 1973/london royal opera house
participation in gala performance marking britain's entry into the european community
wolf kennst du das land?/orchestral version
conductor colin davis

5 january 1973/salisbury
liederabend
pianist geoffrey parsons

8 january 1973/trieste
liederabend
pianist geoffrey parsons

25 january 1973/paris
liederabend
pianist geoffrey parsons

28 january 1973/manchester
royal philharmonic orchestra concert
conductor sir charles groves

1 february 1973/croydon fairfield halls
liederabend
pianist geoffrey parsons

schubert an sylvia/ das lied im grünen/ gretchen am spinnrade/ schumann suleika
brahms immer leiser wird mein schlummer/ vergebliches ständchen/ liszt die drei zigeuner
grieg mit einer wasserlilie/ mahler um schlimme kinder artig zu machen
wolf auf einer wanderung/ philine/ kennst du das land?
strauss meinem kinde/ muttertändelei/ morgen/ ach was kummer/ zueignung
wolf mein liebster ist so klein/ nein junger herr/ wie lange schon/ ich hab' in penna

5 february 1973/lyon
liederabend
pianist brian lamport

6 february 1973/rueil-malmaison
liederabend
pianist brian lamport

10 february 1973/angers
liederabend

15 february 1973/basel
liederabend

19 february-3 march 1973/far east
this tour consisted of lieder recitals with geoffrey parsons in seoul, taechon and hong kong

18 march 1973/bludenz
liederabend

11 may 1973/rome
liederabend
pianist geoffrey parsons

14 may 1973/messina
liederabend
pianist geoffrey parsons

24 may 1973/paris théatre des champs-élysées
liederabend
pianist geoffrey parsons

27 may 1973/prague
liederabend
pianist geoffrey parsons

27 june 1973/scheveningen circustheater
liederabend
pianist geoffrey parsons
    schubert an die musik/ das lied im grünen/ an sylvia
    schumann suleika/ hochländers abschied/ hochländisches wiegenlied/ der nussbaum/
    die kartenlegerin
    brahms ständchen/ immer leiser wird mein schlummer/ vergebliches ständchen
    wolf kennst du das land?/ philine/ keine gleicht von allen schönen/ die zigeunerin
    strauss meinem kinde/ muttertändelei/ morgen/ hat gesagt bleibt's nicht dabei

20 july 1973/vichy
liederabend

25 august 1973/geneva
participation in concert with yehudi menuhin and nikita magaloff

8 september 1973/saint-jean-de-luz
liederabend
pianist aldo ciccolini

15 september 1973/chateau de veves
liederabend
pianist aldo ciccolini

28 september 1973/barcelona
liederabend
pianist brian lamport

2 october 1973/alicante
liederabend
pianist brian lamport

11 october 1973/northampton
liederabend
pianist brian lamport

14 october 1973/sutton granada cinema
liederabend
pianist brian lamport
> *schubert an sylvia/ suleika I-II/ erntelied*
> *brahms ständchen/ immer leiser wird mein schlummer/ salamander*
> *liszt die drei zigeuner/ grieg mit einer wasserlilie/ mahler um schlimme kinder artig zu machen*
> *strauss 3 ophelis-lieder/ meinem kinde/ hat gesagt bleibt's nicht dabei*
> *wolf kennst du das land?/ philine/ in dem schatten meiner locken/ auf einer wanderung/ auftrag*
> *strauss zueignung/ brahms vergebliches ständchen*

19 october 1973/cambridge
liederabend
pianist brian lamport

21 october 1973/hemel hempstead
liederabend
pianist brian lamport

16 november 1973/munich
liederabend
pianist geoffrey parsons

20 november 1973/london
private recital in hyde park hotel
pianist gerald moore

24 november 1973/london royal festival hall
liederabend
pianist geoffrey parsons
> *schubert an sylvia/ suleika I-II/ gretchen am spinnrade*
> *schumann suleika/ der nussbaum/ die kartenlegerin/ brahms immer leiser wird mein schlummer/*
> *salamander/ liszt die drei zigeuner/ grieg mit einer wasserlilie/ mahler des antonius von padua*
> *fischpredigt*
> *wolf an eine äolsharfe/ denk es o seele/ sonne der schlummerlosen/ keine gleicht von allen schönen*
> *strauss morgen/ meinem kinde/ muttertändelei*
> *wolf mein liebster ist so klein/ ihr jungen leute/ mein liebster hat zu tische mich geladen/*
> *ich hab' in penna/ ich esse nun mein brot/ philine/ nun lass uns frieden schliessen*

28 november 1973/nottingham
liederabend
pianist geoffrey parsons

2 december 1973/bucarest
liederabend
pianist geoffrey parsons

9 december 1973/innsbruck
liederabend
pianist geoffrey parsons

12 december 1973/turin conservatorio
liederabend
pianist geoffrey parsons

17 december 1973/naples
liederabend
pianist geoffrey parsons

18 january 1974/lisbon
liederabend
pianist brian lamport

24 january 1974/hull
liederabend

30 january 1974/new haven
liederabend

1 february 1974/torrance ca
liederabend

3 february 1974/chicago
liederabend

7 february 1974/toronto
liederabend

11 february 1974/lake oxford
liederabend

14 february 1974/appleton
liederabend

17 february 1974/carlisle
liederabend

20 february 1974/glasboro
liederabend

25 february 1974/fulton chapel
liederabend

28 february 1974/palm beach
liederabend

2 march 1974/wankiegan
liederabend

5 march 1974/philadelphia
liederabend

8 march 1974/ames iowa
liederabend

11 march 1974/lawrence
liederabend

29 march 1974/linz
liederabend

29 april 1974/trieste
liederabend

8 may 1974/hemel hempstead
liederabend

11-15 june 1974/paris théatre de la ville
series of five lieder recitals with brian lamport

29 june 1974/nohant
liederabend

5 july 1974/istanbul
liederabend

29 july 1974/aix-en-provence
liederabend

31 july 1974/bournemouth
liederabend

2 august 1974/middlesbrough
liederabend

26-27 august 1974/groningen
liederabend

20 september 1974/bucarest
liederabend
recital repeated on 23 september 1974

26 september 1974/croydon fairfield halls
liederabend
pianist geoffrey parsons
> *schubert frühlingsglaube/ frühlingssehnsucht/ der lindenbaum/ erntelied*
> *schumann widmung/ der nussbaum/ die kartenlegerin*
> *brahms da unten im tale/ wie melodien zieht es/ och modr ich well en ding han*
> *wolf das verlassene mägdlein/ elfenlied/ verborgenheit/ wie glänzt der helle mond/*
> *wandl' ich in dem morgentau/ das köhlerweib ist trunken/ ich hab' in penna*
> *strauss 3 ophelia-lieder/ zueignung/ mozart warnung*

3 october 1974/eastbourne congress theatre
liederabend
pianist geoffrey parsons

6 october 1974/harlow
liederabend
pianist geoffrey parsons

12 october 1974/london royal festival hall
liederabend
pianist geoffrey parsons
> *schubert frühlingsglaube/ frühlingssehnsucht/ der lindenbaum/ der leiermann*
> *schumann wehmut/ waldesgespräch/ der nussbaum*
> *wolf geh geliebter geh jetzt/ trau nicht der liebe/ wandl' ich in dem morgentau/ das verlassene*
> *mägdlein/ kennst du das land?/ philine/ wohl kenn' ich euren stand/ mein liebster singt/*
> *wie lange schon/ du sagst mir dass ich keine fürstin sei/ nein junger herr/ ich hab' in penna*
> *strauss ach was kummer/ schubert seligkeit*

17 october 1974/frankfurt-main
liederabend
pianist geoffrey parsons

20 october 1974/cologne
liederabend
pianist geoffrey parsons

25 october 1974/paris
liederabend
pianist geoffrey parsons

29 october 1974/berlin
liederabend
pianist geoffrey parsons

12 november-10 december 1974/japan
this tour consisted of lieder recitals with geoffrey parsons in tokyo, chibu, sendai, tachiwaka, osaka and fujisawa

15 january 1975/santa barbara
liederabend

18 january 1975/vancouver
liederabend

22 january 1975/seattle
liederabend

26 january 1975/berkeley
liederabend

1 february 1975/los angeles
liederabend

9 february 1975.chicago
liederabend

16 february 1975/new orleans
liederabend

3 march 1975/minneapolis
liederabend

6 march 1975/toronto
liederabend

11 march 1975/new orleans
liederabend

13 march 1975/halifax
liederabend

16 march 1975/towson
liederabend

18 march 1975/new york
liederabend

25 march 1975/atlanta
liederabend

1 april 1975/philadelphia
liederabend

5 april 1975/ottawa
liederabend

7 april 1975/montreal
liederabend

10 april 1975/newark
liederabend

17 april 1975/detroit
liederabend
recital repeated on 19 april 1975

21 april 1975/wellesley
liederabend

27 april 1975/new york
liederabend
recital repeated on 29 april 1975

10 may 1975/milan
liederabend

2 august 1975/monte-carlo
liederabend
pianist brian lamport

26 august 1975/bregenz
liederabend

29 august 1975/villach
liederabend

20 september 1975/stockholm
liederabend
pianist geoffrey parsons

23 september 1975/gothenburg
liederabend

2 october 1975/manchester
liederabend

156
5 october 1975/leeds 9 october 1975/cambridge
liederabend **liederabend**
pianist geoffrey parsons pianist geoffrey parsons

13 october 1975/birminghan
liederabend
pianist geoffrey parsons

18 october 1975/london royal festival hall
liederabend hugo wolf
pianist geoffrey parsons
> *bescheidene liebe/ mörike-lieder: im frühling/ denk es o seele/ heimweh*
> *die zigeunerin/ goethe-lieder: ganymed/ phänomen/ als ich auf dem euphrat schiffte/*
> *philine*
> *wie glänzt der helle mond/ das köhlerweib ist trunken*
> *spanisches liederbuch: geh geliebter geh jrtzt/ bedeckt mich mit blumen/ herr was trägt*
> *der boden hier?/ trau nicht der liebe*
> *italienisches liederbuch: du sagst mir dass ich keine fürstin sei/ o wär dein haus durchsichtig/*
> *wie lange schon/ ich esse nun mein brot/ ich hab' in penna*
> *wandl' ich in dem morgentau/ du denkst mit einem fädchen/ nein junger herr/ kennst du*
> *das land?*

22 october 1975/eastbourne congress theatre
liederabend
pianist geoffrey parsons
> *schubert an die musik/ der lindenbaum/ die forelle/ an sylvia*
> *schumann der nussbaum/ die kartenlegerin*
> *brahms da unten im tale/ vergebliches ständchen/ liszt die drei zigeuner*
> *grieg ich liebe dich/ mit einer wasserlilie/ strauss meinem kinde/ muttertändelei/ morgen*
> *wolf heimweh/ wie glänzt der helle mond/ philine/ du sagst mir dass ich keine fürstin sei/*
> *wie lange schon/ ich esse nun mein brot/ ich hab' in penna*
> *schubert seligkeit/ strauss ach was kummer*

25 october 1975/florence
liederabend
pianist geoffrey parsons

2 november 1975/london royal opera house
liederabend
pianist geoffrey parsons
schwarzkopf replaced victoria de los angeles for this recital
> schubert suleika I-II/ der lindenbaum/ gretchen am spinnrade
> schumann der nussbaum/ die kartenlegerin/ brahms da unten im tale/ vergebliches ständchen
> liszt die drei zigeuner/ grieg mit einer wasserlilie/ mahler des antonius von padua fischpredigt
> wolf kennst du das land?/ heimweh/ wie glänzt der helle mond/ philine/ strauss 3 ophelia-lieder
> wolf trau nicht der liebe/ das verlassene mägdlein/ ich esse nun mein brot/ ich hab' in penna/
> wie lange schon
> schubert seligkeit/ strauss zueignung

10-28 november 1975/paris
series of six themed recitals
pianist geoffrey parsons

16 february 1976/milan
liederabend
pianist geoffrey parsons

29 april 1976/brussels
liederabend
pianist geoffrey parsons

8 may 1976/bordeaux
liederabend
pianist graham johnson

31 may 1976
recital on cruise ship

3 june 1976/helsinki
liederabend

12 june 1976/london wigmore hall
themed recital as part of the wigmore hall seventy-fifth anniversary season
liederabend
pianist geoffrey parsons
> nostalgia: wolf kennst du das land?/ im frühling/ heimweh/ schubert der lindenbaum
> philosophy: strauss ruhe meine seele/ liszt die drei zigeuner/ wolf philine
> young girls in love: schubert gretchen am spinnrade/ wolf das verlassene mägdlein/
> wie lange schon/ strauss ach was kummer
> english poets in german lieder: strauss 3 ophelia-lieder/ wolf sonne der schlummerlosen/
> schubert an sylvia
> peculiat happenings: loewe kleiner haushalt/ wolf das köhlerweib ist trunken/ elfenlied/
> mahler des antonius von padua fischpredigt/ wolf mausfallensprüchlein/ storchenbotschaft
> grieg mit einer wasserlilie/ wolf wie glänzt der helle mond/ strauss hat gesagt bleibt's
> nicht dabei

19 june 1976/echternach
liederabend
recital repeated on 26 june 1976

23 august 1976/edinburgh usher hall
liederabend
pianist geoffrey parsons

158

1 september 1976/san sebastian
liederabend
pianist martin isepp

17 september 1976/bucarest
liederabend

13 october 1976/vienna
liederabend
pianist geoffrey parsons

18 october 1976/hamburg
liederabend
pianist geoffrey parsons

22 october 1976/dresden
liederabend
pianist geoffrey parsons

28 october 1976/paris
liederabend
pianist geoffrey parsons

11 december 1976/blois
liederabend
pianist brian lamport

10 january 1977/stratford-upon-avon
liederabend
pianist geoffrey parsons

18 january 1977/turin
liederabend
pianist geoffrey parsons

21 january 1977/essen
liederabend
pianist geoffrey parsons

27 january 1977/reutlingen
liederabend
pianist geoffrey parsons

1 february 1977/stuttgart
liederabend
pianist geoffrey parsons

8 february 1977/amsterdam concertgebouw
*liederabend *themed recital*
pianist geoffrey parsons
    nostalgia: wolf kennst du das land?/ mahler ich atmet' einen linden suft/ wolf heimweh/ schubert der lindenbaum
    in love with love: wolf die zigeunerin/ schumann der nussbaum/ wolf ich esse nun mein brot/ strauss ach was kummer
    philosophy: liszt die drei zigeuner/ strauss ruhe meine seele/ schubert der einsame/ wolf philine
    sleep and death: wolf an den schlaf/ wolf-ferrari vado di notte come fa la luna/ wolf denk es o seele
    girls in love: wolf wie lange schon/ das verlassene mägdlein/ schubert gretchen am spinnrade
    women in love: wolf o wär dein haus/ trau nicht der liebe/ ich hab' in penna schubert seligkeit

12 february 1977/witten
liederabend
pianist geoffrey parsons

20 february 1977 / london royal opera house
liederabend *themed recital*
pianist geoffrey parsons
> *being alone: schubert der einsame/ an mein klavier/ wolf sonne der schlummerlosem/ fussreise*
> *strange happenings: wolf storchenbotschaft/ nixe binsenfuss/ mausfallensprüchlein/ debussy mandoline/ loewe kleiner haushalt/ wolf das köhlerweib ist trunken*
> *devotion: schumann wismung/ wolf keine gleicht von allen schönen/ jägerlied/ strauss zueignung*
> *compliments alla toscana: du denkst mit einem fädchen/ du sagst mir dass ich keine fürstin sei/ schweig einmal still/ wie lange schon/ verschling' der abgrund*
> *wolf ich hab' in penna/ ich esse nun mein brot/ anon gsätzli/ schubert seligkeit*

25 february 1977 / strassburg
liederabend
pianist geoffrey parsons

26 march 1977 / london camden town hall
liederabend *themed recital*
pianist geoffrey parsons
> *devotion: schumann widmung/ anon drink to me only/ grieg ich liebe dich/ mit einer wasserlilie/ strauss zueignung*
> *recollection and anticipation: schubert der lindenbaum/ dvorak songs my mother taught me/ strauss morgen/ schubert seligkeit*
> *children: mozart sehnsucht nach dem frühlinge/ brahms sandmännchen/ grieg farmyard song/ wolf-ferrari preghiera/ schubert wiegenlied/ strauss meinem kinde/ rachmaninov to the children/ mahler um schlimme kinder artig zu machen*
> *in love with love: schumann der nussbaum/ die kartenlegerin/ strauss ach was kummer strauss heimkehr/ mozart warnung/ ich möchte wohl der kaiser sein*

30 march 1977 / london camden town hall
liederabend *themed recital*
pianist geoffrey parsons
> *philosophy: schubert der einsame/ martini plaisir d'amour/ liszt die drei zigeuner/ purcell what can we poor females do?*
> *young girls in love: schubert gretchen am spinnrade/ mahler rheinlegendchen/ brahms salamander/ strauss hat gesagt bleibt's nicht dabei*
> *women in love: schubert suleika I-II/ schumann wie mit innigstem behagen/ mussorgsky in den pilzen*
> *lollipops: tchaikovsky nur wer die sehnsucht kennt/ debussy mandoline/ anon danny boy/ reger mariae wiegenlied/ anon o du liebs ängeli/ gsätzli*

24 april 1977 / stockholm **liederabend** pianist brian lamport	26 april 1977 / gothenburg **liederabend** pianist brian lamport
28 april 1977 / uppsala **liederabend** pianist brian lamport	31 may 1977 / paris **liederabend** pianist geoffrey parsons

27 september 1977/harrogate
liederabend

1 november 1977/birmingham
liederabend

6 november 1977/sheffield
liederabend

13 november 1977/glasgow
liederabend

19 november 1977/london wigmore hall
liederabend hugo wolf
pianist geoffrey parsons
    mörike-lieder: auf einer wanderung/ auf eine christblume/ das verlassene mägdlein/ nixe binsenfuss/ im frühling/ jägerlied/ an den schlaf/ auftrag
    goethe-lieder: mignon I-III/ kennst du das land?/ philine/ ganymed/ anakreons grab/ epiphanias
    mausfallensprüchlein

26 november 1977/london wigmore hall
liederabend hugo wolf
pianist geoffrey parsons
    spanisches liederbuch: herr was trägt der boden hier?/ wenn du zu den blumen gehst/ geh geliebter geh jetzt!/ köpfchen köpfchen nicht gewimmert/ bedeckt mich mit blumen/ wer tat deinem füsslein weh?/ in dem schatten meiner locken/ trau nicht der liebe
    italienisches liederbuch: auch kleine dinge/ mein liebster singt/ nein junger herr/ wir haben beide lange zeit geschwiegen/ wie lange schon/ nun lass uns frieden schliessem/ du denkst mit einem fädchen/ wohl kenn' ich euren stand/ o wär' dein haus durchsichtig/ mein liebster hat zu tische mich geladen/ du sagst mir dass ich keine fürstin sei/ ich esse nun mein brot/ gesegnet sei das grün/ ich hab' in penna
    wie glänzt der helle mond/ keine gleicht von allen schönen/ das köhlerweib ist trunken

30 november 1977/cambridge university music school
liederabend
pianist geoffrey parsons
    mozart abendempfindung/ sehnsucht nach dem frühlinge/ das veilchen/ ich möchte wohl der kaiser sein
    schubert suleika I-II/ an mein klavier/ gretchen am spinnrade
    schumann der nussbaum/ die kartenlegerin/ brahms immer leiser wird mein schlummer/ vergebliches ständchen
    liszt die drei zigeuner/ grieg mit einer wasserlilie/ mahler um schlimme kinder artig zu machen
    strauss 3 ophelia-lieder/ wolf das verlassene mägdlein/ philine/ ich hab' in penna

5 december 1977/warsaw
liederabend
pianist geoffrey parsons

9 december 1977/posen
liederabend
pianist geoffrey parsons

7 january 1978/berlin
liederabend
pianist geoffrey parsons

10 january 1978/milan conservatorio
liederabend
pianist brian lamport

14 january 1978/florence
liederabend
pianist brian lamport

18 january 1978/turin conservatorio
liederabend
pianist brian lamport

26 january 1978/asolo
liederabend

9 may 1978/brescia
liederabend

18 may 1978/budapest
liederabend

13 june 1978/paris
liederabend

16-17 june 1978/hohenems
liederabend

21 june 1978/oslo
liederabend

5 july 1978/ann arbor
liederabend

6 september 1978/breslau
liederabend

23 september 1978/london wigmore hall
liederabend
pianist geoffrey parsons
mozart abendempfindung/ sehnsucht nach dem frühlinge/ das veilchen/ ich möchte wohl der kaiser sein/ schubert suleika I-II/ gretchen am spinnrade/ das lied im grünen
schumann der nussbaum/ wie mit innigstem behagen/ die kartenlegerin
strauss 3 ophelia-lieder/ wer lieben will muss leiden/ ach was kummer
wolf sonne der schlummerlosen/ keine gleicht von allen schönen/ morgentau/ mausfallensprüchlein/ das köhlerweib ist trunken/ philine/ strauss zueignung

30 september 1978/london wigmore hall
liederabend
pianist geoffrey parsons
wolf mühvoll komm' ich und beladen/ wandl' ich in dem morgentau/ wie glänzt der helle mond/ nachtzauber/ die zigeunerin
schubert nähe des geliebten/ der einsame/ der lindenbaum/ an sylvia
liszt es muss ein wunderbares sein/ die drei zigeuner/ grieg letzter frühling/ mit einer wasserlilie
strauss freundliche vision/ muttertändelei/ hat gesagt bleibt's nicht dabei/ schlechtes wetter
wolf ich esse nun mein brot/ ich hab' in penna

19 march 1979/zürich opernhaus
liederabend
pianist geoffrey parsons
final public singing appearance

The discography: an introduction

The major part of Elisabeth Schwarzkopf's commercial recording career was for the Columbia/EMI company (under the exclusive supervision of her husband Walter Legge), with a very few sessions before 1945 for Telefunken and occasional late forays between 1966 and 1979 into the studios of Deutsche Grammophon, CBS and Decca. For detailed explanation of the many Columbia LP issues and the catalogue prefixes in its territories worldwide, readers are referred to the introduction of my recent discography *Columbia 33CX* (ISBN 1 901395 17 0).

For those commercial recordings, the recording dates are those on which Schwarzkopf herself worked in the studio, although in the case of most larger scale works (operas and oratorios) work with orchestra and other participating soloists may well have extended over a longer period.

Titles of operatic scenes or excerpts are followed after a forward slash by the title of the opera (for example, "Non mi dir/Don Giovanni"), and the same applies to individual songs taken from longer cycles (for example, "Was soll der Zorn/Italienisches Liederbuch"). In most other cases of individual songs, the title is followed in brackets by the first line of the text where this differs from the title (for example, "Meeresstille (Tiefe Stille herrscht im Wasser)").

In addition to commercial recordings, radio broadcasts are included, both those taken at public performance and those recorded in the radio studios for simultaneous or later transmission (many examples of *Lieder* performances were thus documented by the BBC Third Programme and by Dutch Radio, among others). A fair number of these have been subsequently issued, and we may expect more in the future - some even in video form taken from televised concerts.

Particularly valuable amongst the unpublished material is that of Hugo Wolf, for whom Schwarzkopf and Legge worked so tirelessly: the *Italienisches Liederbuch*, for example, exists in an unpublished Dutch Radio version (1953) and an unissued Columbia edition (recorded in 1954 in London's Wigmore Hall – an unusual recording venue for EMI) as well as the familiar cycles for Columbia (1959) and EMI (1965-1967), the latter a joint performance with Dietrich Fischer-Dieskau.

WILLIAM ALWYN (1905-1985)
cantata
london 1954	royal philharmonic and chorus mathieson	unpublished soundtrack recording *used in the motion picture svengali*

THOMAS ARNE (1710-1778)
the lass with the delicate air
berlin	raucheisen	lp: acanta 40 23557
2 january 1945	*sung in german*	cd: acanta 42 43801/archipel ARPCD 0295

when daisies pied
vienna	hudez	cd: testament SBT 2172
7 november 1946		*unpublished columbia 78rpm recording*
london	moore	78: columbia LB 73
2 october 1947		lp: emi RLS 763/1C151 43160-43163M/154 6133
		cd: emi 763 6542/763 7902

where the bee sucks
london	moore	78: columbia LB 73
2 october 1947		lp: emi RLS 763/1C151 43160-43163M/154 6133
		cd: emi 763 6542/763 7902
berlin	raucheisen	lp: melodram MEL 082/discoreale DR 10038
6 march 1958		*incorrectly dated 1953*

JOHANN SEBASTIAN BACH (1685-1750)
mass in b minor
vienna	ferrier, w.ludwig,	cd: foyer 2CF 2022/arkadia CDKAR 212/verona 27073-27074/
15 june 1950	poell, schöffler	archipel ARPCD 0031/guild GHCD 2260-2262
	wiener singverein	*excerpts* cd: verona 27076
	vienna symphony	*rehearsal excerpts*
	karajan	cd: emi 763 6552/763 7902/567 2072/586 8382
london	höffgen, gedda,	lp: columbia 33CX 1121-1123/FCX 291-293/WCX 1121-1123/
23-29 november	rehfuss	C 90337-90339/QCX 10055-10057/angel 3500/world records
1952	philharmonia	T 854-856/emi RLS 746/EX 29 09743/1C181 01791-01793
	karajan	cd: emi 763 5052/567 2072/586 8382/naxos 811 1053-1054
		excerpts
		cd: urania URN 22296
		choruses were recorded in vienna with wiener singverein

matthäus-passion
vienna	höngen, w.ludwig,	unpublished soundtrack recording
november 1948	schmitt-walter,	*film directed by ernst marischka and consisting of images from old master*
	braun	*paintings: an italian language soundtrack was also recorded using*
	wiener singverein	*different singers with rome santa cecilia orchestra and chorus*
	vienna philharmonic	
	karajan	
london	ludwig, pears,	lp: columbia 33CX 1799-1803/SAX 2446-2450/FCX 942-946/
4-12 may 1961	gedda, berry,	SAXF 243-247/QCX 10458-10462/SAXQ 7358-7362/
	fischer-dieskau	C 91200-91203/STC 91200-91203/angel 3599/emi SLS 827/
	hampstead choir	1C191 01312-01315/2C167 01312-01315/
	philharmonia chorus	1C197 54135-54145
	philharmonia	cd: emi 763 0582/567 5382/567 5422
	klemperer	*excerpts*
		lp: columbia 33CX 1881/SAX 2526
		cd: emi CDEMX 2223
		recording completed on 28 november 1961

bach/**magnificat**

rome	dominguez,	cd: archipel ARPCD 0237
21 december	gedda, tadeo	
1953	rai roma chorus	
	and orchestra	
	karajan	

cantata no 51 "jauchzet gott in allen landen"

london	philharmonia	cd: testament SBT 2172
28-31 may 1948	susskind	*unpublished columbia 78rpm recording*

london	philharmonia	78: columbia LX 1334-1336/LX 8756-8758
6 october 1950	gellhorn	lp: columbia C 80628/WSX 578/american columbia ML 4792/ angel seraphim 60013/melodiya M10 43861-43862/ emi 154 6133
		cd: emi 763 2012/567 2062/archipel ARPCD 0237
		alleluja omlt
		cd: emi 585 1052

munich	bavarian radio	lp: melodram MEL 082/discoreale DR 10038
5 october 1951	orchestra	cd: melodram CDM 16501/golden melodram GM 40072/ bella voce BLV 107 201
	jochum	

cantata no 199 "mein herze schwimmt in blut"

london	philharmonia	columbia unpublished
29-30 may 1957	dart	

london	philharmonia	cd: emi 763 6552/763 7902/567 2062
20 may 1958	dart	*unpublished columbia lp recording*

london	philharmonia	cd: testament SBT 1178
24 may 1958	dart	*unpublished columbia lp recording*

cantata no 202 "weichet nur betrübte schatten"

stratford ontario	hart house orchestra	lp: rococo 5374
3 august 1955	neel	cd: archipel ARPCD 0237
		recording incomplete

amsterdam	concertgebouw	lp: discocorp RR 208/RR 537
6 february 1957	klemperer	cd: arkadia CD 727/as-disc AS 533/bella voce 107 201/ emi 567 2062

london	philharmonia	cd: testament SBT 1178
30 may-2 june 1957	dart	*unpublished columbia lp recording*

naples	rai napoli orchestra	cd: melodram CDM 16529
15 april 1958	rapalo	

mein gläubiges herze/cantata no 68

london	parikian, violin	78: columbia LX 1336
13 october 1950	sutcliffe, oboe	lp: american columbia ML 4792
	clark, cello	cd: emi 763 2012/567 2062
	jones, organ	

london	philharmonia	cd: testament SBT 1178
2 june 1957	dart	*unpublished columbia lp recording*

meinem hirten bleib' ich treu/cantata no 92

naples	rai napoli orchestra	cd: melodram CDM 16529/bella voce BLV 107 201
15 april 1958	rapalo	

london	philharmonia	columbia unpublished
24 may 1958	dart	

bach/schafe können sicher weiden/cantata no 208

berlin 7 october 1944	scheck, flute wolf, flute schulz, violin schonecke, cello raucheisen, piano	cd: acanta 42 43128

vienna
1 november 1946
	niedermayer, flute
	reznicek, flute
	maurer, cello
	ahlgrimm,
	harpsichord
		78: columbia LX 1051/LCX 115/GQX 11325
		lp: american columbia ML 4792/emi ALP 143 5501
		cd: emi 763 2012/567 2062/567 6342/istituto discografico
		    italiano IDIS 6447-6448/regis RRC 1167/
		    archipel ARPCD 0237

london 2 june 1957	philharmonia dart	cd: testament SBT 1178 *unpublished columbia lp recording*
london 24 may 1958	philharmonia dart	cd: testament SBT 1178 *unpublished columbia lp recording*

ave maria, arranged by gounod

london 2 october 1947	pougnet, violin moore, piano	cd: testament SBT 2172 *unpublished columbia 78rpm recording*
london 26 may 1957	philharmonia and chorus mackerras	columbia unpublished

LUDWIG VAN BEETHOVEN (1770-1827)
symphony no 9 "choral"

vienna
10-14 december
1947
	höngen, patzak,
	hotter
	wiener singverein
	vienna philharmonic
	karajan
		78: columbia LX 1097-1105/LX 8612-8620/LFX 846-854/
		    LVX 32-40/GQX 11250-11258
		45: american columbia EL 51
		lp: emi RLS 7714/1C137 54370-54373M/1C153 03200-
		    03205/2C153 03200-03205
		cd: emi 761 0762/476 8782/479 9312/arkadia 78544/
		    grammofono AB 78736

bayreuth
29 july 1951
	höngen, hopf,
	edelmann
	bayreuth festival
	orchestra and chorus
	furtwängler
		lp: hmv ALP1286-1287/FALP 381-382/WALP 1286-1287/
		    E 90115-90116/STE 90115-90116/SME 90115-90116/
		    EBE 600 000/SMVP 3048-3049/UVT 3048-3049/
		    FALP 30048-30049/QALP 10116-10117/victor LM 6043/
		    angel 4003/angel seraphim 6068/emi RLS 727/1C147
		    00811-00812/2C153 00811-00812/3C153 00811-00812/
		    1C149 53432-53439M/2C153 52540-52551/2C151
		    53678-53679
		cd: emi 747 0812/769 0812/763 6062/566 9012/567 4962/
		    566 9532/grand slam GS 2009/tahra FURT 1101-1104/
		    naxos 811 1060

lucerne
22 august 1954
	cavelti, haefliger,
	edelmann
	lucerne chorus
	philharmonia
	furtwängler
		lp: private japanese issue MF 18862-18863/cetra LO 530/
		    discocorp RR 390
		cd: arkadia CDLSMH 34006/rodolphe RPC 32522-32524/
		    tahra FURT 1003/FURT 1054-1057/FURT 1101-1104

vienna
26-27 july 1955
	höffgen, haefliger,
	edelmann
	vienna singverein
	philharmonia
	karajan
		lp: columbia 33CX 1391-1392/FCX 448-449/WCX
		    1391-1392/C 90515-90516/QCX 10190-10191/angel
		    3544/world records SM 143-149/emi SLS 5053/1C181
		    01380-01386Y/1C063 01200M/3C053 01200/HZE 107
		cd: emi 763 3102

beethoven / missa solemnis

amsterdam 17 may 1957	merriman, simandy, rehfuss toomkunstkoor concertgebouw klemperer	unpublished radio broadcast *dutch radio*

vienna   ludwig, gedda,   lp: columbia 33CX 1634-1635/FCX 828-829/SAXF 177-178/
12-16 september   zaccaria   QCX 10369-10370/SAXQ 7317-7318/WCX 1634-1635/
1958   wiener singverein   C 91019-91020/STC 91019-91020/angel 3598/world records
    philharmonia   T 914-915/ST 914-915/eterna 820 558-559/emi SLS 5198/
    karajan   CFPD 4420-4421/1C137 00627-00628/1C191 00627-00628/
                             2C181 00627-00628/3C153 00627-00628
                         cd: testament SBT 2126
                         testament edition also contains rehearsal extracts and interview about the
                         recording with schwarzkopf

fidelio *role of marzelline*

london   konetzni, friedrich,   cd: istituto discografico italiano IDIS 6379-6380
24 september 1947   klein, weber,   *excerpts*
    schöffler, alsen   cd: istituto discografico italiano IDIS 6447-6448
    vienna opera chorus   *guest performance by vienna staatsoper*
    vienna philharmonic
    krauss

salzburg   flagstad, patzak,   lp: morgan MOR 5001/mrf records MRF 50/bjr records BJR 112/
5 august 1950   dermota, greindl,   discocorp IGI 328/cetra FE 44
    schöffler, braun   cd: arkadia CDWFE 304/CDWFE 354/verona 27044-27045/
    vienna opera chorus   emi 764 9012/regis RRC 2048
    vienna philharmonic   *excerpts*
    furtwängler   lp: melodram MEL 082/discoreale DR 10037
                         cd: melodram CDM 16501/golden melodram GM 70000

vienna   mödl, windgassen,   cd: walhall WLCD 0063
5 june 1953   schock, edelmann,
    metternich, braun
    wiener singverein
    vienna symphony
    karajan

schwarzkopf also speaks the dialogue sections for marzelline in the 1962 klemperer recording of the opera

o wär' ich schon mit dir vereint / fidelio *marzelline*

london   philharmonia   78: columbia LX 1410/LVX 157
19 october 1950   galliera   45: columbia SCD 2114
                         lp: emi EX 769 7411
                         cd: emi 769 7412/565 5772/585 1052/regis RRC 1167

mir ist so wunderbar / fidelio *marzelline*

london   flagstad, glynne,   lp: ed smith EJS 390
16 may 1951   stephenson   *recording also includes dialogue spoken in english both before and after*
    covent garden   *the quartet*
    orchestra
    rankl

beethoven/abscheulicher wo eilst du hin?/fidelio *leonore*
watford	philharmonia	lp: columbia 33CX 1266/FCX 454/FCX 30093/QCX 10186/
20 september 1954	karajan	WCX 1266/C 90436/angel 35231/emi RLS 7715/
		154 6133/1C137 54364-54367M
		cd: emi 763 2012

ah perfido!, concert aria
watford	philharmonia	lp: columbia 33CX 1278/QCX 10149/WCX 1278/C 90447/
20 september 1954	karajan	angel 35203/emi RLS 7715/1C137 54364-54367M/
		154 6133
		cd: emi 763 2012

das geheimnis (wo blüht das blümchen das nie verblüht?)
berlin	raucheisen	lp: acanta 40 23557
21 september 1944		cd: acanta 42 43801/membram 223067/223080/
		archipel ARPCD 0295

wonne der wehmut (trocknet nicht, tränen der ewigen liebe)
london	moore	columbia unpublished
9 april 1952		

london	moore	columbia unpublished
21 september 1952		

london	moore	columbia unpublished
4-7 july 1953		

london	moore	lp: columbia 33CX 1044/FCX 182/WCX 1044/C 90306/
10 january 1954		angel 35023/melodiya M10 43861-43862/emi RLS 763/
		154 6133/1C151 43160-43163M
		cd: emi 763 6542/763 7902

aix-en-provence	rosbaud	cd: melodram CDM 26524/andromeda ANDRCD 5006
23 july 1954		*incorrectly dated 29 june 1954*

salzburg	moore	cd: emi 566 0842
7 august 1956		

HECTOR BERLIOZ (1803-1869)
la damnation de faust *role of marguérite*
lucerne	vroons, hotter,	lp: cetra FE 21
26 august 1950	pernerstorfer	cd: eklipse EKR 60/archipel ARPCD 0008
	lucerne festival	*excerpts*
	chorus and	cd: istituto discografico italiano IDIS 6447-6448
	orchestra	
	furtwängler	
	sung in german	

london	lloyd, roux,	unpublished radio broadcast
25 june 1957	brannigan	*bbc third programme*
	goldsmiths choir	
	philharmonia	
	freccia	

GEORGES BIZET (1838-1875)
l'amour est enfant de boheme....end of act one/carmen *carmen*
berlin	unpublished soundtrack recording
1939	*taken from the motion picture der ewige klang and sung in german*

je dis que rien ne m'épouvante/carmen *micaela*
london	philharmonia	78: columbia LX 1410/LVX 157
19 october 1950	galliera	45: columbia SCD 2114
		lp: emi ALP 143 5501
		cd: emi 567 6342

pastorale
london	moore	cd: testament SBT 1206
26 june 1957		*unpublished columbia lp recording*

CARL BOHM (1844-1920)
was i hab'
london	moore	columbia unpublished
10-11 june 1957		

london	moore	vhs video: emi MVC 491 4763
1958-1959		dvd video: emi DVA 492 8529
		bbc television

JOHANNES BRAHMS (1833-1897)
ein deutsches requiem
lucerne	hotter	lp: private japanese issue W 24
20 august 1947	lucerne festival chorus and orchestra furtwängler	cd: wing WCD 1-2/french furtwängler society SWF 971-972

vienna	hotter	78: columbia LX 1055-1064/LX 8595-8604/LVX 68-77/ GQX 11239-11248/SL 157/american columbia M 755
21-28 october 1947	wiener singverein vienna philharmonic karajan	lp: emi RLS 7714/1C137 54370-54373M/2C051 43176/ 2C153 03200-03205M
		cd: emi 761 0102/562 8112/562 8122/479 9312/ grammofono AB 78755/arkadia 78545

london	fischer-dieskau	lp: columbia 33CX 1781-1782/SAX 2430-2431/FCX 915-916/SAXF 233-234/QCX 10455-10456/ SAXQ 7355-7356/C 91224-91225/STC 91224-91225/ angel 3624/emi SLS 821/1C153 01295-01296/1C161 00545-00546/2C167 01295-01296/ED 29 02793
26 april 1961	philharmonia chorus and orchestra klemperer	
		cd: emi 747 2382/566 9032/566 9552

ach englische schäferin; ach könnt' ich diesen abend/deutsche volkslieder
berlin	fischer-dieskau	lp: emi AN 163-164/SAN 163-164/SMAC 91487-91488/ 1C153 00054-00055/1C193 00054-00055/angel 3675
28 august-	moore	
11 september		cd: emi 749 5252/585 5022
1965		

brahms/**an die nachtigall (geuss' nicht so laut die liebentflammten lieder)**
berlin   parsons   emi unpublished
12-22 december 1975

blinde kuh (im finstern geh' ich suchen)
berlin   parsons   emi unpublished
12-22 december 1975

vienna   parsons   lp: decca SXL 6493/642 576AW/london (usa) OS 26592
10 january 1979   cd: decca 430 0002

da unten im tale/deutsche volkslieder
berlin   raucheisen   lp: acanta 40 23524/40 23557
20 september 1944   cd: acanta 42 43801/membran 223069/223075

london   moore   columbia unpublished
29 november 1951

london   moore   78: columbia LB 118/LV 59/LD 6
2 december 1951

london   moore   columbia unpublished
4-7 july 1953

london   moore   lp: columbia 33CX 1044/FCX 182/WCX 1044/C 90306/
5 january 1954   angel 35023/emi RLS 763/1C151 43160-43163M/
                                                        154 6133
                                                        cd: emi 763 6352/763 7902/356 5262/
                                                         andromeda ANDRCD 5006

rome   fischer   cd: arkadia CD 535/CDHP 535/archipel ARPCD 0295
21 february 1954

aix-en-provence   rosbaud   cd: melodram CDM 26524/andromeda ANDRCD 5006
23 july 1954   *incorrectly dated 29 july 1954*

hannover   reutter   lp: movimento musica 02 017
2 march 1962   cd: movimento musica 051 015/verona 27025

berlin   moore   lp: emi AN 163-164/SAN 163-164/SMAC 91487-91488/
28 august-   1C153 00054-00055/1C193 00054-00055/angel 3675
11 september 1965   cd: emi 749 5252/585 5022

london   moore   vhs video: emi MVC 491 4763
22 march 1968   dvd video: emi DVA 477 8319/DVA492 8529
                                                     bbc television

dort in den weiden; es ging ein maidlein zarte; es steht ein lind'; es war ein markgraf überm rhein; es wohnet ein fiedler/deutsche volkslieder
berlin   moore   lp: emi AN 163-164/SAN 163-164/SMAC 91487-91488/
28 august-   1C153 00054-00055/1C193 00054-00055/angel 3675
11 september 1965   cd: emi 749 3252/585 5022

es ritt ein ritter; es war eine schöne jüdin; feinsliebchen du sollst nicht barfuss geh'n/deutsche volkslieder
berlin   fischer-dieskau   lp: emi AN 163-164/SAN 163-164/SMAC 91487-91488/
28 august-   moore   1C153 00054-00055/1C193 00054-00055/angel 3675
11 september 1965   cd: emi 749 3252/585 5022

brahms/**feldeinsamkeit** (ich ruhe still im hohen grünen gras)
rome   fischer   cd: arkadia CD 535/CDHP 535/archipel ARPCD 0295
21 february 1954

geheimnis; heimkehr; heimweh
berlin   parsons   emi unpublished
12-22 december 1975

gunhilde lebt' gar still und fromm; guten abend mein tausiger schatz; ich stand auf hohem berge/deutsche volkslieder
berlin   moore   lp: emi AN 163-164/SAN 163-164/SMAC 91487-91488/
28 august-   1C153 00054-00055/1C193 00054-00055/angel 3675
11 september 1965   cd: emi 749 5252/585 5022

immer leiser wird mein schlummer
berlin   parsons   lp: emi ASD 2844/1C063 02331
27 august-   cd: emi 565 8602
8 september 1970

in stiller nacht/deutsche volkslieder
rome   fischer   cd: arkadia CD 535/CDHP 535/archipel ARPCD 0295
21 february 1954

london   moore   columbia unpublished
13 january 1958

london   moore   cd: testament SBT 1206
7 december 1962   *unpublished columbia lp recording*

berlin   moore   lp: emi AN 163-164/SAN 163-164/SMAC 91487-91488/
28 august-   1C153 00054-00055/1C193 00054-00055/angel 3675
11 september 1965   cd: emi 749 5252/585 5022

der jäger (mein lieb ist ein jäger)
berlin   parsons   lp: emi ASD 2844/1C063 02331
27 august-   cd: emi 565 8602
8 september 1970

jungfräulein soll ich mit euch geh'n?/deutsche volkslieder
berlin   moore   lp: emi AN 163-164/SAN 163-164/SMAC 91487-91488/
28 august-   1C153 00054-00055/1C193 00054-00055/angel 3675
11 september 1965   cd: emi 749 5252/585 5022

klage; des liebsten schwur
berlin   parsons   emi unpublished
12-22 december 1975

liebestreu (o versenk' o versenk' dein leid)
rome   fischer   cd: arkadia CD 535/CDHP 535/archipel ARPCD 0295
21 february 1954

hannover   reutter   lp: movimento musica 02 017
2 march 1962   cd: movimento musica 051 015/verona 27025

berlin   parsons   lp: emi ASD 2844/1C063 02331
27 august-   cd: emi 565 8602
8 september 1970

brahms/**das mädchen spricht; mädchenfluch**
berlin parsons emi unpublished
12-22 december 1975

mädchenlied (am jüngsten tag ich aufersteh')
berlin parsons emi unpublished
12-22 december 1975

vienna parsons lp: decca SXL 6943/642 576AW/london (usa) OS 26592
6 january 1979 cd: decca 430 0002

mädchenlied II; mädchenlied III
berlin parsons emi unpublished
12-22 december 1975

maria ging aus wandern/deutsche volkslieder
berlin parsons lp: emi AN 163-164/SAN 163-164/SMAC 91487-91488/
28 august- 1C153 00054-00055/1C193 00054-00055/angel 3675
11 september 1965 cd: emi 749 5252/585 5022

meine liebe ist grün/junge lieder
rome fischer cd: arkadia CD 535/CDHP 535/archipel ARPCD 0295
21 february 1954

berlin parsons emi unpublished
12-22 december 1975

och mod'r ich well en ding han/deutsche volkslieder
london moore lp: emi RLS 154 7003
12 september 1952 *unpublished columbia 78rpm recording*

london moore lp: columbia 33CX 1044/FCX 182/WCX 1044/C 90306/
5 january 1954 angel 35023/emi RLS 763/1C151 43160-43163M
 cd: emi 763 6352/763 7902/356 5262/andromeda
 ANDRCD 5006

der reiter; sagt mir o schönste schäferin/deutsche volkslieder
berlin moore lp: emi AN 163-164/SAN 163-164/SMAC 91487-91488/
28 august- 1C153 00054-00055/1C193 00054-00055/angel 3675
11 september 1965 cd: emi 749 5252/585 5022

sandmännchen (die blümelein sie schlafen)
london chorus lp: columbia 33CX 1482/angel 35580/36750/emi ASD 3798/
1 june 1957 philharmonia 100 4531
 mackerras cd: emi 763 5742

london moore cd: testament SBT 1206
12 march 1962 *unpublished columbia lp recording*

berlin parsons lp: emi ASD 2844/1C063 02331
27 august- *published on cd only in japan*
8 september 1970

der schmied (ich hör' meinen schatz)
berlin parsons emi unpublished
12-22 december 1975

brahms/**schöner augen schöne strahlen; die sonne scheint nicht mehr/deutsche volkslieder**

berlin	moore	lp: emi AN 163-164/SAN 163-164/SMAC 91487-91488/
28 august-		1C153 00054-00055/1C193 00054-00055/angel 3675
11 september 1965		cd: emi 749 5252/585 5022

schwesterlein; soll sich der mond nicht heller scheinen/deutsche volkslieder

berlin	fischer-dieskau	lp: emi AN 163-164/SAN 163-164/SMAC 91487-91488/
28 august-	moore	1C153 00054-00055/1C193 00054-00055/angel 3675
11 september 1965		cd: emi 749 5252/585 5022

ständchen (der mond steht über dem berge)

hannover	reutter	lp: movimento musica 02 017
2 march 1962		cd: movimento musica 051 015/verona 27075
berlin	parsons	lp: emi ASD 2844/1C063 02331
27 august-		cd: emi 763 6542/763 7902/565 8602
8 september 1970		

therese (du milchjunger knabe wie schaust du mich an?)

rome	fischer	cd: arkadia CD 535/CDHP 535/archipel ARPCD 0295
21 february 1954		
vienna	parsons	lp: decca SXL 6943/642 576AW/london (usa) OS 26592
10 january 1979		cd: decca 430 0002

der tod das ist die kühle nacht

rome	fischer	cd: arkadia CD 535/CDHP 535/archipel ARPCD 0295
21 february 1954		
berlin	parsons	emi unpublished
12-22 december 1975		

vergebliches ständchen (guten abend mein schatz)

london	moore	lp: emi RLS 154 7003
12 september 1952		*unpublished columbia 78rpm recording*
london	moore	lp: columbia 33CX 1044/FCX 182/WCX 1044/C 90306/
6 january 1954		angel 35023/emi RLS 763/1C151 43160-43163M
		cd: emi 565 8602/356 5262/andromeda ANDRCD 5006
rome	fischer	cd: arkadia CD 535/CDHP 535/archipel ARPCD 0295
21 february 1954		
new york	reeves	cd: emi 761 0432/notablu 935 0911
25 november 1956		
london	moore	vhs video: emi MVC 491 4763
22 march 1968		dvd video: emi DVA 477 8319/DVA 492 8529
		bbc television
berlin	parsons	lp: emi ASD 2844/1C063 02331
27 august-		cd: emi 565 8602
8 september 1970		

brahms/**von ewiger liebe** (dunkel wie dunkel in wald und in feld)
rome 21 february 1954	fischer	cd: arkadia CD 535/CDHP 535/archipel ARPCD 0295
aix-en-provence 23 july 1954	rosbaud	cd: melodram CDM 26524/andromeda ANDRCD 5006 *incorrectly dated 29 july 1954*
london 30 january 1961	moore	cd: testament SBT 1206 *unpublished columbia lp recording*
london 14 february 1961	moore	columbia unpublished
london 7 december 1962	moore	columbia unpublished
berlin 12-22 december 1975	parsons	emi unpublished

wach' auf mein hort!; wie komm' ich denn zur tür herein?/deutsche volkslieder
berlin 28 august- 11 september 1965	fischer-dieskau moore	lp: emi AN 163-164/SAN 163-164/SMAC 91487-91488/ 1C153 00054-00055/1C193 00054-00055/angel 3675 cd: emi 749 5252/585 5022

wehe so willst du mich wieder?
berlin 12-22 december 1975	parsons	emi unpublished

wie melodien zieht es mir
rome 21 february 1954	fischer	cd: arkadia CD 535/CDHP 535/archipel ARPCD 0295
berlin 27 august- 8 september 1970	parsons	lp: emi ASD 2844/1C063 02331 cd: emi 565 8602

wiegenlied (guten abend gut' nacht)
london 1954		unpublished soundtrack recording *used in the motion picture svengali*
rome 21 february 1954	fischer	cd: arkadia CD 535/CDHP 535/archipel ARPCD 0295
london 7 december 1962	moore	cd: testament SBT 1206 *unpublished columbia lp recording*
berlin 12-22 december 1975	parsons	emi unpublished

BENJAMIN BRITTEN (1913-1976)
hölderlin fragments
london 10 february 1964	parsons	unpublished radio broadcast *bbc third programme*

FERRUCCIO BUSONI (1866-1924)
unter den linden
berlin 20 september 1944	raucheisen	lp: acanta 40 23557 cd: acanta 42 43128/membran 223067/223093

GIACOMO CARISSIMI (1605-1674)
cantatas: detesta la cativa sorte; lungi omai; il mio core; a pie d'un verde alloro

london	seefried	lp: columbia 33CX 1331/FCX 515/WCX 1331/C 90486/
27 may 1955	moore	angel 35290/angel seraphim 60376/emi 2C051 43240/
		HLM 7267
		cd: emi 769 7932

GUSTAVE CHARPENTIER (1860-1950)
depuis le jour/louise *louise*

london	philharmonia	lp: emi RLS 763/1C151 43160-43163M/154 6133
6 may 1950	dobrowen	cd: andromeda ANDRCD 5006
		unpublished columbia 78rpm recording

FREDERIC CHOPIN (1810-1849)
charming boy

nohant	ciccolini	cd: arkadia CDGI 8021
29 june 1969	*sung in german*	

lithuanian song; maiden's wish

berlin	parsons	lp: emi ASD 2634/1C063 02116/angel 36752
20-27 october 1968	*sung in german*	*issued on cd only in japan*

nohant	ciccolini	cd: arkadia CDGI 8021
29 june 1968	*sung in german*	

berlin	parsons	emi unpublished
6-16 april 1970		

PETER CORNELIUS (1824-1874)
der barbier von bagdad *role of margiana*

watford	hoffman, gedda,	lp: columbia 33CX 1400-1401/WCX 1400-1401/
11-14 may 1956	unger, wächter,	C 90885-90886/angel 3553/emi 1C147 01448-01449M/
	prey	REG 2047-2048
	chorus	cd: emi 565 2842
	philharmonia	*recording completed in london on 16 may 1956*
	leinsdorf	

duets: heimatgedanken; scheiden

berlin	greindl	cd: acanta 42 43128/membran 223067/223082
16 november 1944	raucheisen	

CLAUDE DEBUSSY (1862-1918)
pelléas et mélisande *role of mélisande*

rome	sciutti, haefliger,	lp: cetra ARK 6/rodolphe RP 12393-12395
19 december 1954	roux, petri,	cd: arkadia CDKAR 218/urania URN 22267
	calabrese	
	rai roma orchestra	
	karajan	

mandoline

berlin	moore	lp: columbia CX 5268/SAX 5268/1C187 01307-01308/
22-27 august 1965		angel 36345/emi RLS 154 6133
		cd: emi 763 6542/763 7902

JOHN DOWLAND (1563-1626)
come again, sweet love doth now invite
vienna	hudez	lp: emi ALP 143 5501/154 6133
26 october 1946		cd: emi 567 6342
		unpublished columbia 78rpm recording

ANTONIN DVORAK (1841-1904)
te deum
london	boyce	unpublished radio broadcast
26 may 1954	bbc chorus	*bbc third programme*
	bbc symphony	
	sargent	

where art thou father?/the spectre's bride
london	bbc symphony	unpublished radio broadcast
26 may 1954	sargent	*bbc third programme*
	sung in english	

moravian duets
london	seefried	lp: columbia 33CX 1331/FCX 515/WCX 1331/C 90486/
25-27 may 1955	moore	angel 35290/angel seraphim 60376/emi 2C051 43240/
	sung in german	HLM 7267
		cd: emi 769 7932

songs my mother taught me
london	moore	45: columbia SEL 1589/ESL 6255
9 april 1956	*sung in english*	lp: columbia 33CX 1404/SAX 2265/FCX 664/SAXF 145/
		WCX 1404/C 90545/angel 35383
		cd: emi 565 8602/356 5262
		recording completed on 19 may 1956

CESAR FRANCK (1822-1890)
panis angelicus
london	chorus	lp: columbia 33CX 1482/angel 35580/36750/
25 may 1957	philharmonia	emi ASD 3798/100 4531
	mackerras	cd: emi 763 5742

WALTER GIESEKING (1895-1956)
kinderlieder, song cycle
london	gieseking	cd: emi 763 6553/763 7902
16 april 1955		*unpublished columbia lp recording*

TOMMASO GIORDANI (1733-1806)
caro mio ben
london	moore	columbia unpublished
11 june 1957		

london	moore	columbia unpublished
21 june 1957		

CHRISTOPH WILLIBALD GLUCK (1714-1787)
orfeo ed euridice *role of euridice*

new york 4 april 1967	popp, fischer-dieskau american opera society chorus and orchestra	unpublished radio broadcast

einem bach der fliesset

berlin 20 september 1944	raucheisen	lp: acanta 40 23557 cd: acanta 42 43801/membran 223067/223093/ archipel ARPCD 0295
london 25 november 1951	moore	columbia unpublished
london 9 april 1952	moore	columbia unpublished
london 10 december 1952	moore	columbia unpublished
london 21 september 1953	moore	columbia unpublished
london 4 january 1954	moore	lp: columbia 33CX 1044/FCX 182/WCX 1044/C 90306/ angel 35023/emi RLS 763/1C151 43160-43163M cd: emi 763 6532/763 7902
aix-en-provence 23 july 1954	rosbaud	cd: melodram CDM 26524/andromeda ANDRCD 5006 *incorrectly dated 29 july 1954*
new york 25 november 1956	reeves	cd: emi 761 0432/notablu 935 0911
london 25 october 1961	moore	unpublished video recording *bbc television*

FREDERICK GLUCK
in einem kühlen grunde, arranged by mackerras

london 1 june 1957	chorus philharmonia mackerras	lp: columbia 33CX 1482/angel 35580/36750/ emi ASD 3798/100 4531 cd: emi 763 5742

EDVARD GRIEG (1843-1907)
erstes begegnen (des ersten sehens wonne)
berlin   parsons   lp: emi ASD 2844/1C063 02331
27 august-   cd: emi 565 8602
8 september 1970

farmyard song (come out snow-white lambkin!)
london   moore   45: columbia SEL 1600/ESL 6274
13 april 1956   lp: columbia 33CX 1404/SAX 2265/FCX 664/SAXF 145/
                                             WCX 1404/C 90545/angel 35385
                                             cd: emi 565 8602/356 5262

ich liebe dich (du mein gedanke, du mein sein und werden!)
london   moore   45: columbia SEL 1600/ESL 6274
12 april 1956   lp: columbia 33CX 1404/SAX 2265/FCX 664/SAXF 145/
                                             WCX 1404/C 90545/angel 35383
                                             cd: emi 356 5262

berlin   parsons   lp: emi ASD 2634/1C063 02116/angel 36752
20-27 october 1968   cd: emi 565 8602

berlin   parsons   emi unpublished
6-16 april 1970

lauf der welt (an jedem abend geh' ich aus)
berlin   parsons   lp: emi ASD 2844/1C063 02331
27 august-   cd: emi 565 8602
8 september 1970

letzter frühling (ja noch einmal ist das wunder geschehn)
berlin   parsons   lp: emi ASD 2634/1C063 02116/angel 36752
20-27 october 1968   cd: emi 565 8602

berlin   parsons   emi unpublished
6-16 april 1970

mit einer primula veris (mag dir du zartes frühlingskind)
berlin   parsons   lp: emi ASD 2844/1C063 02331
27 august-   cd: emi 565 8602
8 september 1970

mit einer wasserlilie (sieh marie was ich bringe!)
berlin   parsons   lp: emi ASD 2634/1C063 02116/angel 36752
20-27 october 1968   cd: emi 565 8602

berlin   parsons   emi unpublished
6-16 april 1970

ein schwan (mein schwan mein stiller)
vienna   parsons   lp: decca SXL 6943/642 576AW/london (usa) OS 26592
9 january 1979   cd: decca 430 0002

zur rosenzeit (ihr verblühet süsse rosen)
berlin   parsons   lp: emi ASD 2844/1C063 02331
27 august-   cd: emi 565 8602
8 september 1970

FRANZ GROTHE (1908-1982)
songs: heimatlied; die lerche und der geiger
berlin   unpublished soundtrack recording
1943   *used in the motion picture der ewige klang*

FRANZ XAVER GRUBER (1787-1863)
stille nacht, heilige nacht

vienna 3 march 1949	vienna opera chorus vienna philharmonic	78: columbia LC 32 lp: emi ALP 143 5501
london 3 october 1952	covent garden and hampstead choirs philharmonia pritchard *sung in english*	78: columbia LB 131 45: columbia SCD 2112
london 25 may 1957	chorus philharmonia mackerras	columbia unpublished
london 30 june- 1 july 1957	chorus philharmonia mackerras	lp: columbia 33CX 1482/angel 35580/36750/ emi ASD 3798/100 4531 cd: emi 763 5742

REYNALDO HAHN (1875-1947)
si mes vers avaient des ailes

london 10 april 1956	moore	45: columbia SEL 1589/ESL 6255/ESBF 17122 lp: columbia 33CX 1404/SAX 2265/FCX 664/ SAXF 145/WCX 1404/C 90545/angel 35383/ emi 154 6133 cd: emi 763 6542/763 7902/356 5262

GEORGE FRIDERIC HANDEL (1685-1759)
messiah/soprano soloist

london 24-25 february 1964	hoffman, gedda, hines philharmonia chorus philharmonia klemperer	lp: emi AN 146-148/SAN 146-148/SLS 915/ 2C167 00036-00039/angel 3657 cd: emi 763 6212 *excerpts* lp: emi ALP 2288/ASD 2288/1C063 01430/ SMC 80936/angel 36324 *recording completed on 12-14 march 1964*

he shall feed his flock/messiah

hamburg 6 december 1952	ndr orchestra schüchter *sung in german*	lp: melodram MEL 082/discocorp RR 208/RR 537/ discoreale DR 10037 cd: melodram CDM 16501/golden melodram GM 70000

eracle *role of iole*

milan 29 december 1958	barbieri, corelli, hines, bastianini la scala chorus and orchestra matacic	lp: ed smith EJS 395/di stefano GDS 3001/hope records HOPE 239 cd: golden melodram GM 50022
new york 2 december 1960	ludwig, berry, ludgin, verreau american opera society chorus and orchestra rescigno *sung in english*	unpublished radio broadcast *excerpts* lp: discocorp RR 208

handel/**my father!**/eracle *iole*
detroit	detroit symphony	lp: rococo 5374
18 february 1960	paray	
	sung in english	

v'adoro pupille/**giulio cesare** *cleopatra*
paris	orchestre national	cd: golden melodram GM 40072
3 march 1959	rosenthal	*incorrectly dated 1953*

detroit	detroit symphony	lp: rococo 5374
18 february 1960	paray	

caro selve/**atalanta**
aix-en-provence	rosbaud	cd: melodram CDM 26524/andromeda ANDRCD 5006
23 july 1954		*incorrectly dated 29 july 1954*

salzburg	moore	cd: emi 566 0842
7 august 1956		

new york	reeves	cd: emi 761 0432/notablu 935 0911
25 november 1956		

sweet bird that shuns the noise of folly/**l'allegro, il pensoroso ed il moderato**
vienna	vienna symphony	cd: radio österreich CD 28
30 april 1944	weisbach	
	sung in german	

vienna	niedermayer, flute	78: columbia LX 1010
2 november 1946	vienna philharmonic	45: columbia SEL 1585
	krips	lp: emi ALP 143 5501/154 6133
		cd: emi 763 2012/567 6342/dutton CDLX 7029/
		istituto discografico italiano IDIS 6447-6448/
		regis RRC 1167

FRANZ JOSEF HAYDN (1732-1809)
scena di berenice
scheveningen	netherlands	lp: discocorp RR 208
25 june 1958	chamber orchestra	
	goldberg	

an den vetter; daphnens einziger fehler
london	de los angeles	lp: emi AN 182-183/SAN 182-183/SLS 926/143 5941
20 february 1967	fischer-dieskau	cd: emi 749 2382/CDEMX 2233/567 9902/567 9942
	moore	

she never told her love
hilversum	antonietti	unpublished radio broadcast
9 june 1952		*vara*

RICHARD HEUBERGER (1850-1914)
gehen wir ins chambre séparée/der opernball

london	philharmonia	45: columbia SEL 1648/ESL 6267
4 july 1957	ackermann	lp: columbia 33CX 1570/SAX 2283/SAXF 158/
		angel 35696/3754/emi ASD 2807/CCPM 130 600/
		SVP 1180/2C053 00478/100 4781
		cd: emi 747 2842/565 5772/566 9892/567 0042
montreal	cbc orchestra	dvd video: video artists international VAI 4390
3 july 1963	boskovsky	*canadian television*

ENGELBERT HUMPERDINCK (1854-1921)
hänsel und gretel *role of gretel*

london	grümmer, ilosvay,	lp: columbia 33CX 1096-1097/FCX 286-287/QCX
27 june-	schürhoff,	10048-10049/LALP 207-208/WCX 1096-1097/
2 july 1953	felbermayer,	C 90327-90328/angel 3506/world records OC 187-188/
	metternich	emi SLS 5145/EX 769 2931
	choirs	cd: emi 763 2932/567 0612/567 1452/naxos 811 0897-8
	philharmonia	*excerpts*
	karajan	45: columbia SEL 1694
		lp: columbia 33CX 1819/WSX 545/C 80528/world
		records OH 189
		cd: emi 763 6572/763 7902/585 1052/urania URN 22296
milan	jurinac, streich,	cd: datum DAT 12314/walhall WLCD 0080
6 february 1954	palombini,	*excerpts*
	panerai	cd: legato LCD 197
	rai milano chorus	
	and orchestra	
	karajan	
	sung in italian	

suse liebe suse....brüderchen komm' tanz mit mir!/hänsel und gretel *gretel*

london	seefried	78: columbia LX 1036-1037
26-27 september	philharmonia	lp: american columbia RO 5417/emi RLS 763/
1947	krips	1C151 43160-43163M
		cd: emi 769 7932/567 6342/istituto discografico italiano
		IDIS 6447-6448/regis RRC 1167/preiser 20044

der kleine sandmann bin ich; abends will ich schlafen geh'n/hänsel und gretel
sandmännchen and gretel

london	seefried	78: columbia LX 1037
26 september 1947	philharmonia	lp: emi RLS 763/1C151 43160-43163M
	krips	cd: emi 567 6342/regis RRC 1167/preiser 20044

weihnachten

london	chorus	lp: columbia 33CX 1482/angel 35580/36750/
26 may 1957	philharmonia	ASD 3798/100 4531
	mackerras	cd: emi 763 5742

winterlied

berlin	raucheisen	lp: acanta 40 23557
20 november 1944		cd: acanta 42 43128/membran 223067/223093

ADOLF JENSEN (1837-1879)
mürmelndes lüftchen

london	moore	45: columbia SEL 1600/ESL 6274
13 april 1956		lp: columbia 33CX 1404/SAX 2265/FCX 664/SAXF 145/
		WCX 1404/C 90545/angel 35383
		cd: emi 565 8602/356 5262

YRVO KILPINEN (1892-1959)
kleines lied/lieder der liebe

vienna	parsons	decca unpublished
3 january 1979		

ERICH WOLFGANG KORNGOLD (1897-1957)
glück das mir verblieb/die tote stadt *marietta*

hamburg	ndr orchestra	lp: melodram MEL 088
6 december 1952	schüchter	cd: golden melodram GM 70000

FRANZ LEHAR (1870-1948)
meine lippen sie küssen so heiss/giuditta

london	chorus	45: columbia SEL 1648/ESL 6267
4-5 july 1957	philharmonia	lp: columbia 33CX 1570/SAX 2283/SAXF 158/angel 35696/
	ackermann	emi ASD 2807/SVP 1180/CCPM 130 600/100 4781/
		2C053 00478
		cd: emi 747 2842/566 9892/567 0042

heut' noch werd' ich ehefrau; hoch evoe angele!/der graf von luxemburg

london	chorus	45: columbia SEL 1652/ESL 6270
2-3 july 1957	philharmonia	lp: columbia 33CX 1570/SAX 2283/SAXF 158/angel 35696/
	ackermann	emi ASD 2807/SVP 1180/CCPM 130 600/100 4781/
		2C053 00478
		cd: emi 747 2842/566 9892/567 0042

das land des lächelns *role of lisa*

london	loose, gedda,	lp: columbia 33CX 1114-1115/WSX 535-536/
19-21 april 1953	kunz	C 80514-80515/angel 3507/emi SXDW 3044/
	bbc chorus	1C149 03047-03048/1C147 03580-03581
	philharmonia	cd: emi 763 5232/585 8222/567 5292/naxos 811.1016-1017
	ackermann	*excerpts*
		lp: columbia 33CX 1712/WSX 563/C 80587/emi SLS 5250/
		RLS 763/1C151 43160-43163M
		recording completed on 28 june 1953

das land des lächelns/querschnitt (scenes)

berlin	glawitsch	78: telefunken E 3115
17 august 1940	orchester des	45: telefunken UE45-3115
	deutschen	cd: teldec 3984 284062
	opernhauses	cd: hänssler classics 94501
	lütze	

lehar/**die lustige witwe** *role of hanna glawari*

london
16-21 april 1953
	loose, gedda,
	kunz
	bbc chorus
	philharmonia
	ackermann
		lp: columbia 33CX 1051-1052/QCX 10050-10051/
		    VCX 515-516/WCX 1051-1052/WSX 537-528/
		    C 90310-90311/C 80516-80517/angel 3501/emi
		    SXDW 3045/1C149 03116-03117M
		cd: emi 769 5202/585 8222/567 5292/naxos 811.1007/
		    regis RRC 1163
		excerpts
		78: columbia LX 1597
		45: columbia SEL 1559/SCD 2083/SCB 113/SCBQ 3019
		lp: columbia 33CX 1712/WSX 563/C 80507/emi
		    RLS 763/1C151 43160-43163M/1C147 03580-03581
		cd: emi 763 6572/763 7902/andromeda ANDRCD 5006/
		    regis RRC 1167

london
2-12 july 1962
	steffek, gedda,
	wächter
	philharmonia
	chorus and
	orchestra
	matacic
		lp: emi AN 101-102/SAN 101-102/EX 29 07973/
		    SLS 823/1C153 00001-00002/2C153 00001-00002/
		    2C181 00001-00002/angel 3630
		cd: emi 747 1788/567 3702/567 3672
		excerpts
		lp: emi ALP 2252/ASD 2252/angel 36340/3754

viljalied/die lustige witwe

london 21 december 1961	philharmonia mackerras	unpublished video recording *bbc television*
montreal 3 july 1963	cbc orchestra boskovsky	dvd video: video artists international VAI 4390 *canadian television*

paganini/querschnitt (scenes)

berlin 2 september 1939	glawitsch orchester des deutschen opernhauses otto	78: telefunken E 3041/E 1172 78: capitol (usa) ECL 2501 lp: capitol (usa) P 8033 cd: teldec 3984 284062 cd: hänssler classics 94501

einer wird kommen/der zarewitsch

london
2 july 1957
	philharmonia
	ackermann
		45: columbia SEL 1652/ESL 6270
		lp: columbia 33CX 1570/SAX 2283/SAXF 158/
		    angel 35696/emi ASD 2807/SVP 1180/CCPM
		    130 600/100 4781/2C053 00478
		cd: emi 747 2842/566 9892/567 0042

RICHARD LEVERIDGE (1670-1758)
this great world is a trouble

berlin 1945	raucheisen *sung in german*	lp: acanta 40 23557 cd: acanta 42 43801/archipel ARPCD 0295

FRANZ LISZT (1811-1886)
es muss ein wunderbares sein
nohant	ciccolini	cd: arkadia CDGI 8021
29 june 1969		

die drei zigeuner
berlin	parsons	lp: emi ASD 2634/1C063 02116/angel 36752
20-27 october 1968		cd: emi 565 8602

nohant	ciccolini	cd: arkadia CDGI 8021
29 june 1969		

amsterdam	parsons	cd: bella voce BLV 107 002
8 february 1977		*also unpublished video recording*

o lieb' solang du lieben kannst!
london	moore	columbia unpublished
21 june 1957		

CARL LOEWE (1796-1869)
abendstunde (die amsel flötet)
berlin	raucheisen	lp: melodiya M10 41285-41286/5289-73/discocorp
9 march 1943		IGI 385/RR 208/acanta 40 23534/40 23557
		cd: acanta 42 43801/membran 223067/223072

abschied (niemals dich wieder zu sehen)
berlin	piltti	lp: melodiya M10 41285-41286/5289-73/discocorp
27 june 1942	raucheisen	IGI 385/RR 208

an sami (als er sami mit dir)
berlin	piltti	lp: melodram MEL 082/acanta 40 23534/discoreale
27 june 1942	raucheisen	DR 10038
		cd: membran 223067/223071

blume der ergebung (ich bin die blum' im garten)
berlin	raucheisen	lp: melodiya M10 41285-41286/5289-73/discocorp
9 march 1943		IGI 385/RR 208/acanta 40 23534
		cd: membran 223067/223069

die freude (es flattert um die quelle)
berlin	piltti	lp: acanta 40 23534
27 june 1942	raucheisen	cd: membran 223067/223071

frühling (der frühling begrüsset die junge natur)
berlin	raucheisen	lp: melodiya M10 41285-41286/5289-73/discocorp
9 march 1943		IGI 385/RR 208/melodram MEL 082/discoreale
		DR 10038/acanta 40 23534/40 23557
		cd: membran 223067/223071

frühlingsankunft (es ist mein herz verengt verdorrt)
berlin	raucheisen	lp: melodiya M10 41285-41286/5289-73/discocorp
9 march 1943		IGI 385/RR 208/melodram MEL 082/discoreale
		DR 10038/acanta 40 23534/40 23557
		cd: membran 223067/223072

das glockenspiel (das glockenspiel der fantasie)
berlin	raucheisen	lp: acanta 40 23534
9 march 1943		cd: membran 223067/223070

ihr spaziergang (will die holde sich ergeben)
berlin	raucheisen	lp: acanta 40 23534
9 march 1943		cd: membran 223067/223068

loewe/**irrlichter; kind und mädchen**
berlin raucheisen lp: acanta 40 23534
2 january 1945 cd: membran 223067/223069
kleiner haushalt (einen haushalt klein und fein)
berlin parsons lp: emi ASD 2634/1C063 02116/angel 36752
20-27 october 1968 cd: emi 763 6542/763 7902

berlin parsons emi unpublished
6-16 april 1970
liebesliedchen (winter vorbei, herzchen mein liebchen!)
berlin piltti lp: melodiya M10 41285-41286/5289-73/discocorp
27 june 1942 raucheisen IGI 385/RR 208
märz (es ist ein schnee gefallen)
berlin piltti lp: melodiya M10 41285-41286/5289-73/discocorp
27 june 1942 raucheisen IGI 385/RR 208/melodram MEL 088/scandia
SLP 546/acanta 40 23534
cd: membran 223067/223071/istituto discografico
italiano IDIS 6447-6448
o süsse mutter
berlin raucheisen lp: melodiya M10 41285-41286/5289-73/discocorp
9 march 1943 IGI 385/RR 208/acanta 40 23534
cd: membran 223067/223069
sonnenlicht (noch ahnt man kaum der sonne licht)
berlin piltti lp: melodiya M10 41285-41286/discocorp IGI 385/
27 june 1942 raucheisen RR 208
die sylphide (liebes leichtes luft'ges ding!)
berlin raucheisen lp: acanta 40 23534/40 23557
9 march 1943 cd: membran 223067/223068
tom der reimer (der reimer thomas lag am bach)
vienna parsons decca unpublished
4 january 1979
die verliebte schäferin; vogelgesang
berlin raucheisen lp: acanta 40 23534
9 march 1943 cd: membran 223067/223068
die wandelnde glocke (es war ein kind das wollte nie)
vienna parsons lp: decca SXL 6943/642 576AW/london (usa)
3 january 1979 OS 26592
cd: decca 430 0002
zeislein (zeislein wo ist dein häuslein?)
berlin raucheisen lp: acanta 40 23534
2 january 1945 cd: membran 223067/223069

GUSTAV MAHLER (1860-1911)
symphony no 2 "resurrection"

london 15 march 1962	rössel-majdan philharmonia chorus and orchestra klemperer	lp: columbia 33CX 1829-1830/SAX 2473-2474/FCX 948-949/ SAXF 948-949/C 91268-91269/STC 91268-91269/angel 3634/emi SLS 806/1C163 00570-00571/1C193 00570- 00571/2C165 52519-52526/CCA 948-949/100 5703 cd: emi 769 6622/567 2352/567 2552

symphony no 4

scheveningen 6 june 1952	concertgebouw walter	cd: globe GLO 6900/GLO 6905/q-disc MCCL 97018
vienna 29 may 1960	vienna philharmonic walter	lp: discocorp BWS 705 cd: music and arts CD 705/CD 4705/wing WCD 1-2 *final movement only* cd: verona 27075
london 25 april 1961	philharmonia klemperer	lp: columbia 33CX 1793/SAX 2441/FCX 941/SAXF 259/ QCX 10473/C 91191/STC 91191/angel 35829/angel seraphim 60359/emi ASD 2799/1C063 00553/ 2C069 00553/2C165 52519-52526/CVB 941/100 5534 cd: emi 769 6672/567 0352

des knaben wunderhorn/ *see individual songs*

des antonius von padua fischpredigt/des knaben wunderhorn

berlin 21-29 april 1966	parsons	lp: emi ASD 2404/1C187 01307-01308/angel 36545/3754 cd: emi 763 6542/763 7902

ich atmet' einen linden duft/rückert-lieder

vienna 29 may 1960	vienna philharmonic walter	lp: discocorp BWS 705/RR 208/RR 537 cd: music and arts CD 705/CD 4705/verona 27075
berlin 21-29 april 1966	parsons	lp: emi ASD 2404/1C187 01307-01308/angel 36545 cd: emi 763 6542/763 7902
amsterdam 8 february 1977	parsons	cd: bella voce BLV 107 002 *also unpublished video recording*

ich bin der welt abhanden gekommen/rückert-lieder

vienna 29 may 1960	vienna philharmonic walter	lp: discocorp BWS 705/RR 208/RR 537 cd: music and arts CD 705/CD 4705/verona 27025

das irdische leben/des knaben wunderhorn

london 8-12 march 1968	london symphony szell	lp: emi SAN 218/ASD 143 4424/1C065 00098/ 2C069 00098/angel 36547 cd: emi 747 2772/567 2362/567 2562

lied des verfolgten im turm/des knaben wunderhorn

london 8-12 march 1968	fischer-dieskau london symphony szell	lp: emi SAN 218/ASD 143 4424/1C065 00098/ 2C069 00098/angel 36547 cd: emi 747 2772/567 2362/567 2562

mahler/**lob des hohen verstandes**/des knaben wunderhorn

berlin	parsons	lp: emi ASD 2404/1C187 01307-01308/angel 36547
21-29 april 1966		cd: emi 763 6542/763 7902/565 8602

london	london symphony	lp: emi SAN 218/ASD 143 4424/1C065 00098/
8-12 march 1968	szell	2C069 00098/angel 36547
		cd: emi 747 2772/567 2362/567 2562

london	moore	unpublished video recording
22 march 1968		*bbc television*

rheinlegendchen/des knaben wunderhorn

london	london symphony	lp: emi SAN 218/ASD 143 4424/1C065 00098/
8-12 march 1968	szell	cd: emi 747 2772/567 2362/567 2562

der schildwache nachtlied; verlor'ne müh'/des knaben wunderhorn

london	fischer-dieskau	lp: emi SAN 218/ASD 143 4424/1C065 00098/
8-12 march 1968	london symphony	2C069 00098/angel 36547
	szell	cd: emi 747 2772/567 2362/567 2562

um schlimme kinder artig zu machen/lieder und gesänge aus der jugendzeit

berlin	parsons	lp: emi ASD 2634/1C063 02116/angel 36752
20-27 october 1968		cd: emi 763 6542/763 7902

wo die schönen trompeten blasen/des knaben wunderhorn

vienna	vienna philharmonic	lp: discocorp BWS 705/RR 208/RR 537
29 may 1960	walter	cd: music and arts CD 705/CD 4705/verona 27075

london	fischer-dieskau	lp: emi SAN 218/ASD 143 4424/1C065 00098/
8-12 march 1968	london symphony	2C069 00098/angel 36547
	szell	cd: emi 747 2772/567 2362/567 2562

JOHANN PAUL MARTINI (1741-1816)
plasir d'amour

aix-en-provence	rosbaud	cd: melodram CDM 26524/andromeda ANDRCD 5006
23 july 1954		*incorrectly dated 29 july 1954*

london	moore	45: columbia SEL 1589/ESL 6255
12 april 1956		lp: columbia 33CX 1404/SAX 2265/FCX 664/SAXF 145/
		WCX 1404/C 90545/angel 35383/emi 154 6133
		cd: emi 763 6542/763 7902/356 5262

JOSEPH MARX (1882-1964)
venezianisches wiegenlied

vienna	parsons	decca unpublished
9-10 january 1979		

NIKOLAY MEDTNER (1880-1951)
elfenliedchen; im vorübergehen
london   medtner   78: columbia LX 1423
22 november 1950   cd: emi 754 8392/565 8602

the rose; when roses fade
london   medtner   78: columbia LX 1423
22 november 1950   *sung in english*   cd: emi 754 8392/565 8602

glückliche fahrt; meeresstille; die quelle; selbstbetrug
london   medtner   78: columbia LX 1424
22 november 1950   cd: emi 754 8392/565 8602

aus lila (so tanzet und springet!)
london   medtner   78: columbia LX 1425
16 october 1950   cd: emi 754 8392/585 8602

the muse; the waltz
london   medtner   78: columbia LX 1425
16 october 1950   *sung in english*   cd: emi 754 8392/585 8602

einsamkeit; präludium; winternacht
london   medtner   78: columbia LX 1426
16 october 1950   cd: emi 754 8392/585 8602

FELIX MENDELSSOHN-BARTHOLDY (1809-1847)
auf flügeln des gesanges
london   moore   45: columbia SEL 1589/ESL 6255/SCD 2149
11 april 1956   lp: columbia 33CX 1404/SAX 2265/FCX 664/
                 SAXF 145/WCX 1404/C 90545/angel 35383
                 cd: emi 585 8602/356 5262

CARL MILLOECKER (1842-1899)
ich schenk' mein herz; was ich im leben beginne/die dubarry
london   philharmonia   lp: columbia 33CX 1507/SAX 2283/SAXF 158/
5 july 1957   ackermann   angel 35696/3754/emi ASD 2807/SVP 1180/
                 100 4781
                 cd: emi 747 2842/566 9892/567 0042

CLAUDIO MONTEVERDI (1567-1643)
madrigals: io son pur vezzosetta pastorella; ardo e scoprir; baci cari; dialogo di ninfa e pastore
london   seefried   lp: columbia 33CX 1331/FCX 515/WCX 1331/
27 may 1955   moore   C 90486/angel 35290/angel seraphim 60376/
                 emi 2C051 43240/HLM 7267
                 cd: emi 769 7932

THOMAS MORLEY (1557-1602)
it was a lover and his lass
vienna   hudez   cd: testament SBT 2172
7 november 1946   *unpublished columbia 78rpm recording*

WOLFGANG AMADEUS MOZART (1756-1791)

bastien und bastienne *role of bastienne*

berlin	sinimberghi,	unpublished soundtrack recording
1939	hausschild	*television production which probably no longer survives*
	berlin philharmonic	
	gebhardt	

betulia liberata *role of amital*

turin	pirazzini, valletti,	lp: melodram MEL 211
30 may 1952	christoff	cd: nuova era NE 2377/memories HR 4222
	rai torino chorus	*excerpts*
	and orchestra	lp: ed smith records EJS 276
	rossi	cd: istituto discografico italiano IDIS 6447-6448

zeffiretti lusinghieri/idomeneo *ilia*

london	philharmonia	45: columbia SEL 1515
16 september 1952	pritchard	lp: columbia 33CX 1069/FCX 183/QCX 10058/WCX 1069/ C 90321/angel 35021/world records T 583/emi 2C051 43222
		cd: emi 747 9502/763 7082/476 8442/476 8452/preiser 93444
turin	rai torino	lp: cetra LMR 5018/melodram MEL 047/MEL 088/ discocorp RR 208
1 december 1952	orchestra	
	rossi	cd: melodram CDM 16529/cetra CDMR 5018/wahlall WLCD 0150/istituto discografico italiano IDIS 6447-6448/ golden melodram GM 70000

l'amero saro costante/il re pastore *aminta*

vienna	sedlak, violin	78: columbia LX 1096/LFX 1018
2 november 1946	vienna philharmonic	lp: emi RLS 763/1C151 43160-43163M
	krips	cd: emi 763 7502/476 8442/476 8452/grandi voci alla scala GVS 19/andromeda ANDRCD 5006/preiser 93444

mozart/**cosi fan tutte** *role of fiordiligi*

london
13-20 july 1954
	merriman, otto,
	simoneau, panerai,
	bruscantini
	chorus
	philharmonia
	karajan
		lp: columbia 33CX 1262-1264/QCX 10146-10148/FCX 484-486/
		    WCX 1262-1264/C 90432-90434/angel 3522/world records
		    OC 195-197/emi RLS 7709/1C147 01748-01750M/
		    2C153 01748-01750/3C153 01748-01750/
		    1C197 54200-54208M
		cd: emi 769 6352/567 0642/567 1382/336 7892/naxos 811 1232-4
		excerpts
		lp: columbia WSX 557/C 80574/world records OH 198/
		    emi 1C063 00838
		cd: emi CDEMX 2211/urania URN 22296
		recording completed on 6 november 1954

milan
27 january 1956
	merriman, sciutti,
	alva, panerai,
	calabrese
	la scala chorus
	and orchestra
	cantelli
		lp: discocorp IGI 326/cetra LO 13/estro armonico EA 029/
		    pantheon C 87662/stradivarius STR 13597-13599
		cd: stradivarius STR 73597-73599/walhall WLCD 0164/
		    living stage LS 40351 45

salzburg 24 august 1958	ludwig, sciutti, alva, panerai, schmidt vienna opera chorus vienna philharmonic böhm	unpublished video recording *austrian television* *excerpts* lp: gioielli della lirica GML 052 cd: orfeo C394 201B/C408 955R
salzburg 27 july 1960	ludwig, sciutti, kmentt, prey, dönch vienna opera chorus vienna philharmonic böhm	lp: melodram MEL 708/movimento musica 03 026 *excerpts* lp: melodram MEL 082/MEL 088 cd: melodram CDM 16501/gala GL 100 501
salzburg 1 august 1961	ludwig, sciutti, kmentt, prey dönch vienna opera chorus vienna philharmonic böhm	unpublished video recording *austrian television*
salzburg 8 august 1962	ludwig, sciutti, kmentt, prey, dönch vienna opera chorus vienna philharmonic böhm	cd: arkadia CDMP 455/gala GL 100 503

london
10-18 september
1962
	ludwig, steffek,
	kraus, taddei,
	berry
	philharmonia
	chorus and
	orchestra
	böhm
		lp: emi AN 103-106/SAN 103-106/SLS 901/SLS 5028/
		    1C163 01182-01184/2C167 01182-01184/angel 3631
		cd: emi 769 3302/567 3822/567 3792
		excerpts
		lp: emi ALP 2265/ASD 2265/ASD 3915/SXLP 30457/
		    1C063 00838/YKM 5002/angel 36167/36948/3754
		cd: emi 565 5772/585 1052

mozart / come scoglio / cosi fan tutte *fiordiligi*

new york 25 november 1956	reeves	cd: emi 761 0432/notablu 935 0911
paris 3 march 1959	orchestre national rosenthal	cd: golden melodram GM 40072 *incorrectly dated 1953*

per pieta / cosi fan tutte *fiordiligi*

naples 10 october 1961	rai napoli orchestra franci	cd: melodram CDM 16529

soave sia il vento / cosi fan tutte *fiordiligi*

london 20 february 1967	de los angeles fischer-dieskau moore	emi unpublished

l'amore e un ladroncello / cosi fan tutte *dorabella*

paris 3 march 1959	orchestre national rosenthal	cd: golden melodram GM 40072 *incorrectly dated 1953*
naples 10 october 1961	rai napoli orchestra franci	cd: melodram CDM 16529
blossom 28 july 1968	cleveland orchestra szell	lp: rococo 5374 cd: arkadia CDGPI 745/golden melodram GM 40072

don giovanni *role of donna elvira*

london 27 september 1947	cebotari, güden, tauber, kunz, schöffler vienna opera chorus vienna philharmonic krips *sung in german*	unpublished radio broadcast *bbc third programme* *excerpts from this performance published by ed smith,* *historia and eklipse do not involve the participation* *of donna elvira*

salzburg
27 july 1950
	welitsch, seefried,
	dermota, kunz,
	gobbi, greindl
	vienna opera chorus
	vienna philharmonic
	furtwängler
		lp: ed smith EJS 419/olympic 9109/discocorp RR 407/
		    turnabout THS 65154-65156/melodram MEL 713
		cd: priceless D 16581/laudis LCD 34001/emi 566 5672
		excerpts
		lp: melodram MEL 082/MEL 088/discoreale
		    DR 10037
		cd: melodram CDM 16501/golden melodram GM 70000
		olympic issue included part of the 1953 performance listed below

salzburg
27 july 1953
	grümmer, berger,
	dermota, edelmann,
	siepi, arié
	vienna opera chorus
	vienna philharmonic
	furtwängler
		cd: rodolphe RPC 32527-32530/virtuoso 269 9052/
		    gala GL 100 602/archipel ARPCD 0162/
		    orfeo C624 043D
		excerpts
		cd: istituto discografico italiano IDIS 6447-6448

mozart/don giovanni/concluded

salzburg
6 august 1954
	grümmer, berger,
	dermota, edelmann,
	siepi, ernster
	vienna opera chorus
	vienna philharmonic
	furtwängler
		lp: morgan MOR 5302/discocorp MORG 003/cetra LO 7/
		    foyer FO 1017/emi EX 29 06673
		cd: music and arts CD 003/cetra CDE 1050/arkadia
		    CD 509/CDHP 509/emi 763 8602/336 7992
		final scene of the opera missing from this recording and is spliced in
		from the 1953 performance listed previously

london 2-4 october 1959	sutherland, sciutti, alva, taddei, wächter, frick philharmonia chorus and orchestra klemperer	columbia unpublished *recording incomplete due to illness of conductor*

london
7-15 october 1959
	sutherland, sciutti,
	alva, taddei,
	wächter, frick
	philharmonia
	chorus and
	orchestra
	giulini
		lp: columbia 33CX 1717-1720/SAX 2369-2372/FCX
		    875-878/SAXF 192-195/QCX 10394-10397/
		    SAXQ 7288-7291/WSX 518-521/C 91059-91062/
		    SAXW 9503-9506/STC 91059-91062/angel 3605/
		    emi SLS 5083/1C165 00504-00507/
		    2C165 00504-00507
		cd: emi 747 2608/556 2322/567 8692/567 8732
		excerpts
		lp: columbia 33CX 1918/SAX 2559/C 80714/STC 80714/
		    angel 36948/3754/emi ASD 2915/SXLP30300/YKM
		    5002/1C037 03069/1C061 02056/2C061 02056
		cd: emi 763 0782/565 5772/566 5672/585 1052
		recording completed on 24 november 1959

london 18 october 1959	sutherland, sciutti, alva, taddei, wächter, frick philharmonia chorus and orchestra davis	unpublished radio broadcast *bbc third programme*

salzburg
3 august 1960
	l.price, sciutti,
	valletti, berry,
	wächter, zaccaria
	vienna opera chorus
	vienna philharmonic
	karajan
		lp: historical recording enterprises HRE 247/movimento
		    musica 03 001
		cd: movimento musica 013 6012/curcio OP 6/arkadia
		    CDKAR 225
		excerpts
		cd: orfeo C394 201B/C408 955R

new york 29 january 1966	stich-randall, elias, peerce, g..evans, siepi, ghiuselev metropolitan opera chorus and orchestra rosenstock	unpublished metropolitan opera broadcast

mozart/**mi tradi/don giovanni** *donna elvira*

london 26 september 1947	philharmonia krips	78: columbia LX 1210/american columbia 72640D 45: columbia SEL 1511 lp: emi RLS 763/1C151 43160-43163M cd: preiser 93444/andromeda ANDRCD 5006/ emi 476 8442
london 16 september 1952	philharmonia pritchard	columbia unpublished
turin 1 december 1952	rai torino orchestra rossi	lp: cetra LMR 5018/discocorp RR 508 cd: cetra CDMR 5018/melodram CDM 16529
london 25 october 1961	philharmonia mackerras	vhs video: emi MVC 491 4763 dvd video: emi DVA 477 8319/DVA 492 8529
blossom 28 july 1968	ckeveland orchestra szell	lp: rococo 5374 cd: arkadia CDGPI 745/golden melodram GM 70004

non mi dir/don giovanni *donna anna*

london
4 july 1952
	philharmonia
	pritchard
		45: columbia SEL 1515/SEBQ 124/ESBF 122
		lp: columbia 33CX 1069/FCX 183/QCX 10058/
		    WCX 1069/C 90321/angel 35021/world records
		    T 583/emi RLS 763/1C151 43160-43163M/
		    2C051 43222
		cd: emi 747 9502/763 7082/476 8442/476 8452/notablu
		    935 0911/preiser 93444/grandi voci alla scala GVS 19/
		    andromeda ANDRCD 5006

batti batti; vedrai carino/don giovanni *zerlina*

london
1-2 july 1952
	philharmonia
	pritchard
		78: columbia LB 145
		45: columbia SEL 1511
		lp: columbia 33CX 1069/FCX 183/QCX 10058/
		    WCX 1069/C 90321/angel 35021/world records
		    T 583/emi 2C051 43222
		cd: emi 747 9502/763 7082/476 8442/476 8452/
		    preiser 93444

die entführung aus dem serail *role of konstanze*

vienna
4-6 september 1944
	loose, dermota,
	klein, alsen
	vienna opera chorus
	vienna philharmonic
	moralt
		lp: melodram MEL 047
		cd: gala GL 100 501/urania URN 22134
		excerpts
		lp: urania URLP 7036/saga XIG 8011/ST 7011/5911/
		    FDY 2143/STFDY 2143/rococo 5374/discoreale
		    DR 10037/melodram MEL 082/MEL 088/
		    historia H 677-678/acanta BB 23119
		cd: melodram CDM 16501/golden melodram GM 70000/
		    istituto discografico italiano IDIS 6447-6448/
		    preiser 90345/cantus classics CACD 500 104
		*many early lp editions of martern aller arten incorrectly described
		the singer as maria cebotari*

mozart/**martern aller arten/die entführung aus dem serail** *konstanze*

vienna	vienna philharmonic	lp: emi RLS 763/RLS 7714/1C151 43160-43163M/
23 october 1946	karajan	1C137 54370-54373M/154 6133
		cd: emi 763 7082/476 8442/476 8452/notablu 935 0923/
		preiser 93444/andromeda ANDRCD 5006/
		golden melodram GM 70004/urania URN 22296
		unpublished columbia 78rpm recording

traurigkeit ward mir zum lose/die entführung aus dem serail *konstanze*

vienna	vienna philharmonic	78: columbia LX 1249/LZX 241
31 october 1946	krips	lp: american columbia ML 4649/emi RLS 763/154 6133/
		1C151 43160-43163M
		cd: emi 763 7082/476 8442/476 8452/andromeda
		ANDRCD 5006/ preiser 93444

le nozze di figaro *role of contessa almaviva*

milan	seefried, jurinac,	unpublished radio broadcast
28 december 1948	höfermayer, taddei	*excerpts*
	vienna opera chorus	lp: melodram MEL 088
	vienna philharmonic	cd: golden melodram GM 70000/istituto discografico
	karajan	italiano IDIS 6447-6448
vienna	seefried, jurinac,	78: columbia LWX 410-425/SL 114
17-21 june 1950	london, kunz	lp: columbia 33CX 1007-1009/QCX 10002-10004/
	vienna opera chorus	FCX 174-176/VCX 503-505/WCX 1007-1009/
	vienna philharmonic	C 90292-90294/emi 1C147 01751-01753M/2C165
	karajan	01751-01753M/1C197 54200-54208M
		cd: emi 769 6392/567 0682/567 1422/336 7792
		excerpts
		78: columbia LX 1575
		lp: columbia 33CX 1558/C 80531/C 70373/emi RLS 764/
		1C137 43187-43189M/angel 35326
		cd: emi 763 6572/763 7902/istituto discografico italiano
		IDIS 6447-6448/regis RRC 1167
naples	loose, zareska,	cassette tape: lyric distribution (usa) ALD 1992
3 february 1951	stabile, badioli	
	san carlo chorus	
	and orchestra	
	böhm	
salzburg	seefried, güden,	lp: ed smith records GMR 999/discocorp IGI 343/
7 august 1953	schöffler, kunz	cetra LO 8/FE 27
	vienna opera chorus	cd: rodolphe RPC 32527-32530/eklipse EKRCD 59/
	vienna philharmonic	emi 566 0802
	furtwängler	*excerpts*
	sung in german	lp: melodram MEL 082
		cd: melodram CDM 16501/orfeo C394 201B/C408 955R
		it is possible that the original lp edition by ed smith was taken from
		a later performance on 11 august 1953

mozart/le nozze di figaro/concluded

milan
4 february 1954
	seefried, jurinac,
	petri, panerai
	la scala chorus
	and orchestra
	karajan
		lp: cetra LO 70
		cd: melodram CDM 37075/arkadia CDKAR 225/istituto
		    discografico italiano IDIS 6428-6429/walhall
		    WLCD 0134
		excerpts
		lp: gioielli della lirica GML 030

salzburg 30 july 1957	seefried, ludwig, fischer-dieskau, kunz vienna opera chorus vienna philharmonic böhm	lp: melodram MEL 709 cd: di stefano GDS 31019/gala GL 100 601/orfeo C296 932S *excerpts* lp: melodram MEL 047 cd: virtuoso 269 7152/verona 27092-27094
salzburg 4 august 1958	seefried, ludwig, fischer-dieskau, kunz vienna opera chorus vienna philharmonic böhm	unpublished radio broadcast *austrian radio* *excerpts* cd: orfeo C335 931B

london
16-27 september
1959
	moffo, cossotto,
	wächter, taddei
	philharmonia
	chorus and
	orchestra
	giulini
		lp: columbia 33CX 1732-1735/SAX 2381-2384/
		    FCX 862-865/SAXF 114-117/QCX 10419-10422/
		    SAXQ 7320-7323/C 91184-91186/STC 91194-91186/
		    angel 3608/emi SLS 5152/1C165 00514-00517/
		    2C165 00514-00517/3C165 00514-00517/1C147
		    01751-01753/1C191 03464-03466
		cd: emi 763 2662/358 6022
		excerpts
		lp: columbia 33CX 1934/SAX 2573/C 80859/SMC 80859/
		    angel 35640/3754/emi CVT 3558/YKM 5002/SXLP
		    30303/1C061 01392/1C063 00839/2C061 01392/
		    1C147 30636-30637
		cd: emi 763 4092/565 5772/585 1052
		recording completed on 21 november 1959

london 6 february 1961	söderström, berganza, blanc, corena philharmonia chorus and orchestra giulini	unpublished radio broadcast *bbc third programme*
amsterdam 3 july 1961	sciutti, malagu, prey, taddei netherlands chamber choir residentieorkest giulini	cd: verona 27092-27094

mozart/**porgi amor**/**le nozze di figaro** *contessa almaviva*

london	philharmonia	lp: columbia 33CX 1069/FCX 183/QCX 10058/
4 july 1952	pritchard	WCX 1069/C 90321/angel 35021/world records
		T 583/emi RLS 763/1C151 43160-43163M/2C051
		43222
		cd: emi 763 7082/476 8442/476 8452/grandi voci alla scala
		GVS 19/ notablu 935 0911/andromeda ANDRCD 5006/
		preiser 93444

hamburg	ndr orchestra	lp: melodram MEL 082/discoreale DR 10037
6 december 1952	schüchter	cd: golden melodram GM 70000

stuttgart	sdr orchestra	cd: hänssler classics 93152
6 april 1959	schuricht	vhs video: emi MVC 491 4763
		dvd video: emi DVA 477 8319/DVA 492 8529

dove sono/**le nozze di figaro** *contessa almaviva*

london	philharmonia	lp: columbia 33CX 1069/FCX 183/QCX 10058/
9 september 1952	pritchard	WCX 1069/C 90321/angel 35021/world records
		T 583/emi RLS 763/1C151 43160-43163M/
		2C051 43222
		cd: emi 763 7082/476 8442/476 8452/grandi voci alla scala
		GVS 19/andromeda ANDRCD 5006/preiser 93444

deh vieni non tardar/**le nozze di figaro** *susanna*

london	philharmonia	lp: columbia 33CX 1069/FCX 183/QCX 10058/
2 july 1952	pritchard	WCX 1069/C 90321/angel 35021/world records
		T 583/emi RLS 763/1C151 43160-43163M/
		2C051 43222
		cd: emi 747 6502/763 7082/565 5772/476 8442/
		476 8452/notablu 935 0911/grandi voci alla scala GVS 19/
		andromeda ABDRCD 5006/preiser 93444

turin	rai torino orchestra	cd: melodram CDM 16529
1 december 1952	rossi	

blossom	cleveland orchestra	lp: rococo 5374
28 july 1968	szell	cd: arkadia CDGPI 745/golden melodram GM 70004

non so piu/**le nozze di figaro** *cherubino*

london	philharmonia	lp: columbia 33CX 1069/FCX 183/QCX 10058/
2 july 1952	pritchard	WCX 1069/C 90321/angel 35021/world records
		T 583/emi 2C051 43222
		cd: emi 747 6502/763 7082/585 1052/476 8442/
		476 8452/preiser 93444

mozart/**voi che sapete/le nozze di figaro** *cherubino*

london
1 july 1952
	philharmonia
	pritchard
		lp: columbia 33CX 1069/FCX 183/QCX 10058/
		    WCX 1069/C 90321/angel 35021/world records
		    T 583/emi 2C051 43222
		cd: emi 747 6502/763 7082/476 8442/476 8452/
		    preiser 93444

london 16 january 1958	goldsborough orchestra mackerras	lp: voce VOCE 116 *ornamented version of the aria*

die zauberflöte *role of pamina*

rome 19 december 1953	streich, gedda, taddei, petri rai roma chorus and orchestra karajan *sung in italian*	cd: myto MCD 89007/walhall WLCD 0017 *excerpts* cd: arkadia CD 535/CDHP 535

private 78rpm test recordings (six sides) of pamina's role in english, accompanied at the piano by norman feasey and also including dialogue, were made by schwarzkopf in march 1948 prior to her covent garden début in the part: these are now published on cd by testament SBT 2172

die zauberflöte *role of erste dame*

london 24 march- 7 april 1964	janowitz, popp, ludwig, höffgen, gedda, berry, frick, crass philharmonia chorus and orchestra klemperer	lp: emi AN 137-139/SAN 137-139/SLS 912/1C157 00031-00033/2C165 00031-00033/angel 3651 cd: emi 769 9712/555 1732/567 3882/567 3852 *excerpts* lp: emi ALP 2314/ASD 2314/ESD 100 3261 cd: emi 763 4512/769 0562/565 5682

ach ich fühl's/die zauberflöte *pamina*

london 12 april 1948	philharmonia braithwaite *sung in english*	lp: emi ALP 143 5501/RLS 154 6133 cd: emi 763 7082/476 8442 *unpublished columbia 78rpm recording*
london 5 july 1952	philharmonia pritchard	columbia unpublished

turin
1 december 1952
	rai torino orchestra
	rossi
		lp: cetra LMR 5018/discocorp RR 208/melodram
		    MEL 047/MEL 088
		cd: cetra CDMR 5018/gala GL 100 501/istituto
		    discografico italiano IDIS 6447-6448

bei männern welche liebe fühlen/die zauberflöte *pamina*

vienna 9 december 1947	kunz vienna philharmonic karajan	columbia unpublished

mozart/abendempfindung (abend ist's, die sonne ist verschwunden)

london 11 september 1952	moore	78: columbia LX 1580
london 4-7 july 1953	moore	columbia unpublished
london 6 january 1954	moore	lp: columbia 33CX 1044/FCX 182/WCX 1044/C 90306/ angel 35023/angel seraphim 60044/emi HQM 1072/ RLS 763/1C151 43160-43163M/melodiya M10 43861-43862 cd: emi 356 5262
aix-en-provence 23 july 1954	rosbaud	cd: melodram CDM 26524/andromeda ANDRCD 5006 *incorrectly dated 29 july 1954*
london 13-16 april 1955	gieseking	lp: columbia 33CX 1321/FCX 30116/WCX 1321/C 90478/ angel 35270/emi ASD 3858/2C061 01578/3C153 52700-52705M cd: emi 747 3262/763 7022/574 8032/353 2262
new york 25 november 1956	reeves	cd: emi 761 0432/notablu 935 0911
hilversum 11 february 1957	de nobel	unpublished radio broadcast *vara*
ascona 6 october 1967	parsons	cd: ermitage ERM 109
berlin 27 august- 8 september 1970	parsons	lp: emi ASD 2844/1C063 02331 *published on cd only in japan*

alma grande e nobil core, concert aria

london 10-18 march 1968	london symphony szell	lp: emi ASD 2493/1C063 01959/2C069 01959/angel 36643 cd: emi 747 9502/763 7022/574 8032

als luise die briefe ihres ungetreuen liebhabers (erzeugt von heisser fantasie)

london 13 april 1955	gieseking	lp: columbia 33CX 1321/FCX 30116/WCX 1321/C 90478/ angel 35270/emi ASD 3858/2C061 01578/3C153 52700-52705M/melodiya M10 43861-43862 cd: emi 747 3262/763 7022/353 2262
new york 25 november 1956	reeves	cd: emi 761 0432
hilversum 11 february 1957	de nobel	unpublished radio broadcast *vara*
amsterdam 22 december 1957	de nobel	cd: verona 27021

mozart/die alte (zu meiner zeit bestand noch recht und billigkeit)

london
14 april 1955
	gieseking	lp: columbia 33CX 1321/FCX 30116/WCX 1321/C 90478/
		    angel 35270/emi ASD 3858/2C061 01578/3C153
		    52700-52705M
		cd: emi 763 7022/353 2262

an chloe (wenn die lieb' aus deinen blauen hellen augen)

london
13-16 april 1955
	gieseking	lp: columbia 33CX 1321/FCX 30116/WCX 1321/C 90478/
		    angel 35270/emi ASD 3858/2C061 01578/3C153
		    52700-52705M
		cd: emi 747 3262/763 7022/353 2262

caro bell' idol mio, canon

london 20 february 1967	de los angeles, fischer-dieskau moore	emi unpublished

ch' io mi scordi di te?, concert aria

london 9 may 1955	anda, piano philharonia ackermann	cd: testament SBT 1178 *unpublished columbia lp recording*
amsterdam 6 february 1957	curcio, piano concertgebouw klemperer	cd: q-disc MCL 97018
paris 3 march 1959	orchestre national rosenthal	cd: golden melodram GM 40072 *incorrectly dated 1953*
naples 10 october 1961	rai napoli orchestra franci	cd: melodram CDM 16529
london 10-18 march 1968	brendel, piano london symphony szell	lp: emi ASD 2493/1C063 01959/2C069 01959/angel 36643 cd: emi 747 9502/763 7022

dans un bois solitaire

london
14 april 1955
	gieseking	lp: columbia 33CX 1321/FCX 30116/WCX 1321/C 90478/
		    angel 35270/melodiya M10 43861-43862/emi ASD 3858/
		    2C061 01578/3C153 52700-52705M
		cd: emi 763 7022/353 2262

new york 25 november 1956	reeves	cd: emi 761 0432
hilversum 11 february 1957	de nobel	unpublished radio broadcast *vara*
amsterdam 22 december 1957	de nobel	unpublished radio broadcast *vara*

die ihr des unermesslichen weltalls

london 10 february 1964	parsons	unpublished radio broadcast *bbc third programme*

mozart/exsultate jubilate

vienna 6 november 1946	vienna philharmonic krips	cd: testament SBT 2172 *unpublished columbia 78rpm recording*
london 26 may 1948	philharmonia susskind	78: columbia LX 1196-1197 lp: columbia C 80628/american columbia ML 4649/ angel seraphim 60013/emi 154 6133 cd: emi 763 2012
london 15-16 september 1952	philharmonia pritchard	columbia unpublished
stratford ontario 3 august 1955	hart house orchestra neel	lp: rococo 5388

im frühlingsanfange; das kinderspiel

london
14 april 1955
	gieseking	lp: columbia 33CX 1321/FCX 30116/WCX 1321/C 90478/
		    angel 35270/emi ASD 3858/2C061 01578/3C153
		    52700-52705M
		cd: emi 747 3262/763 7022/353 2262

die kleine spinnerin (was spinnst du, fragte nachbars fritz)

london
14 april 1955
	gieseking	lp: columbia 33CX 1321/FCX 30116/WCX 1321/C 90478/
		    angel 35270/emi ASD 3858/2C061 01578/3C153
		    52700-52705M/melodiya M10 43861-43862
		cd: emi 747 3262/763 7022/353 2262

london 25 october 1961	moore	unpublished video recording *bbc television*

das lied der trennung (selbst engel gottes weinen)

london
14 april 1953
	gieseking	lp: columbia 33CX 1321/FCX 30116/WCX 1321/C 90478/
		    angel 35270/emi ASD 3858/2C061 01578/3C153
		    52700-52705M
		cd: emi 763 7022/353 2262

meine wünsche (ich möchte wohl der kaiser sein)

ascona 6 october 1967	parsons	cd: ermitage ERM 109
berlin 24-28 october 1967	parsons	lp: emi ASD 2404/1C187 01307-01308/angel 36545/ angel seraphim 6072 *published on cd only in japan*
london 22 march 1968	moore	unpublished video recording *bbc television*
nohant 29 june 1969	parsons	cd: arkadia CDGI 8021

mozart/un moto di gioia

london 13 april 1955	gieseking	cd: testament SBT 1206 *unpublished columbia lp recording*
new york 25 november 1956	reeves	cd: emi 761 0432
hilversum 11 february 1957	de nobel	unpublished radio broadcast *vara*
amsterdam 22 december 1957	de nobel	cd: verona 27021

nehmt meinen dank

london   philharmonia   cd: emi 763 6552/763 7902
10 april 1955   galliera   *unpublished columbia lp recording*

naples   rai napoli orchestra cd: melodram CDM 16529
15 april 1958   franci

london   london symphony   lp: emi ASD 2493/1C063 01959/2C069 01959/
10-18 march 1968 szell   angel 36643
                                       cd: emi 747 9502/763 7022

oiseaux si tous les ans

berlin   raucheisen   lp: acanta 40 23557
january   *sung in german*   cd: acanta 42 43801/membran 223067/223 093/
1945   archipel ARPCD 0295

london   gieseking   lp: columbia 33CX 1321/FCX 30116/WCX 1321/C 90478/
14 april 1955   angel 35270/emi ASD 3858/2C061 01578/3C153
                                           52700-52705M/melodiya M10 43861-43862
                                       cd: emi 747 3262/763 7022/353 2262

la partenza, trio

london   de los angeles   lp: emi AN 182-183/SAN 182-183/SLS 926/EX 29 04353
20 february 1967 fischer-dieskau   cd: emi 565 0612/567 9902/567 9942
                 moore

piu non si trovano, trio

london   de los angeles   lp: emi AN 182-183/SAN 182-183/SLS 926/EX 29 04353/
20 february 1967 fischer-dieskau   ASD 143 5941
                 moore   cd: emi 749 2382/CDEMX 2233/567 9902/567 9942

ridente la calma

london   gieseking   lp: columbia 33CX 1321/FCX 30116/WCX 1321/C 90478/
14 april 1955   angel 35270/emi ASD 3858/2C061 01578/3C153
                                           52700-52705M/melodiya M10 43861-43862
                                       cd: emi 747 3262/763 7022/585 1052/353 2262

mozart/**sehnsucht nach dem frühlinge (komm' lieber mai!)**
london   gieseking   lp: columbia 33CX 1321/FCX 30116/WCX 1321/C 90478/
14-16 april 1955   angel 35270/emi ASD 3858/2C061 01578/3C153
                                           52700-52705M
                                       cd: emi 747 3262/763 7022/353 2262

das traumbild (wo bist du, bild, das vor mir stand?)
london   gieseking   lp: columbia 33CX 1321/FCX 30116/WCX 1321/C 90478/
14 april 1955   angel 35270/emi ASD 3858/2C061 01578/3C153
                                           52700-52705M
                                       cd: emi 763 7022/353 2262

vado ma dove?, concert aria
london   london symphony   lp: emi ASD 2493/1C063 01959/2C069 01959/angel
10-18 march 1968   szell   36643
                                       cd: emi 747 9502/763 7022

das veilchen (ein veilchen auf der wiese stand)
london   moore   cd: testament SBT 2172
21 may 1948   *unpublished columbia 78rpm recording*

london   gieseking   lp: columbia 33CX 1321/FCX 30116/WCX 1321/C 90478/
13 april 1955   angel 35270/emi ASD 3858/2C061 01578/3C153
                                           52700-52705M
                                       cd: emi 763 7022/353 2262

ascona   parsons   cd: ermitage ERM 109
6 october 1967

berlin   parsons   lp: emi ASD 2404/1C187 01307-01308/angel 36545/
24-28 october 1968   angel seraphim 6072
                                       cd: emi 565 8602

die verschweigung (sobald damötas chloen sieht)
berlin   raucheisen   lp: acanta 40 23557
january   cd: acanta 42 43801/membran 223 067/223 093/
1945   archipel ARPCD 0295

london   gieseking   columbia unpublished
13-16 april 1955   *except for lp release in japan*

mozart/warnung (männer suchen stets zu naschen)

london 2 october 1947	moore	78: columbia LB 73/LD 2 lp: american columbia ML 4649 cd: emi 565 8602
aix-en-provence 23 july 1954	rosbaud	cd: melodtam CDM 26524/andromeda ANDRCD 5006 *incorrectly dated 29 july 1954*
london 14 april 1955	gieseking	columbia unpublished
salzburg 7 august 1956	moore	cd: emi 566 0842
london 26 june 1957	moore	cd: testament SBT 1206 *unpublished columbia lp recording*
ascona 6 october 1967	parsons	cd: ermitage ERM 109
london 22 march 1968	moore	unpublished video recording *bbc television*
toronto 15 february 1970	orchestra rich	lp: rococo 5388 *televised concert*

der zauberer (ihr mädchen flieht damöten ja!)

london 29 november 1951	moore	78: columbia LB 118/LW 59/LD 2 cd: emi 565 8602
london 4-7 july 1953	moore	columbia unpublished
london 5 january 1954	moore	lp: columbia 33CX 1044/FCX 182/WCX 1044/C 90306/ angel 35023/emi RLS 763/1C151 43160-43163M cd: emi 567 6342/356 5262
london 13 april 1955	gieseking	lp: columbia 33CX 1321/FCX 30116/WCX 1321/C 90478/ angel 35270/emi ASD 3858/2C061 01578/3C153 52700-52705M cd: emi 747 3262/763 7022/353 2262
berlin 27 august- 8 september 1970	parsons	lp: emi ASD 2844/1C063 02331 cd: emi 565 8602

die zufriedenheit (was frag' ich viel nach geld und gut?)

london 14 april 1955	gieseking	lp: columbia 33CX 1321/FCX 30116/WCX 1321/C 90478/ angel 35270/emiu ASD 3858/2C061 01578/3C153 52700-52705M cd: emi 747 3262/763 7022/353 2262

MODEST MUSSORGSKY (1839-1881)
death of boris/boris godunov *feodor*
london	christoff	78: hmv DB 21097
19 may 1949	covent garden	45: victor EHA 11
	chorus	lp: hmv BLP 1003/WBLP 1003/E 70018/ORLP 5002/
	dobrowen	emi RLS 735/1C147 03336-03337M
		cd: emi 764 2522

gathering mushrooms
berlin	parsons	lp: emi ASD 2404/1C187 01307-01308M/angel 36545
24-28 october	*sung in german*	cd: emi 565 8602
1967		

JACQUES OFFENBACH (1819-1880)
les contes d' hoffmann *role of giulietta*
paris	de los angeles,	lp: emi AN 154-156/SAN 154-156/SLS 918/1C165
1-11 september	d'angelo, fauré,	00045-00047/2C167 12866-12868/angel 3667
1964	gedda, ghiuselev,	cd: emi 763 2222/567 9792/567 9832
	blanc, london	*excerpts*
	duclos choir	lp: emi SXLP 30538/1C063 01967
	conservatoire	cd: emi CDCFP 4602
	orchestra	
	cluytens	

CARL ORFF (1895-1982)
die kluge *title role*
london	christ, kuen,	lp: columbia 33CX 1446-1447/SAX 2257-2258/WSX
22-26 may 1956	frick, cordes,	510-511/C 90284-90285/STC 90284-90285/angel
	prey, kusche,	3551/emi 1C137 43291-43293/arabesque 8021-8022
	neidlinger	cd: emi 763 7122
	philharmonia	*excerpts*
	sawallisch	lp: columbia 33CX 1810/SAX 2456/emi 1C063 00719
		cd: emi 767 1872

ALESSANDRO PARISOTTI (1835-1913)
se tu m' ami *previously attributed to pergolesi*
aix-en-provence	rosbaud	cd: melodram CDM 26524/andromeda ANDRCD 5006
23 july 1954		*incorrectly dated 29 july 1954*

london	moore	columbia unpublished
12 april 1956		

salzburg	moore	cd: emi 566 0842
7 august 1956		

london	moore	cd: testament SBT 1206
21 june 1957		*unpublished columbia lp recording*

amsterdam	de nobel	unpublished radio broadcast
22 december 1957		*vara*

HANS PFITZNER (1969-1949)
songs with orchestra: immer leiser wird mein schlummer; verrat
vienna	vienna symphony	cd: radio österreich CD 28
30 april 1944	weisbach	

GIACOMO PUCCINI (1858-1924)
mi chiamano mimi/la boheme *mimi*

vienna 6 november 1948	vienna philharmonic karajan	lp: emi ALP 143 5501/154 6133 cd: emi 763 5572/566 3932/566 4832 *unpublished columbia 78rpm recording*
london 24 april 1959	philharmonia rescigno	lp: columbia CX 5286/SAX 5286/emi SXDW 3049/ 1C181 52291-52292/2C181 52291-52292/angel 36434/3754 cd: emi 567 6342

donde lieta usci/la boheme *mimi*

vienna 6 november 1948	vienna philharmonic karajan	columbia unpublished
london 6 may 1950	philharmonia dobrowen	cd: testament SBT 2172 *unpublished columbia 78rpm recording*
london 18 october 1950	philharmonia galliera	78: columbia LB 110/LW 51/LN 5/GQ 7246 45: columbia SEL 1575/SCD 2141/SCB 101/SCBF 108/ SCBQ 3001/SCBW 101 lp: emi RLS 763/1C151 43160-43163M/154 6133 cd: andromeda ANDRCD 5006
london 23-24 april 1959	philharmonia rescigno	columbia unpublished
london 21 december 1961	philharmonia mackerras	unpublished video recording *bbc television*
london 27 april 1962	philharmonia tonini	columbia unpublished

o soave fanciulla/la boheme *mimi*

berlin 1942	anders orchestra *sung in german*	unpublished soundtrack recording *used in the motion picture nacht ohne abschied*

marcello! finalmente! ...to end of act 3/la boheme *musetta*

berlin 9 december 1941	cebotari, rosvaenge, schmitt-walter rundfunk-sinfonie- orchester steinkopf *sung in german*	cd: preiser 90248 *reichsrundfunk recording which was also allocated grammophon* *catalogue numbers in the sequence 67642-67645*

puccini/o mio babbino caro/gianni schicchi *lauretta*

vienna 6 november 1948	vienna philharmonic karajan	78: columbia LB 85/LV 7/LN 4/GQ 7240 45: columbia SEL 1575 lp: emi RLS 763/1C151 43160-43163M/154 6133 cd: emi 566 3932/566 4832/567 6342/istituto discografico italiano IDIS 6447-6448/regis RRC 1167

london
24 april 1959
	philharmonia
	rescigno
		lp: columbia CX 5286/SAX 5286/emi SXDW 3049/
		    1C181 52291-52292/2C181 52291-52292/angel
		    36434/3754

un bel di/madama butterfly *title role*

london 18 october 1950	philharmonia galliera	78: columbia LX 1370/GQX 11456 45: columbia SCD 2076/SCB 102/SCBQ 3004/SCDW 102 lp: emi RLS 763/1C151 43160-43163M/154 6133 cd: emi 567 6342/andromeda ANDRCD 5006/ regis RRC 1167
hamburg 6 december 1952	ndr orchestra schüchter *sung in german*	lp: melodram MEL 088 cd: golden melodram GM 70000

ancora un passo; con onor muore/madama butterfly *title role*

hamburg 6 december 1952	ndr orchestra and chorus schüchter *sung in german*	lp: melodram MEL 088 cd: golden melodram GM 70000

turandot *role of liu*

milan
9-15 july 1957
	callas, fernandi,
	zaccaria
	la scala chorus
	and orchestra
	serafin
		lp: columbia 33CX 1555-1557/FCX 766-768/QCX
		    10291-10293/WCX 1555-1557/C 90934-90936/
		    angel 3571/emi RLS 741/EX 29 12673/2C153
		    00969-00971/3C163 00969-00971
		cd: emi 747 9718/252 9432/556 3072
		excerpts
		lp: columbia 33CX 1792/C 80578
		cd: emi 763 6572/763 7902

signore ascolta!/turandot *liu*

london 18 october 1950	philharmonia galliera	78: columbia LB 110/LW 51/LN 5 45: columbia SEL 1575/SCB 101/SCBQ 3001/SCBF 108/ SCBW 101 lp: emi RLS 763/1C151 43160-43163M
london 24-25 april 1959	philharmonia rescigno	columbia unpublished
london 25 april 1962	philharmonia tonini	columbia unpublished

puccini/**tu che di gel sei cinta/turandot** *liu*
vienna	vienna philharmonic	columbia unpublished
10 november 1948	karajan	

vienna	vienna philharmonic	78: columbia LB 85/LN 4/GQ 7240
16 march 1949	böhm	45: columbia SEL 1575
		cd: emi 567 6342

london	philharmonia	columbia unpublished
25 april 1959	rescigno	

london	philharmonia	columbia unpublished
25 april 1962	tonini	

HENRY PURCELL (1659-1695)
dido and aeneas *roles of belinda, second lady and attendant spirit*
london	flagstad, mandikian,	45: victor WHMV 1007
15 march 1952	hemsley, lloyd	lp: hmv ALP 1026/FALP 200/victor LHMV 1007/
	mermaid singers	electrola WALP 1026/E 90031/angel seraphim 60346/
	philharmonia	world records SH 117/emi 2C051 03613
	jones	cd: emi 761 0062
		recording completed on 27-28 march 1952; cd edition incorrectly dated october 1952; orchestra described for this recording as mermaid orchestra

hark the echoing air/the fairy queen
amsterdam	de nobel	unpublished radio broadcast
22 december 1957		*vara*

music for a while
berlin	raucheisen	lp: melodram MEL 082/discoreale DR 10038
6 march 1958		*incorrectly dated 1953*

SERGEI RACHMANINOV (1873-1943)
to the children
london	moore	lp: columbia CX 5268/SAX 5268/emi 1C187 01307-01308/
12 january 1958	*sung in english*	angel 36345
		issued on cd only in japan

JEAN-PHILIPPE RAMEAU (1683-1764)
rossignols amoureux/hippolyte et aricie
berlin	raucheisen	lp: acanta 40 23557
7 october 1944	scheck, flute	cd: acanta 42 43801/membran 223 067/223 093/
	sung in german	archipel ARPCD 0295

MAX REGER (1873-1916)
ich glaub', lieber schatz; viola d'amour
berlin	raucheisen	lp: acanta 40 23565/40 23557
9 october 1944		cd: acanta 42 43128/membran 223 067/223 087

die verschmähte (komm' ich längs der grünen wiese)
berlin	raucheisen	lp: acanta 40 23565
9 march 1943		cd: acanta 42 43128/membran 223 067/223 087

waldseligkeit (der wald beginnt zu rauschen)
berlin	raucheisen	lp: acanta 40 23565/40 23557
20 november 1944		cd: acanta 42 43128/membran 223 067/223 087

wiegenlied (schlaf ein mein liebes kindlein du!)
berlin	raucheisen	lp: discocorp IGI 385/RR 208/melodiya M10 41285-
9 march 1943		41286/5289-73/acanta 40 23565/40 23557
		cd: acanta 42 43801/membran 223 067/223 087

GIOACHINO ROSSINI (1792-1868)
sombre foret/guillaume tell
london	philharmonia	columbia unpublished
27 april 1962	tonini	
	sung in italian	

la danza
berlin	raucheisen	lp: acanta 40 23557
7 october 1944		cd: acanta 42 43801/membran 223 067/223 093

duetto buffo di 2 gatti; la regatta veneziana; la pesca
london	de los angeles	lp: emi AN 182-183/SAN 182-183/SLS 926/ASD
20 february 1967	moore	143 5941/EX 29 04353
		cd: emi 749 2382/CDEMX 2233/567 9902/567 9942

GIUSEPPE SAMMARTINI (1700-1775)
weisse schäfchen (im frühling auf der heide)
berlin	raucheisen	lp: acanta 40 23557
7 october 1944		cd: acanta 42 43801/membran 223 067/223 093/
		archipel ARPCD 0295

FLORENT SCHMITT (1870-1958)
aria from psalm 47
paris	orchestre national	cd: golden melodram GM 40072
27 april 1953	and chorus	
	markevitch	

FRANZ SCHUBERT (1797-1828)
ach um deine feuchten schwingen/suleika-lieder

berlin 20-27 october 1968	parsons	lp: emi ASD 2634/1C063 02116/angel 36752 cd: emi 763 6562/763 7902
london 2 december 1968	parsons	cd: eklipse EKRP 4
berlin 6-16 april 1970	parsons	emi unpublished

an den frühling (willkommen schöner jüngling!)

berlin january 1945	raucheisen	lp: acanta 40 23557 cd: acanta 42 43801/membran 223 067/223 083/ archipel ARPCD 0295

an die musik (du holde kunst, in wieviel grauen stunden)

hilversum 9 june 1952	antonietti	unpublished radio broadcast *vara*
london 4 october 1952	fischer	45: columbia SEL 1564/C 50581/electrola E 50157 lp: columbia 33CX 1040/FCX 181/FCX 30307/ QCX 10214/angel 35022/emi ALP 3843/2C053 00404/1C137 53032-53036M cd: emi 747 3262/764 0262/562 7542/562 7732/ 585 1052/586 8292/regis RRC 1167
strassburg 15 june 1960	bonneau	cd: chant du monde LDC 278 899/notablu 935 0911/ golden melodram GM 70004
london 25 october 1961	moore	unpublished video recording *bbc television*
hannover 2 march 1962	reutter	lp: movimento musica 02 017 cd: movimento musica 051 015/verona 27075
london 22 march 1968	moore	unpublished video recording *bbc television*
toronto 15 february 1970	newmark	lp: rococo 5388 *televised concert*

an mein klavier (sanftes klavier, welche entzückungen schaffst du mir!)

salzburg 13 august 1960	moore	cd: stradivarius STR 10009
berlin 21-29 april 1966	parsons	lp: emi ASD 2404/1C187 01307-01308/154 6133/ angel 36545 cd: emi 763 6562/763 7902/562 7542/562 7732

schubert/**an sylvia (was ist sylvia, saget an?)**

london
4 october 1952
	fischer	45: columbia SEL 1564/C 50581/electrola E 50157
		lp: columbia 33CX 1040/FCX 181/FCX 30307/
		    QCX 10214/angel 35022/emi ALP 3843/2C053
		    00404/1C137 53032-53036M
		cd: emi 747 3262/764 0262/562 7542

aix-en-provence 23 july 1954	rosbaud	cd: melodram CDM 26524/andromeda ANDRCD 5006 *incorrectly dated 29 july 1954*
salzburg 7 august 1956	moore	cd: emi 566 0842
new york 25 november 1956	reeves	cd: emi 761 0432/notablu 935 0911
amsterdam 22 december 1957	de nobel	cd: verona 27021
london 12 march 1962	moore	columbia unpublished
ascona 6 october 1967	parsons	cd: ermitage ERM 109
nohant 29 june 1969	ciccolini	cd: arkadia CDGI 8021
berlin 1-10 march 1973	parsons	lp: emi ASD 3124/1C063 02598 *published on cd only in japan*

auf dem wasser zu singen (mitten im schimmer der spiegelnden wellen)

rome 16 february 1952	favaretto	cd: arkadia CD 535/CDHP 535/archipel ARPCD 0295
hilversum 9 june 1952	antonietti	unpublished radio broadcast *vara*

london
4 october 1952
	fischer	45: columbia SEL 1582
		lp: columbia 33CX 1040/FCX 181/FCX 30307/
		    QCX 10214/angel 35022/emi ALP 3843/2C053
		    00404/1C137 53032-53036M/melodiya M10
		    43861-43862
		cd: emi 747 3262/764 0262/562 7542

strassburg 15 june 1960	bonneau	cd: chant du monde LDC 278 899/notablu 935 0911/ golden melodram GM 70004

ave maria/ellens-gesänge

rome 16 february 1952	favaretto	cd: arkadia CD 535/CDHP 535/archipel ARPCD 0295
london 1954	royal philharmonic mathieson	unpublished soundtrack recording *used in the motion picture svengali*

schubert/**du bist die ruh'**

strassburg 15 june 1960	bonneau	cd: chant du monde LDC 278 899/notablu 935 0911/ golden melodram GM 70004 *golden melodram incorrectly describes the song as ungeduld*
london 22 january 1961	moore	cd: testament SBT 1206 *unpublished columbia lp recording*

der einsame (wenn meine grillen schwirren)

aix-en-provence 23 july 1954	rosbaud	cd: melodram CDM 26524/andromeda ANDRCD 5006 *incorrectly dated 29 july 1954*
salzburg 7 august 1956	moore	cd: emi 566 0842
new york 25 november 1956	reeves	cd: emi 761 0432/notablu 935 0911
hilversum 11 february 1957	de nobel	unpublished radio broadcast *vara*
amsterdam 22 december 1957	de nobel	cd: verona 27021
strassburg 15 june 1960	bonneau	cd: chant du monde LDC 278 899/golden melodram GM 70004
hannover 2 march 1962	reutter	lp: movimento musica 02 017 cd: movimento musica 051 015/verona 27075
berlin 22-27 august 1965	moore	lp: columbia CX 5268/SAX 5268/emi 1C187 01307-01308/angel 36345/emi 154 6133 cd: emi 763 6562/763 7902/562 7542/562 7732
ascona 6 october 1967	parsons	cd: ermitage ERM 109
utrecht 26 april 1969	parsons	unpublished radio broadcast *avro*
nohant 29 june 1969	ciccolini	cd: arkadia CDGI 8021
amsterdam 8 february 1977	parsons	cd: bella voce BLV 107 002 *also unpublished video recording*

erlkönig (wer reitet so spät durch nacht und wind?)

berlin 21-29 april 1966	parsons	lp: emi ASD 2404/1C187 01307-01308/154 6133/ angel 36545/3754 cd: emi 763 6562/763 7902/586 8292/562 7542/ 562 7732

schubert/erntelied (sicheln schallen, ähren fallen)

berlin	parsons	lp: emi ASD 3124/1C063 02598/154 6133
1-10 march 1973		*published on cd only in japan*

fischerweise (den fischer fechten sorgen)

strassburg	bonneau	cd: chant du monde LDC 278 899/golden melodram
15 june 1960		GM 70004
salzburg	moore	cd: stradivarius STR 10009
13 august 1960		

die forelle (in einem bächlein helle)

vienna	hudez	78: columbia LB 77/LV 5/LN 9
26 october		lp: emi RLS 763/RLS 766/1C151 43160-43163M/
1946		1C135 78111-78118M
		cd: andromeda ANDRCD 5006
rome	favaretto	cd: arkadia CD 535/CDHP 535/archipel ARPCD 0295
16 february		
1952		
london	moore	columbia unpublished
11-13 september		
1952		
london	moore	cd: testament SBT 1206
11-13 april		*unpublished columbia lp recording*
1964		
berlin	moore	lp: columbia CX 5268/SAX 5268/angel 35345/emi
22-27 october		1C187 01307-01308/154 6133
1965		cd: emi 763 6562/763 7902/562 7542/562 7732
toronto	newmark	lp: rococo 5388
15 february		*televised concert*
1970		

ganymed (wie im morgenglanze du rings mich anglühst)

london	fischer	lp: columbia 33CX 1040/FCX 181/FCX 30307/
7 october		QCX 10214/angel 35022/emi ALP 3843/2C053
1952		00404/1C137 53032-53036M
		cd: emi 747 3262/764 0262/562 7542

geheimnis (sag' an, wer lehrt dich lieder?)

berlin	parsons	emi unpublished
21-29 april		
1966		

schubert/**gretchen am spinnrade** (meine ruh' ist hin, mein herz ist schwer)

london 21 may 1948	moore	cd: testament SBT 2172 *unpublished columbia 78rpm recording*

london
6 october 1952
	fischer	45: columbia SEL 1561/C 50581/electrola E 50157
		lp: columbia 33CX 1040/FCX 181/FCX 30307/
		    QCX 10214/WCX 1040/C 90305/angel 35022/
		    emi ALP 3843/2C053 00404/1C137 53032-53036M
		cd: emi 747 3262/764 0262/562 7542

new york 25 november 1956	reeves	cd: emi 761 0432/notablu 935 0911
hilversum 11 february 1957	de nobel	unpublished radio broadcast *vara*
amsterdam 22 december 1957	de nobel	cd: verona 27021
hannover 2 march 1962	reutter	lp: movimento musica 02 017 cd: movimento musica 051 015/verona 27075
london 2 december 1968	parsons	cd: eklipse EKRP 4
berlin 1-10 march 1973	parsons	lp: emi ASD 3124/1C063 02598/154 6133 cd: emi 763 6562/763 7902
amsterdam 8 february 1977	parsons	cd: bella voce BLV 107 002 *also unpublished video recording*

hänflings liebeswerbung (ahidi, ich liebe!)

berlin 21-29 april 1966	parsons	emi unpublished
berlin 20-27 october 1968	parsons	lp: emi ASD 2634/1C063 02116/angel 36752 cd: emi 763 6562/763 7902
berlin 6-16 april 1970	parsons	emi unpublished

heidenröslein (sah ein knab' ein röslein steh'n)

london 11 june 1957	moore	lp: columbia CX 5268/SAX 5268/angel 36345/ emi 1C187 01307-01308/154 6133 cd: emi 763 6562/763 7902/562 7542/562 7732

schubert/**der hirt auf dem felsen, arrangement by liszt**
london   london   unpublished radio broadcast
12 september 1950   philharmonic   *bbc third programme*
                      cameron

im frühling (hier sitz' ich an des hügels hang)
london   fischer   45: columbia SEL 1582
7 october 1952   lp: columbia 33CX 1040/FCX 181/FCX 30307/QCX
                                                 10214/WCX 1040/C 90305/angel 35022/
                                                 emi ALP 3843/2C053 00404/1C137 53032-53036M/
                                                 melodiya M10 43861-43862
                                             cd: emi 747 3262/764 0262/562 7542

jäger ruhe von der jagd!/ellens-gesänge
amsterdam   de nobel   unpublished radio broadcast
22 december 1957   *vara*

die junge nonne (wie braust durch die wipfel der heulende sturm!)
london   fischer   45: columbia SEL 1570
4 october 1952   lp: columbia 33CX 1040/FCX 181/FCX 30307/QCX
                                                 10214/WCX 1040/C 90305/angel 35022/
                                                 emi ALP 3843/2C053 00404/1C137 53032-53036M
                                             cd: emi 747 3262/764 0262/562 7542/regis RRC 1167

der jüngling an der quelle (leise, rieselnder quell!)
london   moore   cd: testament SBT 1206
22 january 1961   *unpublished columbia lp recording*

london   moore   columbia unpublished
9 march 1962

london   moore   lp: columbia CX 5268/SAX 5268/angel 36345/emi
7 december 1962   1C187 01307-01308
                                             cd: emi 763 6562/763 7902/562 7542/562 7732

lachen und weinen
london   moore   cd: testament SBT 1206
22 january 1961   *unpublished columbia lp recording*

utrecht   parsons   unpublished radio broadcast
26 april 1969   *avro*

die liebe hat gelogen
aix-en-provence   rosbaud   cd: melodram CDM 26524/andromeda ANDRCD 5006
23 july 1954   *incorrectly dated 29 july 1954*

liebe schwärmt auf allen wegen
amsterdam   de nobel   unpublished radio broadcast
22 december 1957   *vara*

strassburg   bonneau   cd: chant du monde LDC 278 899/notablu 935 0911/
15 june 1960   golden melodram GM 70004
                                             golden melodram issue incorrectly described as die liebe hat gelogen

london   moore   cd: testament SBT 1206
22 january 1961   *unpublished columbia lp recording*

berlin   moore   lp: columbia CX 5268/SAX 5268/angel 36345/
22-27 august 1965   emi 1C187 01307-01308
                                             cd: emi 565 8602/562 7542/562 7732

schubert/**liebhaber in allen gestalten (ich wollt', ich wär' ein fisch!)**

london	moore	lp: emi RLS 766/1C135 78111-78118M/154 6133/ ALP 143 5501
21 may 1948		cd: emi 763 6562/763 7902/567 6342/562 7542/ 562 7732
		unpublished columbia 78rpm recording

das lied im grünen (ins grüne, ins grüne, da lockt uns der frühling)

london	fischer	45: columbia SEL 1564/electrola E 50157
4 october 1952		lp: columbia 33CX 1040/FCX 181/FCX 30307/ QCX 10214/WCX 1040/C 90305/angel 35022/ emi ALP 3843/2C053 00404/1C137 53032-53036M/melodiya M10 43861-43862
		cd: emi 747 3262/764 0262/585 1052/562 7542

salzburg	moore	cd: stradivarius STR 10009
13 august 1960		

utrecht	parsons	unpublished radio broadcast
26 april 1969		*avro*

der lindenbaum/winterreise

amsterdam	parsons	cd: bella voce BLV 107 002
8 february 1977		*also unpublished video recording*

litanei (ruh'n in frieden alle seelen)

london	moore	columbia unpublished
11-12 september 1952		

london	moore	columbia unpublished
27 september 1952		

london	moore	lp: columbia 33CX 1044/FCX 182/WCX 1044/ C 90306/angel 35023/emi RLS 763/154 6133/ 1C151 43160-43163M
9 january 1954		cd: emi 562 7542/562 7732/andromeda ANDRCD 5006

meeresstille (tiefe stille herrscht im wasser)

berlin	parsons	lp: emi ASD 3124/1C063 02598/154 6133
1-10 march 1973		cd: emi 763 6562/763 7902

misero pargoletto

berlin	raucheisen	lp: discocorp RR 208/RR 537/melodram MEL 082/ discoreale DR 10038
6 january 1958		*incorrectly dated 1953*

schubert/**der musensohn** (durch wald und feld zu schweifen)
london   moore   cd: testament SBT 2172
2 december 1951   *unpublished columbia 78rpm recording*

rome   favaretto   cd: arkadia CD 535/CDHP 535/archipel ARPCD 0295
16 february 1952

london   fischer   45: columbia SEL 1582/C 50581
6 october 1952   lp: columbia 33CX 1040/FCX 181/FCX 30307/QCX
                                         10214/WCX 1040/C 90305/angel 35022/emi
                                         ALP 3843/2C053 00404/1C137 53032-53036M
                                     cd: emi 747 3262/764 0262/585 1052/562 7542/
                                         regis RRC 1167

nähe des geliebten (ich denke dein, wenn mir der sonne schimmer)
london   fischer   45: columbia SEL 1570/C 50581
4-7 october 1952   lp: columbia 33CX 1040/FCX 181/FCX 30307/QCX
                                         10214/WCX 1040/C 90305/angel 35022/emi
                                         ALP 3843/2C053 00404/1C137 53032-53036M/
                                         melodiya M10 43861-43862
                                     cd: emi 747 3262/764 0262/562 7542

nachtviolen (nachtviolen, dunkle augen)
london   fischer   45: columbia SEL 1582
4 october 1952   lp: columbia 33CX 1040/FCX 181/FCX 30307/QCX
                                         10214/WCX 1040/C 90305/angel 35022/emi
                                         ALP 3843/2C053 00404/1C137 53032-53036M
                                     cd: emi 747 3262/764 0262/585 1052/562 7542

romanze aus rosamunde (der vollmond strahlt)
hilversum   antonietti   unpublished radio broadcast
9 june 1952   *vara*

salzburg   moore   cd: emi 566 0842
7 august 1956

new york   reeves   cd: emi 761 0432/notablu 935 0911
25 november 1956

hilversum   de nobel   unpublished radio broadcast
11 february 1957   *vara*

amsterdam   de nobel   cd: verona 27021
22 december 1957

strassburg   bonneau   cd: chant du monde LDC 278 899/notablu 935 0911/
15 june 1960   golden melodram GM 70004

ascona   parsons   cd: ermitage ERM 109
6 october 1967

utrecht   parsons   unpublished radio broadcast
26 april 1969   *avro*

nohant   ciccolini   cd: arkadia CDGI 8021
29 june 1969

schubert/**seligkeit** (freuden sonder zahl)

vienna 26 october 1946	hudez	78: columbia LB 77/LV 5/LN 9 lp: emi RLS 763/RLS 766/1C151 43160-43163M/ 1C135 78111-78118M cd: andromeda ANDRCD 5006
london 9 april 1956	moore	columbia unpublished
new york 25 november 1956	reeves	cd: emi 761 0432/notablu 935 0911
london 11 june 1957	moore	columbia unpublished
london 26 june 1957	moore	columbia unpublished
strassburg 15 june 1960	bonneau	cd: chant du monde LDC 278 899/golden melodram GM 70004
salzburg 13 august 1960	moore	cd: stradivarius STR 10009
hannover 2 march 1962	reutter	lp: movimento musica 02 017 cd: movimento musica 051 015/verona 27075
london 11 april 1964	moore	columbia unpublished
berlin 22-27 october 1965	moore	lp: columbia CX 5268/SAX 5268/angel 36345/ emi 1C187 01307-01308 cd: emi 562 7542/562 7732
ascona 6 october 1967	parsons	cd: ermitage ERM 109
london 2 december 1968	parsons	cd: eklipse EKRP 4
utrecht 26 april 1969	parsons	unpublished radio broadcast *avro*
nohant 26 june 1969	ciccolini	cd: arkadia CDGI 8021
toronto 15 february 1970	newmark	lp: rococo 5388 *televised concert*
amsterdam 8 february 1977	parsons	cd: bella voce BLV 107 002 *also unpublished video recording*

schubert/**was bedeutet die bewegung?/suleika-lieder**

rome 16 february 1952	favaretto	cd: arkadia CD 535/CDHP 535/archipel ARPCD 0295
berlin 20-27 october 1968	parsons	lp: emi ASD 2634/1C063 02116/angel 35752 cd: emi 763 6562/763 7902
london 2 december 1968	parsons	cd: eklipse EKRP 4
berlin 6-16 april 1970	parsons	emi unpublished

ungeduld/die schöne müllerin

rome 16 february 1952	favaretto	cd: arkadia CD 535/CDHP 535/archipel ARPCD 0295
london 21 september 1952	moore	columbia unpublished

london
10 january 1954
	moore	lp: columbia 33CX 1044/FCX 182/WCX 1044/
		    C 90306/angel 35023/emi RLS 763/1C151
		    43160-43163M
		cd: emi 565 8602/562 7542/562 7732/andromeda
		    ANDRCD 5006

aix-en-provence 23 july 1954	rosbaud	cd: melodram CDM 26524/andromeda ANDRCD 5006 *incorrectly dated 29 july 1954*
salzburg 7 august 1956	moore	cd: emi 566 0842

vedi quanto adoro

salzburg 7 august 1956	moore	cd: emi 566 0842
amsterdam 22 december 1957	de nobel	unpublished radio broadcast *vara*
berlin 6 january 1958	raucheisen	lp: discocorp RR 208/RR 537/melodram MEL 082/ discoreale DR 10038 *incorrectly dated 1953*

schubert/**die vögel** (wie lieblich und fröhlich zu schweben, zu singen)

london
21 may 1948
	moore	lp: emi RLS 766/ALP 143 5501/154 6133/
		    1C135 78111-78118M
		cd: emi 763 6562/763 7902/567 6342/562 7542/
		    562 7732
		unpublished columbia 78rpm recording

aix-en-provence 23 july 1954	rosbaud	cd: melodram CDM 26524/andromeda ANDRCD 5006 *incorrectly dated 29 july 1954*
salzburg 7 august 1956	moore	cd: emi 566 0842
new york 25 november 1956	reeves	cd: emi 761 0432/notablu 935 0911
hilversum 11 february 1957	de nobel	unpublished radio broadcast *vara*
london 21 june 1957	moore	cd: testament SBT 1206 *unpublished columbia lp recording*
amsterdam 22 december 1957	de nobel	cd: verona 27021

wehmut (wenn ich durch wald und fluren geh')

london
6 october 1952
	fischer	45: columbia SEL 1570
		lp: columbia 33CX 1040/FCX 181/FCX 30307
		    QCX 10214/WCX 1040/C 90305/angel 35022/
		    emi ALP 3843/2C053 00404/1C137 53032-53036M
		cd: emi 747 3262/764 0262/562 7542

berlin 1-10 march 1973	parsons	lp: emi ASD 3124/1C063 02598

wiegenlied (schlafe, schlafe, holder süsser knabe!)

london 12 september 1952	moore	cd: testament SBT 2172 *unpublished columbia 78rpm recording*
amsterdam 22 december 1957	de nobel	unpublished radio broadcast *vara*
london 12 april 1964	moore	cd: testament SBT 1206 *unpublished columbia lp recording*

ROBERT SCHUMANN (1810-1856)
auf einer burg/liederkreis op 39

london 10 february 1964	parsons	unpublished radio broadcast *bbc third programme*
berlin april 1974	parsons	lp: emi ASD 3037/1C063 02547/2C069 02547/ angel 37043

aufträge (nicht so schnelle, nicht so schnelle!)

london 29 november 1951	moore	78: columbia LB 122/LW 58/LV 16 lp: emi 154 6133 cd: emi 565 8602
london 4-7 july 1953	moore	columbia unpublished
london 7 january 1954	moore	columbia unpublished
london 10 january 1954	moore	lp: columbia 33CX 1044/FCX 182/WCX 1044/C 90306/ angel 35023/emi RLS 763/1C151 43160-43163M cd: emi 763 6562/763 7902/567 6342/356 5262/ andromeda ANDRCD 5006
aix-en-provence 23 july 1954	rosbaud	cd: melodram CDM 26524/andromeda ANDRCD 5006 *incorrectly dated 29 july 1954*

er und sie (seh' ich das stille tal)

london 20 february 1967	fischer-dieskau moore	lp: emi AN 182-183/SAN 182-183/SLS 926/ASD 143 5941 cd: emi 749 2382/CDEMX 2233/567 9902

frauenliebe und –leben: seit ich ihn gesehen; er der herrlichste von allen; ich kann's nicht fassen; du ring an meinem finger; helft mir ihr schwestern!; süsser freund du blickest mich verwundert an; an meinem herzen, an meiner brust; nun hast du mir den ersten schmerz getan

berlin january 1974	parsons	lp: emi ASD 3037/1C063 02547/2C069 02547/ angel 37043

frühlingsnacht/liederkreis op 39

london 10 february 1964	parsons	unpublished radio broadcast *bbc third programme*
berlin april 1974	parsons	lp: emi ASD 3037/1C063 02547/2C069 02547/ angel 37043

ich denke dein; in der nacht

london 20 february 1967	fischer-dieskau moore	lp: emi AN 182-183/SAN 182-183/SLS 926 cd: emi 567 9902

schumann/**im walde; in der fremde I; in der fremde II; intermezzo/
liederkreis op 39**

london 10 february 1964	parsons	unpublished radio broadcast *bbc third programme*

berlin april 1974	parsons	lp: emi ASD 3037/1C063 02547/2C069 02547/ angel 37043 cd: emi 565 8602

die kartenlegerin (schlief die mutter endlich ein)

ascona 6 october 1967	parsons	cd: ermitage ERM 109

berlin 24-28 october 1967	parsons	lp: emi ASD 2404/1C187 01307-01308/angel 36545 *published on cd only in japan*

liebhabers ständchen (wachst du noch, liebchen?)

london 20 february 1967	fischer-dieskau moore	emi unpublished

lied der suleika (wie mit innigstem behagen)

berlin 22-27 august 1965	moore	lp: emi ASD 2634/1C063 02116/angel 36752 cd: emi 763 6562/763 7902

ascona 6 october 1967	parsons	cd: ermitage ERM 109

nohant 29 june 1969	ciccolini	cd: arkadia CDGI 8021

marienwürmchen/lieder für die jugend

hilversum 9 june 1952	antonietti	unpublished radio broadcast *vara*

mondnacht; schöne fremde/liederkreis op 39

berlin 1944		unpublished soundtrack recording *used in the motion picture der verteidiger hat das wort*

london 10 february 1964	parsons	unpublished radio broadcast *bbc third programme*

berlin april 1974	parsons	lp: emi ASD 3037/1C063 02547/2C069 02547/ angel 37043 *published on cd only in japan*

die stille/liederkreis op 39

london 10 february 1964	parsons	unpublished radio broadcast *bbc third programme*

berlin april 1974	parsons	lp: emi ASD 3037/1C063 02547/2C069 02547/ angel 37043 cd: emi 565 8602

schumann/der nussbaum (es grünet ein nussbaum vor dem haus)

london 29 november 1951	moore	78: columbia LB 122/LW 58/LV 16/LD 6
london 9 january 1954	moore	lp: columbia 33CX 1044/FCX 182/WCX 1044/C 90306/ angel 35023/emi RLS 763/1C151 43160-43163M/ 154 6133 cd: emi 356 5262/andromeda ANDRCD 5006
aix-en-provence 23 july 1954	rosbaud	cd: melodram CDM 26524/andromeda ANDRCD 5006 *incorrectly dated 29 july 1954*
salzburg 7 august 1956	moore	cd: emi 566 0842
new york 25 november 1956	reeves	cd: emi 761 0432/notablu 935 0911
salzburg 13 august 1960	moore	cd: stradivarius STR 10009
ascona 6 october 1967	parsons	cd: ermitage ERM 109
london 22 march 1968	moore	unpublished video recording *bbc television*
nohant 26 june 1969	ciccolini	cd: arkadia CDGI 8021
toronto 15 february 1970	newmark	lp: rococo 5388 *televised concert*
berlin 1-10 march 1973	parsons	lp: emi ASD 3124/1C063 02598 cd: emi 763 6562/763 7902
amsterdam 8 february 1977	parsons	cd: bella voce BLV 107 002 *also unpublished video recording*

tanzlied (eija, wie flattert der kranz!)

london 20 february 1967	fischer-dieskau moore	lp: emi AN 182-183/SAN 182-183/SLS 926/ASD 143 5941 cd: emi 749 2382/CDEMX 2233/567 6342

unterm fenster (wer ist vor meiner kammertür?)

london 20 february 1967	fischer-dieskau moore	emi unpublished

schumann/2 venezianische lieder: leis' rudern hier; wenn durch die piazetta
berlin   moore   lp: columbia CX 5268/SAX 5268/angel 36345/emi
22-27 august 1965   ASD 3124/1C063 02598/1C187 01307-01308/
                                           154 6133
                                       cd: emi 763 6562/763 7902

ascona   parsons   cd: ermitage ERM 109
6 october 1967

volksliedchen (wenn ich früh in den garten geh')
berlin   raucheisen   lp: acanta 40 23557
january   cd: acanta 42 43801/membran 223 067/223 213/
1945   archipel ARPCD 0295

waldesgespräch/liederkreis op 39
london   parsons   unpublished radio broadcast
10 february 1964   *bbc third programme*

berlin   parsons   lp: emi ASD 3037/1C063 02547/2C069 02547/
april 1974   angel 37043
                                       cd: emi 565 8602

wehmut; zwielicht/liederkreis op 39
london   parsons   unpublished radio broadcast
10 february 1964   *bbc third programme*

berlin   parsons   lp: emi ASD 3037/1C063 02547/2C069 02547/
april 1974   angel 37043

widmung (du meine seele, du mein herz!)
london   moore   cd: testament SBT 1206
11 june 1957   *unpublished columbia lp recording*

berlin   moore   lp: columbia CX 5268/SAX 5268/angel 36345/emi
22-27 august 1965   ASD 3124/1C063 02598
                                       cd: emi 565 8602

JEAN SIBELIUS (1865-1957)
luonnotar, for soprano and orchestra
helsinki   helsinki   unpublished radio broadcast
14 june 1955   philharmoinic
                    hannikainen

den förste kyssen; hundra vägar; kaiutar; kyssen; norden
helsinki   szalkiewicz   cd: emi 565 8602
11 june 1955   *sung in german*

säf säf susa; svarta rosor
helsinki   szalkiewicz   cd: emi 565 8602
11 june 1955   *sung in german*

london   moore   45: columbia SEL 1600/ESL 6274
8 april 1956   *sung in german*   lp: columbia 33CX 1404/SAX 2265/FCX 664/
                                           SAXF 145/WCX 1404/C 90545/angel 35385/
                                           emi 154 6133
                                       cd: emi 356 5262
                                       SAX 2265 and SAXF 145 contained only svarta rosor

sibelius/**war det en dröm?**
helsinki	skalkiewicz	cd: emi 565 8602
11 june 1955	*sung in german*	

london	moore	columbia unpublished
8 april 1956	*sung in german*	

RUDOLF SIECZYNSKI (1879-1952)
wien du stadt meiner träume (wien, wien, nur du allein)
london	chorus	45: columbia SEL 1648/ESL 6267/SCD 2128
2 july 1957	philharmonia	lp: columbia 33CX 1570/SAX 2283/SAXF 158/
	ackermann	angel 35696/emi ASD 2807/SVP 1180/CCPM
		130 600/100 4781/2C053 00478
		cd: emi 747 2842/566 9892/567 0042

montreal	cbc orchestra	vhs video: emi MVC 491 4763
3 july 1963	boskovsky	dvd video: emi DVA 492 8529/DVA 477 8319/
		video artists international VAI 4390

FRIEDRICH SILCHER (1789-1860)
die lorelei, arranged by mackerras
london	chorus	columbia unpublished
25-26 may 1957	philharmonia	
	mackerras	

london	chorus	columbia unpublished
30 june 1957	philharmonia	
	mackerras	

BEDRICH SMETANA (1824-1884)
alone at last....ah bitterness!/the bartered bride
london	philharmonia	lp: columbia CX 5286/SAX 5286/angel 36434/
14 december 1956	schmidt	emi SXDW 3049/1C181 52291-52292/
	sung in german	2C181 52291-52292
		cd: emi 769 5012/565 5772/567 6342/585 1052

GOTTFRIED STOELZEL (1690-1749)
bist du bei mir/*previously attributed to bach*
london	moore	78: columbia LX 1580
11 september 1952		

london	moore	columbia unpublished
4-7 july 1953		

london	moore	lp: columbia 33CX 1044/FCX 182/WCX 1044/
4 january 1954		C 90306/angel 35023/emi 1C151 43160-43163M/
		RLS 763
		cd: emi 763 6542/763 7902/567 2062/585 1052/
		567 2062

aix-en-provence	rosbaud	cd: melodram CDM 26524/andromeda
23 july 1954		ANDRCD 5006
		incorrectly dated 29 july 1954

salzburg	moore	cd: emi 566 0842/archipel ARPCD 0237
7 august 1956		

JOHANN STRAUSS (1825-1899)
nuns' chorus and laura's song/casanova *laura*
london	chorus	45: columbia SEL 1642/ESL 6263/SCD 2128
2-3 july 1957	philharmonia	lp: columbia 33CX 1570/SAX 2283/SAXF 158/angel
	ackermann	35696/emi ASD 2807/YKM 5014/SVP 1180/
		CCPM 130 600/100 4781/2C053 00478
		cd: emi 747 2842/566 9892/567 0042

die fledermaus *role of rosalinde*
london	streich, gedda,	lp: columbia 33CX 1309-1310/QCX 10183-10184/
26-30 april 1955	krebs, christ,	WSX 533-534/C 80512-80513/angel 3539/
	dönch	emi RLS 728/1C149 00427-00428/2C181
	chorus	00427-00428
	philharmonia	cd: emi 769 5312/567 0742/567 1532/naxos 811 1036-7
	karajan	*excerpts*
		lp: columbia 33CX 1516/WSX 602/C 80110/emi
		RLS 763/1C151 43160-43163M/1C047 01953
		cd: emi 763 6572/763 7902/565 5772/andromeda
		ANDRCD 5006/urania URN 22296

mein herr, was dächten sie von mir?/die fledermaus *rosalinde*
chicago	chicago symphony	cd: chicago symphony great soloists CSOCD 95
16 july 1968	boskovsky	

frühlingstimmen, arrangement
vienna	vienna philharmonic	lp: emi ALP 143 5501/154 6133
31 october 1946	krips	cd: emi 763 6542/763 7902
		unpublished columbia 78rpm recording of first stanza only

g'schichten aus dem wienerwald, arrangement
berlin	raucheisen	lp: acanta 40 23557
9 october 1944		cd: acanta 42 43128/membran 223 067/223 093

eine nacht in venedig *role of annina*
london	loose, gedda,	lp: columbia 33CX 1224-1225/WCX 1224-1225/
25-31 may 1954	kunz, dönch	WSX 531-532/C 90404-90405/C 80510-80511/
	chorus	angel 3530/emi SXDW 3043/1C149 03171-
	philharmonia	03172/5C181 03049-03050
	ackermann	cd: emi 769 5302/567 5322
		excerpts
		lp: emi RLS 763/1C151 43160-43163M/SMVP
		6075/andromeda ANDRCD 5006
		recording completed on 25 september 1954

johann strauss/seht o seht!/eine nacht in venedig *annina*

london	philharmonia	columbia unpublished
4 july 1957	ackermann	

wiener blut *role of gabriele*

london	köth, loose,	lp: columbia 33CX 1186-1187/WCX 1186-1187/WSX
21-31 may 1954	gedda, kunz,	539-540/C 90382-90383/C 80518-80519/angel 3519/
	dönch	emi SXDW 3042/1C149 01380-01381
	chorus	cd: emi 769 5292/567 5322
	philharmonia	*excerpts*
	ackermann	lp: columbia WSX 608/C 80113/emi RLS 763/154 6133/
		1C151 43160-43163M/SMVP 6075/andromeda
		ANDRCD 5006

wiener blut/querschnitt (scenes) *gabriele*

berlin	glawitsch	78: telefunken E 3099/E 1160
16 august 1940	orchester des	cd: hänssler classics 94501
	deutschen	
	opernhauses	
	lütze	

ich war ein echtes wiener blut/wiener blut *gabriele*

montreal	cbc orchestra	dvd video: video artists international VAI 4390
3 july 1963	boskovsky	*canadian televosion*

der zigeunerbaron *role of saffi*

london	köth, sinclair,	lp: columbia 33CX 1329-1330/WSX 541-542/
18-31 may 1954	gedda, kunz,	C 80520-80521/angel 3566/emi SXDW 3046/
	prey	1C149 03051-03052/5C181 03051-03052
	chorus	cd: emi 769 5262/567 5352
	philharmonia	*excerpts*
	ackermann	lp: emi SLS 5250/RLS 763/1C151 43160-43163M
		cd: andromeda ANDRCD 5006
		recording completed on 25 september 1954

saffis lied/der zigeunerbaron *saffi*

london	philharmonia	columbia unpublished
2 july 1957	ackermann	

RICHARD STRAUSS (1864-1949)
ich danke fräulein!....aber der richtige/arabella *title role*

london	felbermayer	lp: columbia 33CX 1226/33CX 1897/FCX 385/WCX 1226/
27-29 september	philharmonia	WSX 571/C 90406/C 80619/angel 35094/world records
1954	matacic	OH 199/emi RLS 751/1C037 03297
		cd: emi 761 0012/585 8252/826 4362/naxos 811 1145
		recordings completed on 6 october 1954

mein elemer!/arabella *title role*

london	felbermayer	45: columbia SEL 1579/SCBW 802/C 30166
27-29 september	philharmonia	lp: columbia 33CX 1226/33CX 1897/FCX 385/WCX 1226/
1954	matacic	WSX 571/C 90406/C 80619/angel 35094/world records
		OH 199/emi RLS 751/1C037 03297/154 6133
		cd: emi 761 0012/585 8252/826 4362/grandi voci GVS 19/
		naxos 811 1145
		recordings completed on 6 october 1954

sie woll'n mich heiraten?....und du wirst mein gebieter sein/arabella *title role*

london	metternich	lp: columbia 33CX 1226/33CX 1897/FCX 385/WCX 1226/
27-29 september	philharmonia	WSX 571/C 90406/C 80619/angel 35094/world records
1954	matacic	OH 199/emi RLS 751/1C037 03297/154 6133
		cd: emi 761 0012/585 8252/826 4362/naxos 811 1145
		recordings completed on 6 october 1954

und jetzt sag' ich ihm adieu/arabella *title role*

london	dickie, berry,	lp: columbia 33CX 1226/33CX 1897/FCX 385/WCX 1226/
27-29 september	pröglhöf	WSX 571/C 90406/C 80619/angel 35094/world records
1954	philharmonia	OH 199/emi RLS 751/1C037 03297
	matacic	cd: emi 585 8252/826 4362/naxos 811 1145
		recordings completed on 6 october 1954

das war sehr gut mandryka!/arabella *title role*

london	metternich	45: columbia SEL 1579/SCBW 802/C 30166
27-29 september	philharmonia	lp: columbia 33CX 1226/33CX 1987/FCX 385/WCX 1226/
1954	matacic	WSX 571/C 90406/C 80619/angel 35094/world records
		OH 199/emi RLS 751/1C037 03297/154 6133
		cd: emi 761 0012/565 5772/585 1052/585 8252/826 4362/
		naxos 811 1145
		recordings completed on 6 october 1954

other scenes from arabella, involving singers nicolai gedda and theodor schlott but not elisabeth schwarzkopf, were also recorded

strauss / **ariadne auf naxos** *role of primadonna / ariadne*

london 30 june- 7 july 1954	seefried, streich, schock, prey, dönch philharmonia karajan	lp: columbia 33CX 1292-1294/FCX 506-508/QCX 10168-10170/WCX 1292-1294/C 90458-90460/ angel 3532/emi RLS 760/EX 769 2961/1C153 03520-03522/2C153 03520-03522 cd: emi 769 2962/555 1762/567 0772/567 1562/ naxos 811.1033-1034/membran 223 241 *excerpts* cd: emi 763 6572/763 7902/565 5772/585 1052

es gibt ein reich / ariadne auf naxos *ariadne*

berlin 8 december 1956	berlin philharmonic karajan	unpublished radio broadcast *rias berlin*

capriccio *role of countess madeleine*

london 2-11 september 1957	ludwig, moffo, gedda, hotter, fischer-dieskau, wächter, schmitt-walter philharmonia sawallisch	lp: columbia 33CX 1600-1602/WCX 1600-1602/ C 90997-90999/angel 3580/world records OC 230-232/emi 143 5243 cd: emi 749 0148/567 3942/567 3912 *excerpts* lp: world records OH 233 cd: emi 763 6572/763 7902
vienna 15 june 1960	goltz, köth, dermota, uhde, berry, schöffler vienna philharmonic böhm	cd: private edition vienna

morgen mittag um elf? / capriccio *countess madeleine*

watford 25-26 september 1953	philharmonia ackermann	lp: columbia 33CX 1107/FCX 294/WCX 1107/ C 90334/angel 35084/38266/emi RLS 751/ 100 8651/2C061 01208 cd: emi 761 0012/585 8252/notablu 935 0923

der rosenkavalier *marschallin*

milan 26 january 1952	della casa, jurinac, pirino, edelmann, kunz la scala chorus and orchestra karajan	cd: legato LCD 197
london 10-22 december 1956	stich-randall, ludwig, gedda, edelmann, wächter chorus philharmonia karajan	lp: columbia 33CX 1492-1495/SAX 2269-2272/ FCX 750-753/CVB 750-753/WCX 1492-1495/ C 90566-90569/SAXW 2269-2272/STC 90566- 90569/angel 3563/emi SLS 810/EX 29 00453/ 1C191 00459-00462/2C165 00459-00462/ 3C165 00459-00462 cd: emi 749 3548/556 1132/567 6052/567 6092/ 377 3572 *excerpts* lp: columbia 33CX 1777/SAX 2423/WCX 1777/ SAXW 2423/C 80661/STC 80661/angel 35645/ 3754/emi 1C063 00720 cd: emi 763 6572/763 7902/565 5772/585 1052/ 567 6342 *556 1132 is a re-mastered edition of the mono tapes*

228
strauss/der rosenkavalier/concluded

london 4 december 1959	steffek, jurinac, macdonald, böhme, lewis covent garden chorus and orchestra solti	unpublished radio broadcast *bbc third programme*
salzburg 27-30 august 1960	rothenberger, jurinac, zampieri, edelmann, kunz vienna opera chorus vienna philharmonic karajan	vhs video: rank 7015E/gig records 555 019/ kultur 1268 laserdisc: king (japan) 485L 2501-2502 dvd video: rca/bmg 74321 840379
salzburg 31 august 1963	rothenberger, jurinac, romani, edelmann, dönch vienna opera chorus vienna philharmonic karajan	lp: movimento musica 04 004/discocorp RR 659
salzburg 1 august 1964	rothenberger, jurinac, lorenzi, edelmann. ferenz vienna opera chorus vienna philharmonic karajan	cd: arkadia CDKAR 227
new york 19 december 1964	raskin, della casa, morell, edelmann, dönch metropolitan opera chorus and orchestra schippers	cd: claque GM 3010-3012 *metropolitan opera broadcast*

da geht er hin, der aufgeblas'ne schlechte kerl!/der rosenkavalier
marschallin

hamburg 6 december 1952	ndr orchestra schüchter	lp: melodram MEL 088 cd: golden melodram GM 70000
san francisco 20 september 1955	bible san francisco opera orchestra leinsdorf	lp: rococo 5388
london 24 october 1961	töpper philharmonia mackerras	dvd video: emi classic archive DVB 490 4419 *excerpt* vhs video: emi MVC 491 4763 dvd video: emi DVA 492 8529/DVA 477 8319 *begins only at kann mich auch an ein mädel erinnern*

strauss/marie theres'!....hab mir's gelobt/der rosenkavalier *marschallin*

stockholm 5 november 1966	dobbs, söderström stockholm opera orchestra varviso	lp: legendary recordings LR 168

mir ist die ehre widerfahren/der rosenkavalier *sophie*

vienna
9 december 1947
	seefried
	vienna philharmonic
	karajan
		78: columbia LX 1225-1226
		lp: columbia (usa) ML 2126/world records SH 286/
		    emi RLS 763/RLS 7714/1C151 43160-43163M/
		    1C137 54370-54373M
		cd: emi 769 7932/567 6342/grandi voci GVS 19/
		    istituto discografico italiano IDIS 6447-6448/
		    regis RRC 1167

4 letzte lieder: frühling; september; beim schlafengehen; im abendrot

hilversum 24 april 1953	omroeporkest nussio	unpublished radio broadcast *avro*

watford
25-26 september
1953
	philharmonia
	ackermann
		lp: columbia 33CX 1107/FCX 294/WCX 1107/
		    C 90334/angel 35084/38266/emi RLS 751/
		    100 8651/2C061 01208
		cd: emi 761 0012/585 8252/notablu 935 0923/
		    naxos 811 1145

london 20 june 1956	philharmonia karajan	cd: emi 763 6552/763 7902/urania URN 22296
new york 5 december 1957	new york philharmonic previtali	unpublished radio broadcast
amsterdam 19 june 1964	concertgebouw szell	cd: audiophile classics APL 101 548 *im abendrot only* cd: globe GLP 6900/GLO 6905

salzburg
15 august 1964
	berlin
	philharmonic
	karajan
		cd: paragon PCD 84008/nuova era 2251-2252/
		    virtuoso 269 7152/dg salzburg festival 415 5082/
		    verona 27075/golden melodram GM 70004

berlin
1-3 september
1965
	berlin radio
	symphony
	szell
		lp: columbia CX 5258/SAX 5258/angel 36347/
		    emi ASD 2888/1C063 00608/2C069 00608/
		    3C065 00608
		cd: emi 747 2762/566 9082/566 9602

blossom 26 july 1968	cleveland orchestra szell	unpublished radio broadcast
london 25 september 1969	london symphony barbirolli	unpublished radio broadcast
louisville 5 february 1971	louisville orchestra mester	unpublished radio broadcast

strauss/ach was kummer, qual und schmerzen!

berlin 21-29 april 1966	parsons	lp: emi ASD 2404/1C187 01307-01308/angel 36545 cd: emi 763 6562/763 7902/565 8602
london 2 december 1968	parsons	cd: eklipse EKRP 4
utrecht 26 april 1969	parsons	unpublished radio broadcast *avro*
nohant 29 june 1969	ciccolini	cd: arkadia CDGI 8021
amsterdam 8 february 1977	parsons	cd: bella voce BLV 107 002 *also unpublished video recording*

all' mein gedanken

berlin 20-27 october 1968	parsons	emi unpublished

das bächlein (du bächlein silberhell und klar)

london 10-18 march 1968	london symphony szell	lp: emi ASD 2493/1C063 01959/2C069 01959/ angel 36643 cd: emi 747 2762/566 9082/566 9602

freundliche vision (nicht im schlafe hab' ich das geträumt)

strassburg 15 june 1960	bonneau	cd: chant du monde LDC 278 899/notablu 935 0923
berlin 1-3 september 1965	berlin radio symphony szell	lp: columbia CX 5258/SAX 5258/angel 36347/ emi ASD 2888/1C063 00608/2C069 00608/ 3C065 00608 cd: emi 747 2762/566 9082/566 9602

die heiligen 3 kön'ge aus morgenland

berlin september 1965	berlin radio symphony szell	lp: columbia CX 5258/SAX 5258/angel 36347/ emi ASD 2888/1C063 00608/2C069 00608/ 3C065 00608 cd: emi 747 2762/566 9082/566 9602

heimkehr (leise schwanken die äste)

vienna 10 january 1979	parsons	decca unpublished

strauss/**hat gesagt, bleibt's nicht dabei (mein vater hat gesagt)**

berlin 1945	raucheisen	lp: acanta 40 23546 cd: acanta 42 43128/membran 223 067/223 078
london 25 november 1951	moore	cd: testament SBT 2172 *unpublished columbia 78rpm recording*
london 9 april 1952	moore	columbia unpublished
london 21 september 1952	moore	columbia unpublished
london 5-6 january 1954	moore	78: columbia LX 1577 lp: columbia 33CX 1044/FCX 182/WCX 1044/C 90306/ angel 35023/emi RLS 763/1C151 43160-43163M/ 154 6133 cd: emi 763 6562/763 7902/356 5262
salzburg 7 august 1956	moore	cd: emi 566 0842
new york 25 november 1956	reeves	cd: emi 761 0432/notablu 935 0923
hilversum 11 february 1957	de nobel	unpublished radio broadcast *vara*
amsterdam 22 december 1957	de nobel	cd: verona 27021
berlin 6 january 1958	raucheisen	lp: melodram MEL 088 *incorrectly dated 1953*
london 25 october 1961	moore	unpublished video recording *bbc television*
hannover 2 march 1962	reutter	lp: movimento musica 02 017
london 22 march 1968	moore	unpublished video recording *bbc television*
utrecht 26 april 1969	parsons	unpublished radio broadcast *avro*
nohant 29 june 1969	ciccolini	cd: arkadia CDGI 8021

strauss/heimliche aufforderung (auf, hebe die funkelnde schale empor!)

london 18 may 1959	moore	columbia unpublished
new york 14 january 1966	gould	cbs unpublished

meinem kinde (du schläfst und sachte neig' ich mich)

hannover 2 march 1962	reutter	lp: movimento musica 02 017
berlin 21-29 april 1966	parsons	lp: emi ASD 2404/1C187 01307-01308/angel 36545 cd: emi 763 6562/763 7902
london 10-18 march 1968	london symphony szell	lp: emi ASD 2493/1C063 01959/2C069 01959/ angel 36643/3754 cd: emi 747 2762/566 9082
london 2 december 1968	parsons	cd: eklipse EKRP 4
nohant 29 june 1969	ciccolini	cd: arkadia CDGI 8021

morgen (und morgen wird die sonne wieder scheinen)

berlin 1945	raucheisen	lp: acanta 40 23546/40 23557 cd: acanta 42 43128/membran 223 067/223 078
new york 14 january 1966	gould	cbs unpublished
paris 7 june 1967	orchestre national klobucar	unpublished video recording *french television*
london 10-18 march 1968	london symphony szell	lp: emi ASD 2493/1C063 01959/2C069 01959/ angel 36643 cd: emi 747 2762/566 9082
nohant 29 june 1969	ciccolini	cd: arkadia CDGI 8021
versailles 30 june 1971	ciccolini	vhs video: emi MVC 491 4763 dvd video: emi DVA 492 8529

muttertändelei (seht mir doch, mein schönes kind!)

berlin
1-3 september 1965
	berlin radio
	symphony
	szell
		lp: columbia CX 5258/SAX 5258/angel 36347/
		    emi ASD 2888/1C063 00608/2C069 00608/
		    3C065 00608
		cd: emi 747 2762/566 9082

london 2 december 1968	parsons	cd: eklipse EKRP 4
utrecht 26 april 1969	parsons	unpublished radio broadcast *avro*

strauss/**die nacht** (aus dem walde tritt die nacht)

berlin 20-27 october 1968	parsons	emi unpublished
berlin 27 august- 8 september 1970	parsons	lp: emi ASD 2844/1C063 02331/154 6133 cd: emi 763 6562/763 7902

3 ophelia-lieder: wie erkenn' ich mein treulieb?; guten morgen, 's ist sankt valentinstag; sie trugen ihn auf der bahre bloss

new york 14 january 1966	gould	lp: cbs 76983/35914 cd: sony SM2K 52657/S2K 60686
berlin 28 october 1967	parsons	lp: emi ASD 2634/1C063 02116/angel 36752 cd: emi 763 6562/763 7902
london 2 december 1968	parsons	cd: emi 565 8602/eklipse EKRP 4
utrecht 26 april 1969	parsons	unpublished radio broadcast *avro*

das rosenband (im frühlingsschatten fand ich sie)

london 10-18 march 1968	london symphony szell	lp: emi ASD 2493/1C063 01959/2C069 01959/ angel 36643 cd: emi 747 2762/566 9082
london 2 december 1968	parsons	cd: eklipse EKRP 4

3 rosenlieder: rote rosen; die erwachte rose; begegnung

january 1959	moore	unpublished radio broadcast *bbc third programme*

schlagende herzen (über wiesen und felder)

berlin 1945	raucheisen	lp: acanta 40 23546/40 23557 cd: acanta 42 43128/membran 223 067/223 078

ständchen (mach' auf doch leise, mein kind!)

amsterdam 22 december 1957	de nobel	unpublished radio broadcast *vara*

strauss/ruhe meine seele (nicht ein lüftchen regt sich leise)

london 8 april 1956	moore	columbia unpublished
salzburg 7 august 1956	moore	cd: emi 566 0842
new york 25 november 1956	reeves	cd: emi 761 0432/notablu 935 0923
hilversum 11 february 1957	de nobel	unpublished radio broadcast
amsterdam 22 december 1957	de nobel	cd: verona 27021
london 18 may 1959	moore	columbia unpublished
strassburg 15 june 1960	bonneau	cd: chant du monde LDC 278 899
hannover 2 march 1962	reutter	lp: movimento musica 02 017
london 10 february 1964	parsons	unpublished radio broadcast *bbc third programme*
london 12 april 1964	moore	cd: testament SBT 1206 *unpublished columbia lp recording*
london 10-18 march 1968	london symphony szell	lp: emi ASD 2493/1C063 01959/2C069 01959/ angel 36643 cd: emi 747 2762/566 9082
nohant 29 june 1969	ciccolini	cd: arkadia CDGI 8021
amsterdam 8 february 1977	parsons	cd: bella voce BLV 107 002 *also unpublished video recording*

strauss/schlechtes wetter (das ist ein schlechtes wetter!)

london 25 november 1951	moore	cd: testament SBT 2172 *unpublished columbia 78rpm recording*
london 9 april 1952	moore	columbia unpublished
london 21 september 1952	moore	columbia unpublished

london
5 january 1954
	moore	78: columbia LX 1577
		lp: columbia 33CX 1044/FCX 182/WCX 1044/C 90306/
		    angel 35023/emi RLS 763/1C151 43160-43163M/
		    154 6133
		cd: emi 763 6562/763 7902/356 5262

salzburg 7 august 1956	moore	cd: emi 566 0842/stradivarius STR 10009
new york 25 november 1956	reeves	cd: emi 761 0432
hilversum 11 february 1957	de nobel	unpublished radio broadcast *vara*
amsterdam 22 december 1957	de nobel	cd: verona 27021
berlin 6 january 1958	raucheisen	lp: melodram MEL 088 *incorrectly dated 1953*
strassburg 15 june 1960	bonneau	cd: chant du monde LDC 278 899/notablu 935 0923
hannover 2 march 1962	reutter	lp: movimento musica 02 017

waldseligkeit (der wald beginnt zu rauschen)

berlin
1-3 september
1965
	berlin radio
	symphony
	szell
		lp: columbia CX 5258/SAX 5258/angel 36347/emi
		    ASD 2888/1C063 00608/2C069 00608/
		    3C065 00608
		cd: emi 747 2762/566 9082

strauss/**wer lieben will, muss leiden**

new york 14 january 1966	gould	cbs unpublished
berlin 21-29 april 1966	parsons	lp: emi ASD 2404/1C187 01307-01308/angel 36545 cd: emi 763 6562/763 7902/565 8602
london 2 december 1968	parsons	cd: eklipse EKRP 4
nohant 29 june 1969	ciccolini	cd: arkadia CDGI 8021

wiegenlied (träume, träume, du mein süsses leben)

london 8 april 1956	moore	cd: testament SBT 1206 *unpublished columbia lp recording*

london
18 may 1956
	moore	45: columbia SEL 1588
		lp: columbia 33CX 1404/SAX 2265/FCX 664/
		    SAXF 145/WCX 1404/C 90545/angel 35383/
		    emi 154 6133
		cd: emi 763 6562/763 7902/356 5262

salzburg 7 august 1956	moore	cd: emi 566 0842
new york 25 november 1956	reeves	cd: emi 761 0432/notablu 935 0923
amsterdam 22 december 1957	de nobel	unpublished radio broadcast *vara*
hannover 2 march 1962	reutter	lp: movimento musica 02 017
london 10-18 march 1968	london symphony szell	lp: emi ASD 2493/1C063 01959/2C069 01959/ angel 36643 cd: emi 747 2762/566 9082

wiegenliedchen (bienchen wiegt sich im sonnenschein)

berlin 20-27 october 1968	parsons	emi unpublished
berlin 27 august- 8 september 1970	parsons	lp: emi ASD 2844/1C063 02331 cd: emi 763 6562/763 7902

strauss/**winterweihe** (**in diesen wintertagen nun sich das licht verhüllt**)
new york   gould   cbs unpublished
14 january 1966

london   london symphony   lp: emi ASD 2493/1C063 01929/2C069 01929/
10-18 march 1968   szell   angel 36643
                                         cd: emi 747 2762/566 9082

zueignung (ja, du weisst es, teure seele!)
london   moore   columbia unpublished
11 june 1957

strassburg   bonneau   cd: chant du monde LDC 278 899
15 june 1960

hannover   reutter   lp: movimento musica 02 017
2 march 1962

london   moore   cd: testament SBT 1206
12 april 1964   *unpublished columbia lp recording*

berlin   berlin radio   lp: columbia CX 5258/SAX 5258/angel 36347/
1-3 september   symphony   emi ASD 2888/1C 063 00608/2C069 00608/
1965   szell   3C065 00608
                                         cd: emi 747 2762/566 9082

utrecht   parsons   unpublished radio broadcast
26 april 1969

IGOR STRAVINSKY (1882-1971)
the rakes's progress *role of anne truelove*
venice   rounseville,   lp: cetra DOC 29
11 september 1951   tourel, o.kraus,   cd: great operatic performances GOP 66355/
                      arié   gala GL 100 567
                      la scala chorus
                      and orchestra
                      stravinsky

pastorale
berlin   parsons   lp: emi ASD 2404/1C187 01307-01308/angel 36545
24-28 october 1967   cd: emi 763 6562/763 7902/565 8602

FRANZ VON SUPPE (1819-1895)
boccacio/querschnitt (scenes) *fiametta*
berlin   glawitsch   78: telefunken E 3029/capitol 89-80109
4 september 1939   orchester des   cd: hänssler classics 94501
                      deutschen
                      opernhauses
                      lütze

hab' ich nur deine liebe/boccacio *fiametta*
london   philharmonia   45: columbia SEL 1652/ESL 6270
4 july 1957   ackermann   lp: columbia 33CX 1570/SAX 2283/SAXF 158/
                                             angel 35696/emi ASD 2807/SVP 1180/
                                             100 4781/2C053 00478
                                         cd: emi 747 2842/566 9892/567 0042

HEINRICH SUTERMEISTER (1910-1995)
messa da requiem *soprano soloist*

rome	tadeo	unpublished radio broadcast
21 december 1953	rai roma chorus	
	and orchestra	
	karajan	

PIOTR TCHAIKOVSKY (1840-1893)
tatiana's letter scene/evgeny onegin *tatiana*

london	london symphony	lp: columbia CX 5286/SAX 5286/angel 36464/
16-17 september	galliera	emi SXDW 3049/1C181 52291-52292/
1966	*sung in german*	2C181 52291-52292
		cd: emi 769 5012

none but the lonely heart

london	moore	45: columbia SEL 1600/ESL 6274
11 april 1956	*sung in german*	lp: columbia 33CX 1404/SAX 2265/FCX 664/
		SAXF 145/WCX 1404/C 90545/angel 35383
		cd: emi 565 8602

pimpimella (non contrastar cogl' uomini fallo per carita!)

berlin	parsons	lp: emi ASD 2404/1C187 01307-01308/angel 36545
24-28 october 1967		cd: emi 763 6542/763 7902

MICHAEL TIPPETT (1905-1998)
a child of our time *soprano soloist*

turin	cavelti, gedda,	unpublished radio broadcast
20 february 1953	petri	
	rai torino chorus	
	and orchestra	
	karajan	

RICHARD TRUNK (1879-1968)
4 heitere lieder: brautwerbung; menuett; schlittenfahrt; vertrag

berlin	raucheisen	lp: acanta 40 23557
20 september 1944		cd: acanta 42 43128/membran 223 067/223 093

die allee; das hemd

berlin	raucheisen	lp: acanta 40 23557
20 september 1944		cd: acanta 42 43801/membran 223 067/223 093

GIUSEPPE VERDI (1813-1901)
messa da requiem *soprano soloist*

paris 30 april 1953	barbieri, berdini, von rohr orchestre national and chorus markevitch	cd: golden melodram GM 40072/tahra TAH 543-544

milan
18-27 june 1954
	dominguez,
	di stefano, siepi
	la scala chorus
	and orchestra
	de sabata
		lp: columbia 33CX 1195-1196/FCX 361-362/QCX
		    10104-10105/WCX 1195-1196/C 90387-90388/
		    angel 3520/emi 100 9373/3C163 00937-0093 34928
		cd: emi 565 5062/teorema THS 121 123-124/naxos
		    811 1049-1050/urania RM 11930
		libera me
		cd: emi 763 6572/763 7902/istituto discografico
		    italiano IDIS 6447-6448

london
16-24 september
1963
	ludwig, gedda,
	ghiaurov
	philharmonia
	chorus and
	orchestra
	giulini
		lp: emi AN 133-134/SAN 133-134/1C165 00629-00630/
		    2C167 00629-00630/3C165 00629-00630/SLS 909/
		    A 91353-91354/STA 91353-91354/angel 3649
		cd: emi 747 2578/566 2502/567 5602/567 5632
		recording completed on 7 april 1964

alzira/concert version for radio *title role*

berlin 1 november 1938	glawitsch, hübner, garavello reichssender chorus and orchestra steiner *sung in german*	cd: myto MCD 962 148/radio years RY 73 *excerpts* cd: istituto discografico italiano IDIS 6447-6448

falstaff *role of alice ford*

london
21-29 june 1956
	moffo, merriman,
	barbieri, alva,
	gobbi, panerai
	chorus
	philharmonia
	karajan
		lp: columbia 33CX 1410-1412/SAX 2254-2256/
		    QCX 10244-10246/WCX 1410-1412/C 90524-
		    90526/angel 3552/emi SLS 5037/SLS 5211/
		    EX 749 6682/1C153 00442-00443/1C165
		    02125-02127/2C167 03951-03952/
		    3C153 00442-00443
		cd: emi 749 6682/567 0832/567 1622/377 3492
		excerpts
		lp: columbia 33CX 1939/SAX 2578/WSX 528/C 80615

salzburg 10 august 1957	moffo, canali, simionato, alva, gobbi, panerai vienna opera chorus vienna philharmonic karajan	cd: arkadia CDKAR 226/andante 3080

verdi/**piangea cantando**/otello *desdemona*

london 22 april 1959	elkins philharmonia rescigno	lp: columbia CX 5286/SAX 5286/angel 36434/3754/ emi 1C181 52291-52292/2C181 52291-52292/ SXDW 3049 cd: emi 567 6342
london 15 october 1967	howells covent garden orchestra downes	unpublished video recording *bbc television*

ave maria/otello *desdemona*

london 5 october 1955	philharmonia galliera	columbia unpublished
london 22 april 1959	philharmonia rescigno	lp: columbia CX 5286/SAX 5286/angel 36434/3754/ emi 1C181 52291-52292/2C181 52291-52292/ SXDW 3049 cd: emi 567 6342
london 15 october 1967	covent garden orchestra downes	unpublished video recording *bbc television*

ah fors e lui!...sempre libera!/la traviata *violetta*

london 12 april 1948	philharmonia braithwaite *sung in english*	78: columbia LX 1079 cd: testament SBT 2172

madamigella valery?...dite alle giovane/la traviata *violetta*

london 1 october 1953	panerai philharmonia galliera	lp: emi EX 29 10753 cd: emi 574 2672 *unpublished columbia lp recording*

addio del passato/la traviata *violetta*

london 19 october 1950	philharmonia galliera	78: columbia LX 1370/GQX 11456 45: columbia SCD 2076/SCB 102/SCBW 102/ SCBF 107/SCBQ 3004 lp: emi RLS 763/1C151 43160-43163M cd: andromeda ANDRCD 5006
london 25 april 1959	philharmonia rescigno	columbia unpublished
london 25 april 1962	philharmonia tonini	columbia unpublished

lo spazzocamino

berlin 20 september 1944	raucheisen *sung in german*	lp: acanta 40 23557 cd: acanta 42 43801/membran 223 067/223 093

BERNHARD VLIES (1770)
wiegenlied (schlafe mein prinzchen)

london	moore	cd: testament SBT 1206
14 april 1956		*unpublished columbia lp recording*

RICHARD WAGNER (1813-1883)
götterdämmerung *role of woglinde*

bayreuth	varnay, mödl,	cd: testament SBT 4175/golden melodram GM 10067
4 august 1951	siewert, aldenhoff,	audiophile lp: testament SBTLP 6175
	uhde, weber	*unpublished decca lp recording*
	bayreuth festival	
	chorus and orchestra	
	knappertsbusch	
bayreuth	varnay, mödl,	columbia unpublished
15 august 1951	siewert, aldenhoff,	
	uhde, weber	
	bayreuth festival	
	chorus and orchestra	
	karajan	

einsam in trüben tagen/lohengrin *elsa*

london	philharmonia	lp: columbia 33CX 1658/SAX 2300/FCX 821/
28 april 1956	susskind	angel 35806/world records T 520/ST 520/
		emi SXDW 3049
		cd: emi 769 5012/565 5772/585 1052

euch lüften, die mein klagen...to end of scene 2/lohengrin *elsa*

london	hoffman, czerwenka	columbia unpublished
9 may 1956	philharmonia	
	susskind	
london	ludwig	lp: columbia 33CX 1658/SAX 2300/FCX 821/
25 may 1958	philharmonia	angel 35806/world records T 520/ST 520/
	wallberg	emi SXDW 3049
		cd: emi 769 5012/567 6342

die meistersinger von nürnberg *role of eva*

bayreuth	malaniuk, hopf,	78: columbia LX 1465-1498/LX 8851-8884
july-august	unger, edelmann,	lp: columbia 33CX 1021-1025/FCX 128-133/
1951	dalberg, kunz	VCX 523-527/WCX 501-505/C 90275-90279/
	bayreuth festival	angel seraphim 6030/emi RLS 7708/143 3903/
	chorus and orchestra	1C153 43390-43394M
	karajan	cd: emi 763 5002/naxos 811 0872-0875
		excerpts
		cd: urania URN 22296
		recorded at dress rehearsal and various public performances
bayreuth	malaniuk, hopf,	cd: arkadia CDKAR 224/membran 221 743
5 august 1951	unger, edelmann,	
	dalberg, kunz	
	bayreuth festival	
	chorus and orchestra	
	karajan	

guten abend meister!/die meistersinger von nürnberg *eva*

london	edelmann	columbia unpublished
14 december 1956	philharmonia	
	schmidt	

wagner/**das rheingold** *role of woglinde*

bayreuth 31 july 1951	malaniiuk, siewert, brivkalne, fritz, windgassen, kuen, s.björling bayreuth festival orchestra knappertsbusch	decca unpublished

bayreuth 11 august 1951	malaniuk, siewert, brivkalne, fritz, windgassen, kuen, s.björlimg bayreuth festival orchestra karajan	lp: melodram MEL 516 cd: melodram CDM 26107/arkadia CDKAR 216/ walhall WLCD 0034 *excerpts* lp: melodram MEL 088

weia! waga! woge, du welle!/**das rheingold** *wellgunde*

berlin
24 may 1941
	scheppan, schilp,
	hann
	orchester des
	deutschen
	opernhauses
	rother
		lp: acanta 22 21486/40 23502/discoreale
		    DR 10037/ melodram MEL 082
		cd: melodram CDM 16501/golden melodram
		    GM 70000

**lugt schwestern!; abendlich strahlt der sonne auge....to end /
das rheingold** *wellgunde*

berlin 24 may 1941	scheppan, schilp, hann, aldenhoff, nissen orchester des deutschen opernhauses rother	lp: acanta 22 21486/40 23502/discoreale DR 10037

dich teure halle!/**tannhäuser** *elisabeth*

london
27 april 1956
	philharmonia
	susskind
		lp: columbia 33CX 1658/SAX 2300/FCX 821/
		    angel 35806/world records T 520/ST 520/
		    emi SXDW 3049
		cd: emi 769 5012/585 1052

allmächt'ge jungfrau!/**tannhäuser** *elisabeth*

london
27 april 1956
	philharmonia
	susskind
		lp: columbia 33CX 1658/SAX 2300/FCX 821/
		    angel 35806/world records T 520/ST 520/
		    emi SXDW 3049
		cd: emi 769 5012

wagner/**tot denn alles!/tristan und isolde** *brangäne*
london	weber	78: columbia LX 8892
16 september 1951	philharmonia	lp: emi 1C177 00933-00934M
	schüchter	cd: testament SBT 1171

schmerzen/wesendonk-lieder
london	moore	columbia unpublished
30 january 1961		
london	moore	columbia unpublished
14 february 1961		

träume/wesendonk-lieder
london	moore	columbia unpublished
30 january 1961		
london	moore	cd: testament SBT 1206
14 february 1961		*unpublished columbia lp recording; dated by testament as 27 february 1961*
london	moore	lp: emi SAN 255/1C065 01861/154 6133/ angel 36640
7 december 1962		cd: emi 763 6542/763 7902/567 9902

WILLIAM WALTON (1902-1983)
troilus and cressida, scenes *role of cressida*
is cressida a slave?; slowly it all comes back; how can i sleep?; if one last doubt remain; now close your arms; from isle to isle chill waters; all's well!; diomede! father!
london	lewis, sinclair	lp: columbia 33CX 1313/QCX 10173/angel 35278/ world records OH 217
18-20 april 1955	philharmonia	cd: emi 764 1992
	walton	*recording completed on 16 may 1955*

CARL MARIA VON WEBER (1786-1826)
abu hassan *role of fatima*
berlin	witte, bohnen	lp: urania URLP 7029/UR 7029/URLP 57029/ vox OPBX 149/opera society OPS 1/classics club 108/saga XID 5055/FDY 2065/ STFDY 2065/varese sarabande VC 81093
18-19 december	rundfunk-sinfonie-	
1944	orchester	
	and chorus	
	l.ludwig	cd: urania ULS 5153/forlane UCD 16572/ preiser 90209/20044
		excerpts
		lp: melodram MEL 082/discoreale DR 10038
		cd: melodram CDM 16501/golden melodram GM 70000/istituto discografico italiano IDIS 6447-6448
		preiser issues also include spoken dialogue

weber/**und ob die wolke/der freischütz** *agathe*

london	philharmonia	lp: columbia 33CX 1658/SAX 2300/FCX 821/
27 april 1956	susskind	angel 35806/3754/world records T 520/ST 520/
		emi SXDW 3049
		cd: emi 769 5012/grandi voci GVS 19

leise leise/der freischütz *agathe*

london	philharmonia	lp: columbia 33CX 1658/SAX 2300/FCX 821/
28 april 1956	susskind	angel 35806/world records T 520/ST 520/
		emi SXDW 3049
		cd: emi 769 5012/565 5772/567 6342/585 1052

ozean du ungeheuer!/oberon *rezia*

london	philharmonia	columbia unpublished
27 april 1956	susskind	

mille volte mio tesoro; va ti consolo, addio/italian duets

berlin	piltti	lp: melodiya M10 41285-41286/5289-73/
27 june 1942	raucheisen	discocorp IGI 385/RR 208/scandia SLP 546

se il mio ben/italian duets

berlin	piltti	lp: melodiya M10 41285-41286/5289-73/
27 june 1942	raucheisen	discocorp IGI 385/RR 208/scandia SLP 546/
		acanta 40 23566
		cd: acanta 42 43128/membran 223 067/223 072

HUGO WOLF (1860-1903)

ach des knaben augen/spanisches liederbuch

berlin	moore	lp: deutsche grammophon SLPM 139 329-139 330/
16-17 december		2707 035/2726 071
1966		cd: deutsche grammophon 421 9342/457 7262
		recordings completed on 2-10 january 1967

ach im maien war's/spanisches liederbuch

london	parsons	cd: eklipse EKRP 4
2 december 1968		

als ich auf dem euphrat schiffte/goethe-lieder

london	moore	columbia unpublished
9 june 1957		

london	moore	columbia unpublished
30 january 1961		

london	moore	columbia unpublished
9 march 1962		

london	moore	lp: columbia 33CX 1946/SAX 2589/angel 36308/
4 december 1962		emi SLS 5197/1C161 53747-53748
		cd: emi 565 8602

an eine äolsharfe/mörike-lieder

berlin	parsons	lp: emi ASD 3124/1C063 02598/154 6133
1-8 september		cd: emi 763 6532/763 7902
1970		

wolf/an den schlaf/mörike-lieder

berlin 1-10 march 1973	parsons	lp: emi ASD 3124/1C063 02598 *published on cd only in japan*
amsterdam 8 february 1977	parsons	cd: bella voce BLV 107 002 *also unpublished video recording*

anakreons grab/goethe-lieder

salzburg
12 august 1953
	furtwängler	lp: cetra FE 30/melodram MEL 088/discocorp
		    IGI 385/RR 208/emi ALP 2114/1C063 01915M/
		    143 5491/angel seraphim 60179
		cd: cetra CDC 21/priceless D 18355/virtuoso
		    269 7152/269 7312/emi 567 5702

london 6 april 1956	moore	columbia unpublished
london 4 july 1956	moore	columbia unpublished

london
10 june 1957
	moore	lp: columbia 33CX 1657/SAX 2333/FCX 837/SAXF 256/
		    angel 35909/emi SLS 5197/1C161 53748-53749/
		    1C037 03725

amsterdam 22 december 1957	de nobel	unpublished radio broadcast *vara*
salzburg 27 july 1958	moore	cd: emi 764 9052
london 2 december 1968	parsons	cd: eklipse EKRP 4

auch kleine dinge/italienisches liederbuch

hilversum 23 april 1953	de nobel	unpublished radio broadcast *ncrv*
london 12-21 april 1954	moore	columbia unpublished *recordings completed in june, july and september 1954*
london 5 september 1954	moore	unpublished radio broadcast *bbc third programme*
london 1-7 april 1958	moore	columbia unpublished
london 19-23 december 1959	moore	lp: columbia 33CX 1714/SAX 2366/angel 35883 cd: emi 565 8602/585 1052

auf ein altes bild/mörike-lieder

london 6 january 1977	parsons	lp: decca SXL 6943/642 576AW/london OS 26592 cd: decca 430 0002

wolf/auf eine christblume/mörike-lieder

salzburg 27 july 1958	moore	cd: emi 764 9052
berlin 27 august- 8 september 1970	parsons	lp: emi ASD 2844/1C063 02331 *issued on cd only in japan*

auf einer wanderung/mörike-lieder

berlin 1-10 march 1973	parsons	lp: emi ASD 3124/1C063 02598 cd: emi 763 6532/763 7902

auftrag/mörike-lieder

berlin 1-10 march 1973	parsons	lp: emi ASD 3124/1C063 02598 cd: emi 565 8602

bedeckt mich mit blumen/spanisches liederbuch

london 7 april 1951	moore	cd: testament SBT 2172 *unpublished columbia 78rpm recording*

salzburg
12 august 1953
	furtwängler	lp: cetra FE 30/melodram MEL 088/discocorp
		    IGI 385/RR 208/emi ALP 2114/1C063 01915M/
		    143 5491/angel seraphim 60179
		cd: cetra CDC 21/proceless D 18355/virtuoso 269
		    7312/emi 567 5702

new york 25 november 1956	reeves	cd: emi 761 0432/notablu 935 0923
salzburg 27 july 1958	moore	cd: emi 764 9052
hannover 2 march 1962	reutter	lp: movimento musica 02 017 cd: movimento musica 051 015
salzburg 17 august 1963	moore	cd: emi 565 7492
berlin 16-17 december 1966	moore	lp: deutsche grammophon SLPM 139 329-139 330/ 2707 035/2726 071 cd: deutsche grammophon 421 9342/457 7262 *recordings completed on 2-10 january 1967*
vienna 9 january 1979	parsons	decca unpublished

begegnung/mörike-lieder

berlin 1-10 march 1973	parsons	lp: emi ASD 3124/1C063 02598 cd: emi 763 6532/763 7902

bei einer trauung/mörike-lieder

london 14 january 1977	parsons	lp: decca SXL 6943/642 576AW/london OS 26592 cd: decca 430 0002

wolf/die bekehrte/goethe-lieder

london 11 april 1951	moore	cd: testament SBT 2172 *unpublished columbia 78rpm recording*
salzburg 12 august 1953	furtwängler	lp: cetra FE 30/emi ALP 2114/1C063 01915M/143 5491/ angel seraphim 60179 cd: cetra CDC 21/priceless D 18355/virtuoso 269 7152/ 269 7312/emi 567 5702
london 5 april 1956	moore	columbia unpublished
london 9-10 june 1957	moore	lp: columbia 33CX 1657/SAX 2333/FCX 857/SAXF 256/ angel 35909/emi SLS 5197/1C161 53748-53749/ 1C037 03725 cd: emi 763 6532/763 7902

bitt' ihn, o mutter!/spanisches liederbuch

berlin 16-17 december 1966	moore	lp: deutsche grammophon SLPM 139 329-139 330/ 2707 035/2726 071 cd: deutsche grammophon 421 9342/457 7262 *recordings completed on 2-10 january 1967*

blumengruss/goethe-lieder

salzburg 12 august 1953	furtwängler	lp: cetra FE 30/emi ALP 2114/1C063 01915M/143 5491/ angel seraphim 60179 cd: cetra CDC 21/priceless D 18355/virtuoso 269 7152/ 269 7312/emi 567 5702
london 4 april 1955	moore	columbia unpublished
london 4-6 april 1956	moore	columbia unpublished
london 11 january 1958	moore	lp: columbia 33CX 1657/SAX 2333/FCX 857/SAXF 256/ angel 35909/emi SLS 5197/1C161 53748-53749/ 1C037 03725 cd: emi 565 8602
salzburg 27 july 1958	moore	cd: emi 764 9052

denk' es, o seele/mörike-lieder

berlin 1-8 september 1970	parsons	lp: emi ASD 3124/1C063 02598/154 6133 cd: emi 763 6532/763 7902
amsterdam 8 february 1977	parsons	cd: bella voce BLV 107 002 *also unpublished video recording*

wolf/die ihr schwebt um diese palmen/spanisches liederbuch

berlin 16-17 december 1966	moore	lp: deutsche grammophon SLPM 139 329-139 330/ 2707 035/2726 071 cd: deutsche grammophon 421 9342/457 7262 *recordings completed on 2-10 january 1967*

du milchjunger knabe/alte weisen

salzburg 27 july 1958	moore	cd: emi 764 9052/stradivarius STR 10009
london 15 april 1961	moore	lp: columbia 33CX 1946/SAX 2589/angel 36308/ emi SLS 5197/1C161 53747-53748

du denkst, mit einem fädchen mich zu fangen/italienisches liederbuch

london 2 april 1951	moore	cd: testament SBT 2172 *unpublished columbia 78rpm recording*
london 18 june 1951	moore	columbia unpublished
hilversum 23 april 1953	de nobel	unpublished radio broadcast *ncrv*
london 12-21 april 1954	moore	columbia unpublished *recordings completed in june, july and september 1954*
london 5 september 1954	moore	unpublished radio broadcast *bbc third programme*
london 1-7 april 1958	moore	columbia unpublished
london 19-23 december 1959	moore	lp: columbia 33CX 1714/SAX 2366/angel 35883 cd: emi 565 8602
london 10 february 1964	parsons	unpublished radio broadcast *bbc third programme*
berlin 12-13 september 1965	moore	lp: emi AN 210-211/SAN 210-211/1C165 08171-01872/ angel 3703 cd: emi 763 7322/562 6502/562 6512 *recordings completed in march 1966 and september 1967*

wolf/du sagst mir, dass ich keine fürstin sei/italienisches liederbuch

hilversum 23 april 1953	de nobel	unpublished radio broadcast *ncrv*
london 12-21 april 1954	moore	columbia unpublished *recordings completed in june, july and september 1954*
salzburg 19 august 1957	moore	cd: emi 565 7492
london 1-7 april 1958	moore	columbia unpublished
london 19-23 december 1959	moore	lp: columbia 33CX 1714/SAX 2366/angel 35883 cd: emi 565 8602
london 10 february 1964	parsons	unpublished radio broadcast *bbc third programme*
berlin 12-13 september 1965	moore	lp: emi AN 210-211/SAN 210-211/1C165 08171-08172/ angel 3703 cd: emi 763 7322/562 6502/562 6512 *recordings completed in march 1966 and september 1967*

eide, so die liebe schwur/spanisches liederbuch

berlin 16-17 december 1966	moore	lp: deutsche grammophon SLPM 139 329-139 330/ 2707 035/2721 071 cd: deutsche grammophon 421 9342/457 7262 *recordings completed on 2-10 january 1967*

wolf/elfenlied/mörike-lieder

london 7 april 1951	moore		cd: testament SBT 2172 *unpublished columbia 78rpm recording*
london 19 june 1951	moore		columbia unpublished
salzburg 12 august 1953	furtwängler		lp: cetra FE 30/emi ALP 2114/1C063 01915M/143 5491/ angel seraphim 60179 cd: cetra CDC 21/priceless D 18355/virtuoso 269 7152/ 269 7312/emi 567 5702
london 10 april 1956	moore		45: columbia SEL 1588/SELW 1805/C 50502 lp: columbia 33CX 1404/SAX 2265/FCX 664/SAXF 145/ WCX 1404/C 90545/angel 35383 cd: emi 763 6532/763 7902/356 5262
new york 25 november 1956	reeves		cd: emi 761 0432/notablu 935 0923
salzburg 19 august 1957	moore		cd: emi 565 7492
amsterdam 22 december 1957	de nobel		unpublished radio broadcast *vara*
london 17 january 1977	parsons		lp: decca SXL 6943/642 576AW/london OS 26592 cd: decca 430 0002

fussreise/mörike-lieder

london 6 january 1977	parsons		lp: decca SXL 6943/642 576AW/london OS 26592 cd: decca 430 0002

wolf/epiphanias/goethe-lieder

london 2 april 1951	moore	cd: testament SBT 2172 *unpublished columbia 78rpm recording*
london 18 june 1951	moore	columbia unpublished

salzburg
12 august 1953
	furtwängler	lp: cetra FE 30/emi ALP 2114/1C063 01915M/143 5491/
		  angel seraphim 60179
		cd: cetra CDC 21/priceless D 18355/virtuoso 269 7152/
		  269 7312/emi 567 5702

london 4 april 1955	moore	columbia unpublished

london
4-7 april 1956
	moore	lp: columbia 33CX 1657/SAX 2333/FCX 837/SAXF 256/
		  angel 35909/emi SLS 5197/1C161 53748-53749/
		  1C037 03725
		cd: emi 565 8602

frühling übers jahr/goethe-lieder

london 4 april 1955	moore	columbia unpublished

london
4-7 april 1956
	moore	lp: columbia 33CX 1657/SAX 2333/FCX 837/SAXF 256/
		  angel 35909/emi SLS 5197/1C161 53748-53749/
		  1C037 03725
		cd: emi 565 8602

amsterdam 22 december 1957	de nobel	unpublished radio broadcast *vara*
salzburg 27 july 1958	moore	cd: emi 764 9052

ganymed/goethe-lieder

london
6-8 april 1956
	moore	lp: columbia 33CX 1657/SAX 2333/FCX 837/SAXF 256/
		  angel 35909/emi SLS 5197/1C161 53748-53749/
		  1C037 03725
		cd: emi 763 6532/763 7902/notablu 935 0911

salzburg 27 july 1958	moore	cd: emi 764 9052

der gärtner/mörike-lieder

berlin 1-10 march 1973	parsons	lp: emi ASD 3124/1C063 02598 *issued on cd only in japan*

gebet/mörike-lieder

london 7 january 1977	parsons	decca unpublished

wolf/geh' geliebter, geh' jetzt!/spanisches liederbuch

salzburg 19 august 1957	moore	cd: emi 565 7492
strassburg 15 june 1960	bonneau	cd: chant du monde LDC 278 899/notablu 935 0911
berlin 16-17 december 1966	moore	lp: deutsche grammophon SLPM 139 329-139 330/ 2707 035/2726 071 cd: deutsche grammophon 421 9342/457 7262 *recordings completed on 2-10 january 1967*

der genesene an die hoffnung/mörike-lieder

salzburg 19 august 1957	moore	cd: emi 565 7492
london 23 december 1959	moore	columbia unpublished
vienna 6 january 1979	parsons	decca unpublished

gesang weylas/mörike-lieder

berlin 21-29 april 1966	parsons	emi unpublished

gesegnet sei das grün/italienisches liederbuch

hilversum 23 april 1953	de nobel	unpublished radio broadcast *ncev*
london 12-21 april 1954	moore	columbia unpublished *recordings completed in june, july and september 1954*
london 5 september 1954	moore	unpublished radio broadcast *bbc third programme*
london 1-7 april 1958	moore	columbia unpublished
london 19-23 december 1959	moore	lp: columbia 33CX 1714/SAX 2366/angel 35883 cd: emi 565 8602
berlin 12-13 september 1965	moore	lp: emi AN 210-211/SAN 210-211/1C165 01871-01872/angel 3703 cd: 763 7322/562 6502/562 6512 *recordings completed in march 1966 and september 1967*

wolf/gleich und gleich/goethe-lieder

london 4 april 1956	moore	lp: columbia 33CX 1657/SAX 2333/FCX 837/SAXF 256/ angel 35909/emi SLS 5197/1C161 53748-53749/ 1C037 03725 cd: emi 565 8602
amsterdam 22 december 1957	de nobel	unpublished radio broadcast *vara*

heimweh/mörike-lieder

london 13 january 1977	parsons	decca unpublished
amsterdam 8 february 1977	parsons	cd: bella voce BLV 107 002 *also unpublished video recording*
vienna 8 january 1979	parsons	lp: decca SXL 6943/642 576AW/london OS 26592 cd: decca 430 0002

herr, was trägt der boden hier?/spanisches liederbuch

salzburg 12 august 1953	furtwängler	lp: cetra FE 30/emi ALP 2114/1C063 01915M/143 5491/ angel seraphim 60179 cd: cetra CDC 21/priceless D 18355/virtuoso 269 7312/ emi 567 5702
new york 25 november 1956	reeves	cd: emi 761 0432/notablu 935 0923
strassburg 15 june 1960	bonneau	cd: chant du monde LDC 278 899
hannover 2 march 1962	reutter	lp: movimento musica 02 017 cd: movimento musica 051 015
salzburg 17 august 1963	moore	cd: emi 565 7492
vienna 7 january 1979	parsons	decca unpublished

heut' nacht erhob ich mich/italienisches liederbuch

london 12-21 april 1954	moore	columbia unpublished *recordings completed in june, july and september 1954*

hochbeglückt in deiner liebe/goethe-lieder

london 10 june 1957	moore	columbia unpublished
london 9 march 1962	moore	lp: columbia 33CX 1946/SAX 2589/angel 36308/ emi SLS 5197/1C161 53747-53748 cd: 565 8602

wolf/ich esse nun mein brot nicht trocken mehr/italienisches liederbuch

hilversum 23 april 1953	de nobel	unpublished radio broadcast *ncrv*
london 12-21 april 1954	moore	columbia unpublished *recordings completed in june, july and september 1954*
london 5 september 1954	moore	unpublished radio broadcast *bbc third programme*
salzburg 19 august 1957	moore	cd: emi 565 7492
london 1-7 april 1958	moore	columbia unpublished
london 19-23 december 1959	moore	lp: columbia 33CX 1714/SAX 2366/angel 35883 cd: emi 565 8602
berlin 12-13 september 1965	moore	lp: emi AN 210-211/SAN 210-211/1C165 01871-01872/angel 3703 cd: emi 763 7322/562 6502/562 6512 *recordings completed in march 1966 and september 1967*
amsterdam 8 february 1977	parsons	cd: bella voce BLV 107 002 *also unpublished video recording*

wolf/ich hab' in penna einen liebsten wohnen/italienisches liederbuch

hilversum 23 april 1953	de nobel	unpublished radio broadcast *ncrv*
london 12-21 april 1954	moore	columbia unpublished *recordings completed on june, july and september 1954*
new york 25 november 1956	reeves	cd: emi 761 0432
salzburg 19 august 1957	moore	cd: emi 565 7492
amsterdam 22 december 1957	de nobel	unpublished radio broadcast *vara*
london 1-7 april 1958	moore	columbia unpublished
london 19-23 december 1959	moore	lp: columbia 33CX 1714/SAX 2366/angel 35883 cd: emi 565 8602/585 1052
london 10 february 1964	parsons	unpublished radio broadcast *bbc third programme*
berlin 12-13 september 1965	moore	lp: emi AN 210-211/SAN 210-211/1C165 01871-01872/angel 3703 cd: emi 763 7322/562 6502/562 6512 *recordings completed in march 1966 and september 1967*
amsterdam 8 february 1977	parsons	cd: bella voce BLV 107 002 *also unpublished video recording*

ich liess mir sagen/italienisches liederbuch

london 1-7 april 1958	moore	columbia unpublished
london 19-23 december 1959	moore	lp: columbia 33CX 1714/SAX 2366/angel 35883 cd: emi 565 8602
berlin 12-13 september 1965	moore	lp: emi AN 210-211/SAN 210-211/1C165 01871-01872/angel 3703 cd: emi 763 7322/562 6502/562 6512 *recordings completed in march 1966 and september 1967*

wolf/ihr jungen leute, die ihr zieht ins feld/italienisches liederbuch

hilversum 23 april 1953	de nobel	unpublished radio broadcast *ncrv*
london 12-21 april 1954	moore	columbia unpublished *recordings completed in junem july and september 1954*
london 1-7 april 1958	moore	columbia unpublished
london 19-23 december 1959	moore	lp: columbia 33CX 1714/SAX 2366/angel 35883 cd: emi 565 8602
berlin 12-13 september 1965	moore	lp: emi AN 210-211/SAN 210-211/1C165 01871-01872/angel 3703 cd: emi 763 7322/562 6502/562 6512 *recordings completed in march 1966 and september 1967*

im frühling/mörike-lieder

salzburg
12 august 1953
	furtwängler	lp: cetra FE 30/emi 143 5491/melodram MEL 088/
		  discocorp IGI 385/RR 208
		cd: cetra CDC 21/priceless D 18355/virtuoso
		  269 7152/269 7312/emi 567 5702

london 6 april 1954	moore	cd: testament SBT 2172 *unpublished columbia lp recording*
salzburg 27 july 1958	moore	cd: emi 764 9052
london 2 december 1968	parsons	cd: eklipse EKRP 4
utrecht 26 april 1969	parsons	unpublished radio broadcast *avro*
berlin 27 august- 8 september 1970	parsons	lp: emi ASD 2844/1C063 02331/154 6133 cd: emi 763 6532/763 7902

wolf/in dem schatten meiner locken/spanisches liederbuch

london 11 april 1951	moore	columbia unpublished

salzburg
12 august 1953
	furtwängler	lp: cetra FE 30/emi 143 5491/melodram MEL 088/
		    discocorp IGI 385/RR 208
		cd: cetra CDC 21/priceless D 18355/virtuoso 269 7312/
		    emi 567 5702

aix-en-provence 23 july 1954	rosbaud	cd: melodram CDM 26524 *incorrectly dated 29 july 1954*
london 10 april 1956	moore	45: columbia SEL 1588/SELW 1805/C 50502 lp: columbia 33CX 1404/SAX 2265/FCX 664/SAXF 145/ WCX 1404/C 90545/angel 35383 cd: emi 565 8602/585 1052/356 5262
new york 25 november 1956	reeves	cd: emi 761 0432/notablu 935 0923
salzburg 19 august 1957	moore	cd: emi 565 7492
salzburg 27 july 1958	moore	cd: emi 764 9052
strassburg 15 june 1960	bonneau	cd: chant du monde LDC 278 899
hannover 2 march 1962	reutter	lp: movimento musica 02 017 cd: movimento musica 051 015
berlin 16-17 december 1966	moore	lp: deutsche grammophon SLPM 139 329-139 330/ 2707 035/2726 071 cd: deutsche grammophon 421 9342/457 7262 *recordings completed on 2-10 january 1967*
ascona 6 october 1967	parsons	cd: ermitage ERM 109
london 22 march 1968	moore	unpublished video recording *bbc television*
london 2 december 1968	parsons	cd: eklipse EKRP 4
utrecht 26 april 1969	parsons	unpublished radio broadcast *avro*
nohant 26 june 1969	ciccolini	cd: arkadia CDGI 8021

wolf/jägerlied/mörike-lieder

london 7 january 1977	parsons	lp: decca SXL 6943/642 576AW/london OS 26592 cd: decca 430 0002
vienna 2 january 1979	parsons	decca unpublished

keine gleicht von allen schönen

berlin 1-10 march 1973	parsons	lp: emi ASD 3124/1C063 02598 cd: emi 565 8602

klinge, klinge, mein pandero!/spanisches liederbuch

salzburg 19 august 1957	moore	cd: emi 565 7492
berlin 16-17 december 1966	moore	lp: deutsche grammophon SLPM 139 329-139 330/ 2707 035/2726 071 cd: deutsche grammophon 421 9342/457 7262 *recordings completed on 2-10 january 1967*

köpfchen, köpfchen, nicht gewimmert/spanisches liederbuch

berlin 16-17 december 1966	moore	lp: deutsche grammophon SLPM 139 329-139 330/ 2707 035/2726 071 cd: deutsche grammophon 421 9342/457 7262 *recordings completed on 2-10 january 1967*

das köhlerweib ist trunken/alte weisen

salzburg 27 july 1958	moore	cd: emi 764 9052/stradivarius STR 10009
london 15-16 january 1961	moore	cd: testament SBT 1206 *unpublished columbia lp recording; incorrectly dated as 4 december 1962*
london 3-7 december 1962	moore	lp: columbia 33CX 1946/SAX 2589/angel 36308/ emi SLS 5197/1C161 53747-53748

der knabe und das immlein/mörike-lieder

salzburg 17 august 1963	moore	cd: emi 565 7492

wolf/lebe wohl!/mörike-lieder

salzburg
12 august 1953
	furtwängler	lp: cetra FE 30/emi ALP 2114/1C063 01915M/
		   143 5491/angel seraphim 60179
		cd: cetra CDC 21/priceless D 18355/virtuoso
		   269 7152/269 7312/emi 567 5702

aix-en-provence 23 july 1954	rosbaud	cd: melodram CDM 26524 *incorrectly dated 29 july 1954*
salzburg 17 august 1963	moore	cd: emi 565 7492
berlin 24-28 october 1967	parsons	lp: emi ASD 2404/1C187 01307-01308/angel 36545 cd: emi 565 8602
london 5 january 1977	parsons	lp: decca SXL 6943/642 576AW/london OS 26592 cd: decca 430 0002

liebe mir im busen/spanisches liederbuch

berlin 16-17 december 1966	moore	lp: deutsche grammophon SLPM 139 329-139 330/ 2707 035/2726 071 cd: deutsche grammophon 421 9342/457 7262 *recordings completed on 2-10 january 1967*

lied vom winde/mörike-lieder

salzburg 27 july 1958	moore	cd: emi 764 9052

man sagt mir, deine mutter woll' es nicht/italienisches liederbuch

hilversum 23 april 1953	de nobel	unpublished radio broadcast *ncrv*
london 12-21 april 1954	moore	columbia unpublished *recordings completed in june, july and september 1954*
london 1-7 april 1958	moore	columbia unpublished
london 19-23 december 1959	moore	lp: columbia 33CX 1714/SAX 2366/angel 35883 cd: emi 565 8602
berlin 12-13 september 1965	moore	lp: emi AN 210-211/SAN 210-211/1C165 01871-01872/angel 3703 cd: emi 763 7322/562 6502/562 6512 *recordings completed in march 1966 and september 1967*

wolf/mausfallensprüchlein/mörike-lieder

london 7 april 1951	moore	cd: testament SBT 2172 *unpublished columbia 78rpm recording*
london 9 april 1952	moore	columbia unpublished
london 21-27 september 1952	moore	columbia unpublished
london 8 october 1952	moore	78: columbia LX 1577
london 19 december 1952	moore	columbia unpublished
london 4-7 july 1953	moore	columbia unpublished
london 5 january 1954	moore	columbia unpublished

london
11 january 1954
	moore	45: columbia SELW 1805/C 50202
		lp: columbia 33CX 1044/FCX 182/WCX 1044/
		    C 90306/angel 35023/emi 154 6133/RLS 763/
		    1C161 43160-43163M
		cd: emi 565 8602/567 6342/356 5262

salzburg 27 july 1958	moore	cd: emi 764 9052/585 1052
strassburg 15 june 1960	bonneau	cd: chant du monde LDC 278 899/notablu 935 0923
london 16 january 1961	moore	lp: columbia 33CX 1946/SAX 2589/angel 36308/ emi SLS 5197/1C161 53747-53748 cd: emi 763 6532/763 7902
amsterdam 29 june 1962	de nobel	cd: verona 27021/globe GLO 6900/GLO 6902
london 16 january 1977	parsons	decca unpublished
vienna 2 january 1979	parsons	lp: decca SXL 6943/642 576AW/london OS 26592 cd: decca 430 0002

wolf/**mein liebster hat zu tische mich geladen/italienisches liederbuch**

london 2 april 1951	moore	cd: testament SBT 2172 *unpublished columbia 78rpm recording*
london 18 june 1951	moore	columbia unpublished
hilversum 23 april 1953	de nobel	unpublished radio broadcast *ncrv*
salzburg 12 august 1953	furtwängler	lp: cetra FE 30/melodram MEL 088/discocorp RR 208/emi 143 5491 cd: cetra CDC 21/virtuoso 269 7312/emi 567 5702
london 12-21 april 1954	moore	columbia unpublished *recordings completed in june, july and september 1954*
london 1-7 april 1958	moore	columbia unpublished
london 19-23 december 1959	moore	lp: columbia 33CX 1714/SAX 2366/angel 35883 cd: emi 565 8602
berlin 12-13 september 1965	moore	lp: emi AN 210-211/SAN 210-211/1C165 01871-01872/angel 3703 cd: emi 763 7322/562 6502/562 6512 *recordings completed in march 1966 and september 1967*

wolf/mein liebster ist so klein/italienisches liederbuch

hilversum 23 april 1953	de nobel	unpublished radio broadcast *ncrv*
london 12-21 april 1954	moore	columbia unpublished *recordings completed in june, july and september 1954*
london 1-7 april 1958	moore	columbia unpublished
london 19-23 december 1959	moore	lp: columbia 33CX 1714/SAX 2366/angel 35883 cd: emi 565 8602/585 1052
berlin 12-13 september 1965	moore	lp: emi AN 210-211/SAN 210-211/1C165 01871-01872/angel 3703 cd: emi 763 7322/562 6502/562 6512 *recordings completed in march 1966 and september 1967*

mein liebster singt am haus/italienisches liederbuch

hilversum 23 april 1953	de nobel	unpublished radio broadcast *ncrv*
london 12-21 april 1954	moore	columbia unpublished *recordings completed in june, july and september 1954*
london 1-7 april 1958	moore	columbia unpublished
london 19-23 december 1959	moore	lp: columbia 33CX 1714/SAX 2366/angel 35883 cd: emi 565 8602
berlin 12-13 september 1965	moore	lp: emi AN 210-211/SAN 210-211/1C165 01871-01872/angel 3703 cd: emi 763 7322/562 6502/562 6512 *recordings completed in march 1966 and september*

wolf/**mignon (kennst du das land, wo die zitronen blüh'n?)**/goethe-lieder

aix-en-provence 23 july 1954	rosbaud	cd: melodram CDM 26524 *incorrectly dated 29 july 1954*
london 3 april 1956	moore	columbia unpublished
london 15 april 1956	moore	columbia unpublished
london 3 july 1956	moore	columbia unpublished
salzburg 7 august 1956	moore	cd: emi 566 0842
new york 25 november 1956	reeves	cd: emi 761 0432/notablu 935 0911
london 8 june 1957	moore	lp: columbia 33CX 1657/SAX 2333/FCX 837/ SAXF 256/angel 35909/3754/emi SLS 5197/ 1C161 53747-53748/1C037 03752/154 6133 cd: emi 763 6532/763 7902/585 1052
salzburg 27 july 1958	moore	cd: emi 764 9052
hannover 2 march 1962	reutter	lp: movimento musica 02 017 cd: movimento musica 051 015
amsterdam 29 june 1962	de nobel	cd: verona 27021
london 20 february 1967	moore	lp: emi AN 182-183/SAN 182-183/SLS 926/143 5941 cd: emi 749 2382/CDEMX 2233/567 9902
ascona 6 october 1967	parsons	cd: ermitage ERM 109
london 2 december 1968	parsons	cd: eklipse EKRP 4
utrecht 26 april 1969	parsons	unpublished radio broadcast *avro*
nohant 29 june 1969	ciccolini	cd: arkadia CDGI 8021
amsterdam 8 february 1977	parsons	cd: bella voce BLV 107 002 *also unpublished video recording*

wolf/mignon I (heiss mich nicht reden)/goethe-lieder

london 3 april 1956	moore	lp: columbia 33CX 1657/SAX 2333/FCX 837/ SAXF 256/angel 35909/emi SLS 5197/1C161 53747-53748/1C037 03752/154 6133 cd: emi 763 6352/763 7902
amsterdam 22 december 1957	de nobel	unpublished radio broadcast *vara*
hannover 2 march 1962	reutter	lp: movimento musica 02 017 cd: movimento musica 051 015
amsterdam 29 june 1962	de nobel	cd: verona 27021

mignon II (nur wer die sehnsucht kennt)/goethe-lieder

london 3-4 april 1956	moore	lp: columbia 33CX 1657/SAX 2333/FCX 837/ SAXF 256/angel 35909/emi SLS 5197/1C161 53747-53748/1C037 03752/154 6133 cd: emi 763 6352/763 7902
amsterdam 22 december 1957	de nobel	unpublished radio broadcast *vara*
hannover 2 march 1962	reutter	lp: movimento musica 02 017 cd: movimento musica 051 015
amsterdam 29 june 1962	de nobel	cd: verona 27021

mignon III (so lasst mich scheinen)/goethe-lieder

london 4 april 1956	moore	columbia unpublished
london 15 april 1956	moore	columbia unpublished
london 3 july 1956	moore	columbia unpublished
london 9 june 1957	moore	columbia unpublished
london 11 january 1958	moore	lp: columbia 33CX 1657/SAX 2333/FCX 837/ SAXF 256/angel 35909/emi SLS 5197/1C161 53747-53748/1C037 03752/154 6133 cd: emi 763 6352/763 7902
amsterdam 22 december 1957	de nobel	unpublished radio broadcast *vara*
hannover 2 march 1962	reutter	lp: movimento musica 02 017 cd: movimento musica 051 015
amsterdam 29 june 1962	de nobel	cd: verona 27021

wolf/mir ward gesagt, du reisest in die ferne/italienisches liederbuch

hilversum 23 april 1953	de nobel	unpublished radio broadcast *ncrv*
london 12-21 april 1954	moore	columbia unpublished *recordings completed in june, july and september 1954*
london 1-7 april 1958	moore	columbia unpublished
london 19-23 december 1959	moore	lp: columbia 33CX 1714/SAX 2366/angel 35883 cd: emi 565 8602
berlin 12-13 september 1965	moore	lp: emi AN 210-211/SAN 210-211/1C165 01871-01872/angel 3703 cd: emi 763 7322/562 6502/562 6512 *recordings completed in march 1966 and september 1967*

mögen alle bösen zungen/spanisches liederbuch

london 7 april 1951	moore	cd: testament SBT 2172 *unpublished columbia 78rpm recording*

salzburg
12 august 1953
	furtwängler	lp: cetra FE 30/melodram MEL 088/discocorp
		    RR 208/IGI 385/emi 143 5491
		cd: cetra CDC 21/prrceless D 18355/virtuoso
		    269 7312/emi 567 5702

salzburg 19 august 1957	moore	cd: emi 565 7492
berlin 16-17 december 1966	moore	lp: deutsche grammophon SLPM 139 329-139 330/ 2707 035/2726 071 cd: deutsche grammophon 421 9342/457 7262 *recordings completed on 2-10 january 1967*

morgentau (der frühhauch hat gefächelt)

london 16 january 1961	moore	lp: columbia 33CX 1946/SAX 2589/angel 36308/ emi SLS 5197/1C161 53747-53748 cd: emi 763 6532/763 7902
amsterdam 29 june 1962	de nobel	cd: verona 27021/globe GLO 6900/GLO 6902

wolf/**mühvoll komm' ich und beladen/spanisches liederbuch**

salzburg 27 july 1958	moore	cd: emi 764 9052
berlin 16-17 december 1966	moore	lp: deutsche grammophon SLPM 139 329-139 330/ 2707 035/2726 071 cd: deutsche grammophon 421 9342/457 7262 *recordings completed on 2-10 january 1967*

nachtzauber/eichendorff-lieder

salzburg
12 august 1953
	furtwängler	lp: cetra FE 30/emi ALP 2114/1C063 01915M/
		    143 5491/angel seraphim 60179
		cd: cetra CDC 21/virtuoso 269 7312/istituto
		    discografico italiano IDIS 6447-6448/emi 567 5702

aix-en-provence 23 july 1954	rosbaud	cd: melodram CDM 26524 *incorrectly dated 29 july 1954*
salzburg 7 august 1956	moore	cd: emi 566 0842
new york 25 novenber 1956	reeves	cd: emi 761 0432/notablu 935 0923
salzburg 19 august 1957	moore	cd: emi 565 7492
london 12 january 1958	moore	columbia unpublished
london 20 january 1961	moore	columbia unpublished
hannover 2 march 1962	reutter	lp: movimento musica 02 017 cd: movimento musica 051 015
london 8 march 1962	moore	cd: testament SBT 1206 *unpublished columbia lp recording*

wolf/**nein junger herr, so treibt's man nicht fürwahr!/italienisches liederbuch**

hilversum 23 april 1953	de nobel	unpublished radio broadcast *ncrv*
salzburg 12 august 1953	furtwängler	lp: cetra FE 30/melodram MEL 088/discocorp RR 208/ emi 143 5491 cd: cetra CDCD 21/virtuoso 269 7312/emi 567 5702
london 12-21 april 1954	moore	columbia unpublished *recordings completed in june, july and september 1954*
london 5 september 1954	moore	unpublished radio broadcast *bbc third programme*
salzburg 19 august 1957	moore	cd: emi 565 7492
london 1-7 april 1958	moore	columbia unpublished
london 19-23 december 1959	moore	lp: columbia 33CX 1714/SAX 2366/angel 35883 cd: emi 565 8602
london 10 february 1964	parsons	unpublished radio broadcast *bbc third programme*
berlin 12-13 september 1965	moore	lp: emi AN 210-211/SAN 210-211/1C165 01871-01872/angel 3703 cd: emi 763 7322/562 6502/562 6512 *recordings completed in march 1966 and september 1967*
london 2 december 1968	parsons	cd: eklipse EKRP 4

nimmer will ich dich verlieren/goethe-lieder

london 9 june 1957	moore	columbia unpublished
london 9 march 1962	moore	lp: columbia 33CX 1946/SAX 2589/angel 36308/ emi SLS 5197/1C161 53747-53748 cd: emi 565 6802

nimmersatte liebe/mörike-lieder

salzburg 17 august 1963	moore	cd: emi 565 7492
berlin 21-29 april 1966	parsons	lp: emi ASD 2404/1C187 01307-01308/angel 36545 cd: emi 565 8602
london 16 january 1977	parsons	lp: decca SXL 6943/642 576AW/london OS 26592 cd: decca 430 0002

wolf/**nixe binsenfuss/mörike-lieder**

london 7 april 1951	moore	cd: testament SBT 2172 *unpublished columbia 78rpm recording*	
london 19 june 1951	moore	columbia unpublished	
london 17 january 1977	parsons	decca unpublished	
vienna 8 january 1979	parsons	lp: decca SXL 6943/642 576AW/london OS 26592 cd: decca 430 0002	

nun lass uns frieden schliessen/italienisches liederbuch

hilversum 23 april 1953	de nobel	unpublished radio broadcast *ncrv*	
london 12-21 april 1954	moore	columbia unpublished *recordings completed in june, july and september 1954*	
london 5 september 1954	moore	unpublished radio broadcast *bbc third programme*	
salzburg 19 august 1957	moore	cd: emi 565 7492	
amsterdam 22 december 1957	de nobel	unpublished radio broadcast *vara*	
london 1-7 april 1958	moore	columbia unpublished	
salzburg 27 july 1958	moore	cd: emi 764 9052	
london 19-23 december 1959	moore	lp: columbia 33CX 1714/SAX 2366/angel 35883 cd: emi 565 8602	
strassburg 15 june 1960	bonneau	cd: chant du monde LDC 278 899/notablu 935 0923	
amsterdam 29 june 1962	de nobel	cd: verona 27021/globe GLO 6900/GLO 6902	
london 10 february 1964	parsons	unpublished radio broadcast *bbc third programme*	
berlin 20-27 october 1968	parsons	emi unpublished	

wolf/o wär' dein haus durchsichtig wie ein glas/italienisches liederbuch

hilversum 23 april 1953	de nobel	unpublished radio broadcast *ncrv*
london 12-21 april 1954	moore	columbia unpublished *recordings completed in june, july and september 1954*
london 5 september 1954	moore	unpublished radio broadcast *bbc third programme*
salzburg 19 august 1957	moore	cd: emi 565 7492
london 1-7 april 1958	moore	columbia unpublished
london 19-23 december 1959	moore	lp: columbia 33CX 1714/SAX 2366/angel 35883 cd: emi 565 8602
london 25 october 1961	moore	vhs video: emi MVC 491 4763 dvd video: emi DVA 492 8529
berlin 12-13 september 1965	moore	lp: emi AN 210-211/SAN 210-211/1C165 01871-01872/angel 3703 cd: emi 763 7322/562 6502/562 6512 *recordings completed in march 1966 and september 1967*
london 2 december 1968	parsons	cd: eklipse EKRP 4
amsterdam 8 february 1977	parsons	cd: bella voce BLV 107 002 *also unpublished video recording*

ob auch finstre blicke/spanisches liederbuch

berlin 16-17 december 1966	moore	lp: deutsche grammophon SLPM 139 329-139 330/ 2707 035/2726 071 cd: deutsche grammophon 421 9342/457 7262 *recordings completed on 2-10 january 1967*

phänomen/goethe-lieder

salzburg 12 august 1953	furtwängler	lp: cetra FE 30/emi ALP 2114/1C063 01915M/ 143 5491/angel seraphim 60179 cd: cetra CDC 21/priceless D 18355/virtuoso 269 7152/269 7312/emi 567 5702
london 4 april 1955	moore	columbia unpublished
london 4-7 april 1956	moore	columbia unpublished
salzburg 27 july 1958	moore	cd: emi 764 9052
london 2 december 1968	parsons	cd: eklipse EKRP 4

wolf / philine / goethe-lieder

london 3 april 1956	moore	lp:	columbia 33CX 1657/SAX 2333/FCX 837/ SAXF 256/angel 35909/emi SLS 5197/1C161 53747-53748/1C037 03725/154 6133
		cd:	emi 763 6532/763 7902
salzburg 7 august 1956	moore	cd:	emi 566 0842
new york 25 november 1956	reeves	cd:	emi 761 0432/notablu 935 0923
berlin 6 january 1958	raucheisen	lp: cd:	acanta 40 23580 membran 223 067/223 089
salzburg 27 july 1958	moore	cd:	emi 764 9052
hannover 2 march 1962	reutter	lp: cd:	movimento musica 02 017 movimento musica 051 015
amsterdam 29 june 1962	de nobel	cd:	verona 27021

sagt ihm, dass er zu mir komme / spanisches liederbuch

berlin 16-17 december 1966	moore	lp: cd:	deutsche grammophon SLPM 139 329-139 330/ 2707 035/2726 071 deutsche grammophon 421 9342/457 7262 *recordings completed on 2-10 january 1967*

sagt seid ihr es, feiner herr? / spanisches liederbuch

berlin 16-17 december 1966	moore	lp: cd:	deutsche grammophon SLPM 139 329-139 330/ 2707 035/2726 071 deutsche grammophon 421 9342/457 7262 *recordings completed on 2-10 january 1967*
london 2 december 1968	parsons	cd:	eklipse EKRP 4
utrecht 26 april 1969	parsons		unpublished radio broadcast *avro*

sankt nepomuks vorabend / goethe lieder

london 7 april 1956	moore	lp:	columbia 33CX 1657/SAX 2333/FCX 837/ SAXF 256/angel 35909/emi SLS 5197/1C161 53747-53748/1C037 03725
strassburg 15 june 1960	bonneau	cd:	chant du monde LDC 278 899/notablu 935 0923

wolf/der schäfer/goethe-lieder

london 9 june 1957	moore	columbia unpublished
amsterdam 22 december 1957	de nobel	unpublished radio broadcast *vara*
salzburg 27 july 1958	moore	cd: emi 764 9052
london 30 january 1961	moore	lp: columbia 33CX 1946/SAX 2589/angel 36308/ emi SLS 5197/1C161 53747-53748 cd: emi 565 8602

schlafendes jesuskind/mörike-lieder

salzburg 12 august 1953	furtwängler	lp: cetra FE 30/emi ALP 2114/1C063 01915M/ 143 5491/angel seraphim 60179 cd: cetra CDC 21/priceless D 18355/virtuoso 269 7152/269 7312/emi 567 5702
aix-en-provence 23 july 1954	rosbaud	cd: melodram CDM 26524 *incorrectly dated 29 july 1954*
london 16 january 1977	parsons	decca unpublished

schmerzliche wonnen und wonnige schmerzen/spanisches liederbuch

berlin 16-17 december 1966	moore	lp: deutsche grammophon SLPM 139 329-139 330/ 2707 035/2726 071 cd: deutsche grammophon 421 9342/457 7262 *recordings completed on 2-10 january 1967*

schweig' einmal still!/italienisches liederbuch

london 2 april 1951	moore	cd: testament SBT 2172 *unpublished columbia 78tpm recording*
london 18 june 1951	moore	columbia unpublished
hilversum 23 april 1953	de nobel	unpublished radio broadcast *ncrv*
london 12-21 april 1954	moore	columbia unpublished *recordings completed in june, july and september 1954*
salzburg 19 august 1957	moore	cd: emi 565 7492
london 1-7 april 1958	moore	columbia unpublished
london 19-23 december 1959	moore	lp: columbia 33CX 1714/SAX 2366/angel 35883/ cd: emi 565 8602
berlin 12-13 september 1965	moore	lp: emi AN 210-211/SAN 210-211/1C165 01871-01872/angel 3703 cd: emi 763 7322/562 6502/562 6512 *recordings completed in march 1966 and september 1967*

wolf/**selbstgeständnis/mörike-lieder**

salzburg 17 august 1963	moore	cd: emi 565 7492

berlin 21-29 april 1966	parsons	lp: emi ASD 2404/1C187 01307-01308/angel 36545 cd: emi 565 8602

london 15 january 1977	parsons	lp: decca SXL 6943/642 576AW/london OS 26592 cd: decca 430 0002

sie blasen zum abmarsch/spanisches liederbuch

salzburg 17 august 1957	moore	cd: emi 565 7492

berlin 16-17 december 1966	moore	lp: deutsche grammophon SLPM 139 329-139 330/ 2707 035/2726 071 cd: deutsche grammophon 421 9342/457 7262 *recordings completed on 2-10 january 1967*

singt mein schatz wie ein fink/alte weisen

salzburg 27 july 1958	moore	cd: emi 764 9052/stradivarius STR 10009

london 15 january 1961	moore	lp: columbia 33CX 1946/SAX 2589/angel 36308/ emi SLS 5197/1C161 53747-53748

sonne der schlummerlosen

london 18-20 january 1961	moore	lp: columbia 33CX 1946/SAX 2589/angel 36308/ emi SLS 5197/1C161 53747-53748

london 20 february 1967	moore	lp: emi AN 182-183/SAN 182-183/SLS 926/ 143 5941 cd: emi 749 2382/CDEMX 2233/567 9902

utrecht 26 april 1969	parsons	unpublished radio broadcast *avro*

berlin 1-10 march 1973	parsons	lp: emi ASD 3124/1C063 02598

die spinnerin (o süsse mutter, ich kann nicht spinnen!)

london 17 january 1961	moore	lp: columbia 33CX 1946/SAX 2589/angel 36308/ emi SLS 5197/1C161 53747-53748 cd: emi 763 6532/763 7902

amsterdam 29 june 1962	de nobel	unpublished radio broadcast *vara*

wolf/die spröde/goethe-lieder

london 11 april 1951	moore	cd: testament SBT 2172 *unpublished columbia 78rpm recording*

salzburg
12 august 1953
	furtwängler	lp: cetra FE 30/emi ALP 2114/1C063 01915M/
		    143 5491/angel seraphim 60179
		cd: cetra CDC 21/priceless D 18355/virtuoso
		    269 7152/269 7312/emi 567 5702

london 5 april 1956	moore	columbia unpublished
london 9 june 1957	moore	columbia unpublished

london
11 january 1958
	moore	lp: columbia 33CX 1657/SAX 2333/FCX 837/
		    SAXF 256/angel 35909/emi SLS 5197/1C161
		    53747-53748/1C037 03725
		cd: emi 763 6532/763 7902

storchenbotschaft/mörike-lieder

london 21 may 1948	moore	cd: testament SBT 2172 *unpublished columbia 78rpm recording*
london 6 april 1951	moore	cd: testament SBT 2172 *unpublished columbia 78rpm recording*
salzburg 17 august 1957	moore	cd: emi 565 7492
berlin 20-27 october 1968	parsons	emi unpublished
london 15 january 1977	parsons	lp: decca SXL 6943/642 576AW/london OS 26592 cd: decca 430 0002
vienna 2 january 1979	parsons	decca unpublished

ein stündlein wohl vor tag/mörike-lieder

london 15 january 1977	parsons	decca unpublished

wolf/trau' nicht der liebe/spanisches liederbuch

salzburg 17 august 1963	moore	cd: emi 565 7492
berlin 16-17 december 1966	moore	lp: deutsche grammophon SLPM 139 329-139 330/ 2707 035/2726 071 cd: deutsche grammophon 421 9342/457 7262 *recordings completed on 2-10 january 1967*
ascona 6 october 1967	parsons	cd: ermitage ERM 109
utrecht 26 april 1969	parsons	unpublished radio broadcast *avro*
amsterdam 8 february 1977	parsons	cd: bella voce BLV 107 002 *also unpublished video recording*

tretet ein, hoher krieger!/alte weisen

salzburg 27 july 1958	moore	cd: emi 764 9052/stradivarius STR 10009
london 15 january 1961	moore	cd: testament SBT 1206 *unpublished columbia lp recording*
london 3 december 1962	moore	lp: columbia 33CX 1946/SAX 2589/angel 36545/ emi SLS 5197/1C161 53747-53748

verborgenheit/mörike-lieder

berlin 21-29 april 1966	parsons	lp: emi ASD 2404/1C187 01307-01308/ angel 36545/3754 *issued on cd only in japan*

das verlassene mägdlein/mörike-lieder

berlin 21-29 april 1966	parsons	emi unpublished
london 20 february 1967	moore	lp: emi AN 182-183/SAN 182-183/SLS 926/143 5941 cd: emi 749 2382/CDEMX 2233/567 9902
ascona 6 october 1967	parsons	cd: ermitage ERM 109
london 22 march 1968	moore	unpublished video recording *bbc television*
utrecht 26 april 1969	parsons	unpublished radio broadcast *avro*
london 5 january 1977	parsons	lp: decca SXL 6943/642 576AW/london OS 26592 cd: decca 430 0002
amsterdam 8 february 1977	parsons	cd: bella voce BLV 107 002 *also unpublished video recording*

wolf/verschling' der abgrund meines liebsten hütte!/italienisches liederbuch

hilversum 23 april 1953	de nobel	unpublished radio broadcast *ncrv*
london 12-21 april 1954	moore	columbia unpublished *recordings completed in june, july and september 1954*
salzburg 19 august 1957	moore	cd: emi 565 7492
london 1-7 april 1958	moore	columbia unpublished
london 19-23 december 1959	moore	lp: columbia 33CX 1714/SAX 2366/angel 35883 cd: emi 565 8602/585 1052
berlin 12-13 september 1965	moore	lp: emi AN 210-211/SAN 210-211/1C165 01871-01872/angel 3703 cd: emi 763 7322/562 6502/562 6512 *recordings completed in march 1966 and september 1967*

das vöglein (vöglein am zweig!)

london 17 january 1961	moore	lp: columbia 33CX 1946/SAX 2589/angel 36308/ emi SLS 5197/1C161 53747-53748 cd: emi 763 6532/763 7902
amsterdam 28 june 1962	de nobel	cd: verona 27021/globe GLO 6900/GLO 6902

wandl' ich in dem morgentau/alte weisen

salzburg 27 july 1958	moore	cd: emi 764 9052/stradivarius STR 10009
london 16 january 1961	moore	lp: columbia 33CX 1946/SAX 2589/angel 36308/ emi SLS 5197/1C161 53747-53748 cd: emi 763 6532/763 7902
london 2 december 1968	parsons	cd: eklipse EKRP 4
utrecht 26 april 1969	parsons	unpublished radio broadcast *avro*

was für ein lied soll dir gesungen werden?/italienisches liederbuch

london 2 december 1968	parsons	cd: eklipse EKRP 4

wolf/was soll der zorn, mein schatz?/italienisches liederbuch

hilversum 23 april 1953	de nobel	unpublished radio broadcast *ncrv*
salzburg 12 august 1953	furtwängler	lp: cetra FE 30/emi ALP 2114/1C063 01915M/ 143 5491/angel seraphim 60179 cd: cetra CDC 21/virtuoso 269 7312/emi 567 5702
london 12-21 april 1954	moore	columbia unpublished *recordings completed in june, july and september 1954*
new york 25 november 1956	reeves	cd: emi 761 0432/notablu 935 0923
london 1-7 april 1958	moore	columbia unpublished
london 19-23 december 1959	moore	lp: columbia 33CX 1714/SAX 2366/angel 35883 cd: emi 565 8602
berlin 12-13 september 1965	moore	lp: emi AN 210-211/SAN 210-211/1C165 01871-01872/angel 3703 cd: emi 763 7322/562 5602/562 5612 *recordings completed in march 1966 and september 1967*

wehe der, die mir verstrickte meinen geliebten!/spanisches liederbuch

salzburg 27 july 1958	moore	cd: emi 764 9052
berlin 16-17 december 1966	moore	lp: deutsche grammophon SLPM 139 329-139 330/ 2707 035/2726 071 cd: deutsche grammophon 421 9342/457 7262 *recordings completed on 2-10 january 1967*

weint nicht ihr äuglein!/spanisches liederbuch

berlin 16-17 december 1966	moore	lp: deutsche grammophon SLPM 139 329-139 330/ 2707 035/2726 071 cd: deutschr grammophon 421 9342/457 7262 *recordings completed on 2-10 january 1967*

wolf/wenn du, mein liebster, steigst zum himmel auf/italienisches liederbuch

hilversum 23 april 1953	de nobel	unpublished radio broadcast *ncrv*
london 12-21 april 1954	moore	columbia unpublished *recordings completed in june, july and september 1954*
london 1-7 april 1958	moore	columbia unpublished
london 19-23 december 1959	moore	lp: columbia 33CX 1714/SAX 2366/angel 35883 cd: emi 565 8602
berlin 12-13 september 1965	moore	lp: emi AN 210-211/SAN 210-211/1C165 01871-01872/angel 3703 cd: emi 763 7322/562 5602/562 5612 *recordings completed in march 1966 and september 1967*

wenn du zu den blumen gehst/spanisches liederbuch

berlin 22-27 august 1965	moore	lp: columbia CX 5268/SAX 5268/angel 36345/ emi 1C187 01307-01308 cd: emi 763 6532/763 7902
utrecht 26 april 1969	parsons	unpublished radio broadcast *avro*
nohant 29 june 1969	ciccolini	cd: arkadia CDGI 8021

wolf/wer rief dich denn?/italienisches liederbuch

hilversum 23 april 1953	de nobel	unpublished radio broadcast *ncrv*
london 12-21 april 1954	moore	columbia unpublished *recordings completed in june, july and september 1954*
london 5 september 1954	moore	unpublished radio broadcast *bbc third programme*
salzburg 19 august 1957	moore	cd: emi 565 7492
london 1-7 april 1958	moore	columbia unpublished
london 19-23 december 1959	moore	lp: columbia 33CX 1714/SAX 2366/angel 35883 cd: emi 565 8602
hannover 2 march 1962	reutter	lp: movimento musica 02 017 cd: movimento musica 051 015
amsterdam 29 june 1962	de nobel	cd: verona 27021/globe GLO 6900/GLO 6902
london 10 february 1964	parsons	unpublished radio broadcast *bbc third programme*
berlin 12-13 september 1965	moore	lp: emi AN 210-211/SAN 210-211/1C165 01871-01872/angel 3703 cd: emi 763 7322/562 5602/562 5612 *recordings completed in march 1966 and september 1967*
london 20 february 1967	moore	emi unpublished
london 2 december 1968	parsons	cd: eklipse EKRP 4

wer tat deinem füsslein weh?/spanisches liederbuch

london 11 april 1951	moore	cd: testament SBT 2172 *unpublished columbia 78rpm recording*
salzburg 27 july 1958	moore	cd: emi 764 9052
berlin 16-17 december 1966	moore	lp: deutsche grammophon SLPM 139 329-139 330/ 2707 035/2726 071 cd: deutsche grammophon 421 9342/457 6272 *recordings completed on 2-10 january 1967*

wolf/wie glänzt der helle mond/alte weisen

salzburg 12 august 1953	furtwängler	lp: cetra FE 30/emi ALP 2114/1C063 01915M/ 143 5491/amgel seraphim 60179 cd: cetra CDC 21/virtuoso 269 7312/emi 567 5702
salzburg 27 july 1958	moore	cd: emi 764 9052/stradivarius STR 10009
london 16-18 january 1961	moore	lp: columbia 33CX 1946/SAX 2589/angel 36308/ emi SLS 5197/1C161 53747-53748/154 6133 cd: emi 763 6532/763 7902/notablu 935 0923

wie lange schon war immer mein verlangen/italienisches liederbuch

hilversum 23 april 1953	de nobel	unpublished radio broadcast *ncrv*
salzburg 12 august 1953	furtwängler	lp: cetra FE 30/melodram MEL 088/discocorp RR 208/ emi 143 5491 cd: cetra CDC 21/virtuoso 269 7312/emi 567 5702
london 12-21 april 1954	moore	columbia unpublished *recordings completed in june, july and september 1954*
london 5 september 1954	moore	unpublished radio broadcast *bbc third programme*
london 1-7 april 1958	moore	columbia unpublished
london 19-23 december 1959	moore	lp: columbia 33CX 1714/SAX 2366/angel 35883 cd: emi 565 8602
berlin 12-13 september 1965	moore	lp: emi AN 210-211/SAN 210-211/1C165 01871-01872/angel 3703 cd: emi 763 7322/562 6502/562 6512 *recordings completed in march 1966 and september 1967*
ascona 6 october 1967	parsons	cd: ermitage ERM 109
utrecht 26 april 1969	parsons	unpublished radio broadcast *avro*
amsterdam 8 february 1977	parsons	cd: bella voce BLV 107 002 *also unpublished video recording*

wolf/wie soll ich fröhlich sein?/italienisches liederbuch

hilversum 23 april 1953	de nobel	unpublished radio broadcast *ncrv*	
london 12-21 april 1954	moore	columbia unpublished *recordings completed in june, july and september 1954*	
london 1-7 april 1958	moore	columbia unpublished	
london 19-23 december 1959	moore	lp: columbia 33CX 1714/SAX 2366/angel 35883 cd: emi 565 8602	
berlin 12-13 september 1965	moore	lp: emi AN 210-211/SAN 210-211/1C165 01871-01872/angel 3703 cd: emi 763 7322/562 6502/562 6512 *recordings completed in march 1966 and september 1967*	

wiegenlied im winter (schlaf' ein, mein süsses kind!)

london 17-18 january 1961	moore	lp: columbia 33CX 1946/SAX 2589/angel 36308/ emi SLS 5197/1C161 53747-53748 cd: emi 763 6532/763 7902
amsterdam 29 june 1962	de nobel	cd: verona 27021

wolf/**wiegenlied im sommer** (vom berg hinabgestiegen)

london 2 april 1951	moore	cd: testament SBT 2172 *unpublished columbia 78rpm recording*
london 27 september 1952	moore	columbia unpublished
london 8 october 1952	moore	78: columbia LX 1577
london 19 december 1952	moore	columbia unpublished
salzburg 12 august 1953	furtwängler	lp: cetra FE 30/emi ALP 2114/1C063 01915M/ 143 5491/angel seraphim 60179 cd: cetra CDC 21/virtuoso 269 7312/emi 567 5702
london 10-11 january 1954	moore	lp: columbia 33CX 1044/FCX 182/WCX 1044/ C 90306/angel 35023/emi RLS 763/1C161 43160-43163M/154 6133/melodiya M10 43861-43861 cd: emi 565 8602/585 1052
new york 25 november 1956	reeves	cd: emi 761 0432/notablu 935 0923
strassburg 15 june 1960	bonneau	cd: chant du monde LDC 278 899
london 18 january 1961	moore	columbia unpublished
hannover 2 march 1962	reutter	lp: movimento musica 02 017 cd: movimento musica 051 015
amsterdam 29 june 1962	de nobel	cd: verona 27021
london 7 december 1962	moore	lp: columbia 33CX 1946/SAX 2589/angel 36308/ emi SLS 5197/1C161 53747-53748 cd: emi 763 6532/763 7902
london 2 december 1968	parsons	cd: eklipse EKRP 4
utrecht 26 april 1969	parsons	unpublished radio broadcast *avro*

wolf/wir haben beide lange zeit geschwiegen/italienisches liederbuch

hilversum 23 april 1953	de nobel	unpublished radio broadcast *ncrv*
london 12-21 april 1954	moore	columbia unpublished *recordings completed in june, july and september 1954*
aix-en-provence 23 july 1954	rosbaud	cd: melodram CDM 26524 *incorrectly dated 29 july 1954*
london 5 september 1954	moore	unpublished radio broadcast *bbc third programme*
new york 25 november 1956	reeves	cd: emi 761 0432/notablu 935 0923
london 1-7 april 1958	moore	columbia unpublished
london 19-23 december 1959	moore	lp: columbia 33CX 1714/SAX 2366/angel 35883 cd: emi 565 8602
berlin 12-13 september 1965	moore	lp: emi AN 210-211/SAN 210-211/1C165 01871-01872/angel 3703 cd: emi 763 7322/562 6502/562 6512 *recordings completed in march 1966 and september 1967*
london 2 december 1968	parsons	cd: eklipse EKRP 4

wohl kenn' ich euren stand/italienisches liederbuch

hilversum 23 april 1953	de nobel	unpublished radio broadcast *ncrv*
london 12-21 april 1954	moore	columbia unpublished *recordings completed in june, july and september 1954*
london 1-7 april 1958	moore	columbia unpublished
london 19-23 december 1959	moore	lp: columbia 33CX 1714/SAX 2366/angel 35883 cd: emi 565 8602
berlin 12-13 september 1965	moore	lp: emi AN 210-211/SAN 210-211/1C165 01871-01872/angel 3703 cd: emi 763 7322/562 6502/562 6512 *recordings completed in march 1966 and september 1967*

wolf/wunden trägst du, mein geliebter!/spanisches liederbuch

berlin 16-17 december 1966	moore	lp: deutsche grammophon SLPM 139 329-139 330/ 2707 035/2726 071 cd: deutsche grammophon 421 9342/457 7262 *recordings completed on 2-10 january 1967*

die zigeunerin/eichendorff-lieder

salzburg 12 august 1953	furtwängler	lp: cetra FE 30/melodram MEL 088/discocorp IGI 385/ RR 208/emi 143 5491 cd: cetra CDC 21/virtuoso 269 7312/emi 567 5702/ istituto discografico italiano IDIS 6447-6448
aix-en-provence 23 july 1954	rosbaud	cd: melodram CDM 26524 *incorrectly dated 29 july 1954*
london 10 april 1956	moore	columbia unpublished
salzburg 7 august 1956	moore	cd: emi 566 0842
new york 25 november 1956	reeves	cd: emi 761 0432/notablu 935 0923
london 10 april 1957	moore	cd: testament SBT 1206 *unpublished columbia lp recording*
salzburg 19 august 1957	moore	cd: emi 565 7492
berlin 1 march 1958	raucheisen	lp: acanta 40 23580 cd: membran 223 067/223 088
london 20-21 january 1961	moore	columbia unpublished
hannover 2 march 1962	reutter	lp: movimento musica 02 017 cd: movimento musica 051 015
london 8 march 1962	moore	columbia unpublished
amsterdam 29 june 1962	de nobel	cd: verona 27021/globe GLO 6900/GLO 6902
london 4 december 1962	moore	columbia unpublished
berlin 22-27 august 1965	moore	lp: columbia CX 5268/SAX 5268/angel 36345/ 3754/emi 1C187 01307-01308 cd: emi 763 6532/763 7902

wolf/die zigeunerin/eichendorff-lieder/concluded

london 20 february 1967	moore	lp: emi AN 182-183/SAN 182-183/SLS 926/143 5941 cd: emi 749 2382/CDEMX 2233/567 9902
ascona 6 october 1967	parsons	cd: ermitage ERM 109
london 2 december 1968	parsons	cd: eklipse EKRP 4
nohant 26 june 1969	ciccolini	cd: arkadia CDGI 8021
amsterdam 8 february 1977	parsons	cd: bella voce BLV 107 002 *also unpublished video recording*

zum neuen jahr/mörike-lieder

new york 25 november 1956	reeves	cd: emi 761 0432/notablu 935 0923

zur ruh', zur ruh', ihr müden glieder!

london 21-22 january 1961	moore	columbia unpublished

ERMANNO WOLF-FERRARI (1876-1948)
italian folksongs op 17: dimmi bellino mio; dio ti facesse; giovanetti; giovanottino; vo' fa 'na palazzina

berlin 22-27 august 1965	moore	lp: columbia CX 5268/SAX 5268/angel 36345/ emi 1C187 01307-01308 cd: emi 763 6542/763 7902

italian folksongs op 17: quando a letto vo' la sera

berlin 22-27 august 1965	moore	lp: columbia CX 5268/SAX 5268/angel 36345/ emi 1C187 01307-01308 cd: emi 763 6542/763 7902
ascona 6 october 1967	parsons	cd: ermitage ERM 109

wolf-ferrari/**italian folksongs op 17: quando sara benedetto giorno**
berlin   moore   lp: emi 1C187 01307-01308
22-27 august 1965   *unpublished columbia lp recording*

italian folksongs op 17: vado di notte, come fa la luna
berlin   moore   lp: columbia CX 5268/SAX 5268/angel 36345/
22-27 august 1965   emi 1C187 01307-01308
                                   cd: emi 763 6542/763 7902

amsterdam   parsons   cd: bella voce BLV 107 002
8 february 1977   *also unpublished video recording*

CARL ZELLER (1842-1898)
sei nicht bös'/der obersteiger *title role*
london   philharmonia   45: columbia SEL 1648/ESL 6267
5 july 1957   ackermann   lp: columbia 33CX 1570/SAX 2283/SAXF 158/
                                       angel 35696/3754/emi ASD 2807/SVP 1180/
                                       100 4781/CFP 4277/SEOM 13
                                   cd: emi 747 2842/566 9892/567 0042

montreal   cbc orchestra   dvd video: video artists international VAI 4390
3 july 1963   boskovsky   *canadian television*

ich bin die christel von der post/der vogelhändler *christel*
london   philharmonia   45: columbia SEL 1642/ESL 6263
3 july 1957   ackermann   lp: columbia 33CX 1570/SAX 2283/SAXF 158/
                                       angel 35696/3754/emi ASD 2807/SVP 1180/
                                       100 4781
                                   cd: emi 747 2842/566 9892/567 0042

schenkt man sich rosen im tirol/der vogelhändler
london   philharmonia   45: columbia SEL 1642/ESL 6263
3 july 1957   ackermann   lp: columbia 33CX 1570/SAX 2283/SAXF 158/
                                       angel 35696/emi ASD 2807/SVP 1180/100 4781
                                   cd: emi 747 2842/566 9892/567 0042

montreal   cbc orchestra   dvd video: video artists international VAI 4390
3 july 1963   boskovsky   *canadian television*

HERMANN ZILCHER (1881-1948)
rokoko-suite: an den menschen; der frühling; abendständchen; die nacht; die alte; mailied
berlin   raucheisen   lp: acanta 40 23557
january 1945   richartz, violin cd: acanta 42 43801/membran 223 067/223 093
                  steiner, cello

TRADITIONAL AND MISCELLANEOUS
alleluia, arranged by o'connor morris
london moore columbia unpublished
13-14 april 1956

london moore columbia unpublished
19 may 1956

die beruhigte, bavarian folksong
berlin raucheisen lp: acanta 40 23557
january 1945 cd: acanta 42 43801/membran 223 067/223 093

london moore 78: columbia LB 112
3 april 1951 lp: emi ALP 143 5501/154 6133

danny boy, arranged by weatherly
london moore lp: columbia CX 5268/SAX 5268/angel 36345/
13 january 1958 emi 154 6133
cd: emi 763 6542/763 7902

drink to me only, arranged by quilter
london moore columbia unpublished
12 april 1956

london moore 45: columbia SEL 1589/ESL 6255/SCD 2149
19 may 1956 lp: columbia 33CX 1404/SAX 2265/FCX 664/
SAXF 145/WCX 1404/C 90545/angel 35383/
emi 154 6133
cd: emi 763 6542/763 7902

berlin raucheisen lp: melodram MEL 082/discoreale DR 10038
6 march 1958 *incorrectly dated 1953*

london moore vhs video: emi MVC 491 4763
25 october 1961 dvd video: emi DVA 477 8319/DVA 492 8529

london moore unpublished video recording
22 march 1968 *bbc television*

easter alleluia
london philharmonia lp: columbia 33CX 1482/angel 35530/emi ASD 3798
26 may 1957 mackerras cd: emi 763 5742

es ist ein ros' entsprungen
vienna vienna opera 78: columbia LC 33
3 march 1949 chorus
vienna philharmonic

the first nowell
london covent garden 78: columbia LB 131
3 october 1952 and hampstead 45: columbia SCD 2112
choirs lp: legendary recordings LR 136
philharmonia
pritchard

london philharmonia lp: columbia 33CX 1482/angel 35530/36750/
26 may 1957 mackerras emi ASD 3798/100 4531
cd: emi 763 5742

traditional and miscellaneous/continued
gsätzli, swiss folksong

berlin january 1945	raucheisen	lp: acanta 40 23557 cd: acanta 42 43801/membran 223 067/223 093
london 3 april 1951	moore	78: columbia LB 112 lp: emi ALP 143 5501/154 6133 cd: regis RRC 1167
aix-en-provence 23 july 1954	rosbaud	cd: melodram CDM 26524 *incorrectly dated 29 july 1954*
london 5 september 1954	moore	unpublished radio broadcast *bbc third programme*
london 11-12 april 1956	moore	columbia unpublished
london 18-19 may 1956	moore	45: columbia SEL 1588 lp: columbia 33CX 1404/SAX 2265/FCX 664/ SAXF 145/WCX 1404/C 90545/angel 35383 cd: emi 763 6542/763 7902/585 1052
new york 25 november 1956	reeves	cd: emi 761 0432
london 1959	schwarzkopf accompanies herself on guitar	vhs video: emi MVC 491 4763 dvd video: emi DVA 492 8529
london 10 february 1964	parsons	unpublished radio broadcast *bbc third programme*

i saw three ships

london 25 may 1957	chorus philharmonia mackerras	lp: columbia 33CX 1482/angel 35530/36750/ emi ASD 3798/100 4531 cd: emi 763 5742

in dulci jubilo

london 26 may 1957	chorus philharmonia mackerras	lp: columbia 33CX 1482/angel 35530/36750/ emi ASD 3798/100 4531 cd: emi 763 5742

maria auf dem berge, silesian folksong

london 3 april 1951	moore	78: columbia LB 112 lp: emi ALP 143 5501/154 6133 cd: emi 763 6542/763 7902
london 5 september 1954	moore	unpublished radio broadcast *bbc third programme*
london 1 june 1957	chorus philharmonia mackerras	lp: columbia 33CX 1482/angel 35530/emi ASD 3798 cd: emi 763 5742
amsterdam 22 december 1957	de nobel	unpublished radio broadcast *vara*

traditional and miscellaneous/continued
o come all ye faithful

london 3 october 1952	covent garden and hampstead choirs philharmonia pritchard	columbia unpublished
london 30 june 1957	chorus philharmonia mackerras	lp: columbia 33CX 1482/angel 35530/36750/ emi ASD 3798/100 4531 cd: emi 763 5742

o du fröhliche!

vienna 3 march 1949	vienna opera chorus vienna philharmonic	78: columbia LC 33
london 25 may 1957	chorus philharmonia mackerras	lp: columbia 33CX 1482/angel 35530/36750/ emi ASD 3798/100 4531 cd: emi 763 5742

o du liebs ängeli, bernese folksong

berlin january 1945	raucheisen	lp: acanta 40 23557 cd: acanta 42 43801/membran 223 067/223 093
london 3 april 1951	moore	78: columbia LB 112 lp: emi ALP 143 5501/154 6133
london 5 september 1954	moore	unpublished radio broadcast *bbc third ptogramme*
london 12 april 1956	moore	45: columbia SEL 1588 lp: columbia 33CX 1404/SAX 2265/FCX 664/ SAXF 145/WCX 1404/C 90545/angel 35383 cd: emi 763 6542/763 7902

o tannenbaum

vienna 3 march 1949	vienna opera chorus vienna philharmonic	78: columbia LC 32
london 1 june 1957	chorus philharmonia mackerras	columbia unpublished

traditional and miscellaneous/concluded
vesper hymn, arranged by woodman
london moore columbia unpublished
13 april 1956

vom himmel hoch
london	chorus	lp: columbia 33CX 1482/angel 35530/36750/
26 may 1957	philharmonia	emi ASD 3798/100 4531
	mackerras	cd: emi 763 5742

z' lauterbach han i mein strumpf verlor'n, swiss folksong
berlin raucheisen lp: acanta 40 23557
january 1945 cd: acanta 42 43801/membran 223 067/223 093

london moore unpublished radio broadcast
5 september 1954 *bbc third ptogramme*

appendix a/**the operatic performances**
number of appearances in each role, including concert and radio performances; listing does not refer to commercial gramophone recordings

the key roles
marschallin/strauss der rosenkavalier/*125*
fiordiligi/mozart cosi fan tutte/*84*
donna elvira/mozart don giovanni/*84*
contessa almaviva/mozart le nozze di figaro/*72*
gräfin madeleine/strauss capriccio/*18*
alice ford/verdi falstaff/*20*
eva/wagner die meistersinger von nürnberg/*15*

the middle-period mozart roles
susanna/mozart le nozze di figaro/*24*
pamina/mozart die zauberflöte/*26*
ilia/mozart idomeneo/*1*
amital/betulia liberata/*1*

the operatic performances/continued

the other middle-period roles
marzelline/beethoven fidelio/*21*
leonore/beethoven fidelio/*3*
marguérite/berlioz la damnation de faust/*5*
mélisande/debussy pelléas et melisande/*5*
euridice/gluck orfeo ed euridice/*2*
blessed spirit/gluck orfeo ed euridice/*6*
iole/handel eracle/*5*
cleopatra/handel giulio cesare/*1*
marguérite/gounod faust/*5*
gretel/humperdinck hänsel und gretel/*1*
nedda/leoncavallo i pagliacci/*3*
manon/massenet manon/*6*
soprano soloist/orff trionfi/*6*
mimi/puccini la boheme/*37*
cio-cio-san/puccini madama butterfly/*6*
liu/puccini turandot/*2*
rosina/rossini il barbiere di siviglia/*11*
marie/smetana the bartered bride/*4*
sophie/strauss der rosenkavalier/*14*
anne truelove/stravinsky the rake's progress/*7*
violetta/verdi la traviata/*51*
gilda/verdi rigoletto/*21*
woglinde/wagner das rheingold/*2*
woglinde/wagner götterdämmerung/*2*
elsa/wagner lohengrin/*6*
elisabeth/wagner tannhäuser/*1*
agathe/weber der freischütz/*2*

the early roles
pepa/d'albert tiefland/*20*
frasquita/bizet carmen/*26*
gianetta/donizetti l'elisir d'amore/*18*
leonore/flotow alessandro stradella/*3*
dew fairy/humperdinck hänsel und gretel/*19*
lumpensämmlerin/kienzl der evangelimann/*1*
alexei/kusterer katarina/*3*
first page/kusterer katarina/*3*
angela/lortzing prinz caramo/*2*
undine/lortzing undine/*4*
marie/lortzing der waffenschmied/*10*
gretchen/lortzing der wildschütz/*12*
marie/lortzing zar und zimmermann/*3*
nun/marinuzzi palla de mozzi/*10*
lola/mascagni cavalleria rusticana/*15*
konstanze/mozart die entführung aus dem serail/*21*
blondchen/mozart die entführung aus dem serail/*2*
serpetta/mozart la finta giardiniera/*8*
barbarina/mozart le nozze di figaro/*18*
first boy/mozart die zauberflöte/*27*
musetta/puccini la boheme/*16*
lauretta/puccini gianni schicchi/*4*
erika/schultze der schwarze peter/*2*
esmeralda/smetana the bartered bride/*11*
adele/j. strauss die fledermaus/*9*
ida/j. strauss/die fledermaus/*16*
arsena/j. strauss der zigeunerbaron/*23*
zerbinetta/strauss ariadne auf naxos/*11*
noble orphan/strauss der rosenkavalier/*11*
isabella/suppé boccaccio/*6*
alzira/verdi alzira/*1*
page/verdi rigoletto/*3*
ines/verdi il trovatore/*9*
wellgunde/wagner götterdämmerung/*7*
wellgunde/wagner das rheingold/*7*
waldvogel/wagner siegfried/*4*
ortlinde/wagner die walküre/*3*
edelknabe/wagner lohengrin/*5*
blumenmädchen/wagner parsifal/*28*
junger hirt and edelknabe/wagner tannhäuser/*20*
fatima/weber abu hassan/*2*
berta/weber euryanthe/*16*
ännchen/weber der freischütz/*11*
bridesmaid/weber der freischütz/*5*

appendix b/**selection of television interviews and documentaries**

im gespräch mit klaus harprecht/*zweites deutsches fernsehen 1968*

schwarzkopf and legge at home/*dutch television 1976*

pebble mill interview/*bbc television 1982*

face the music/*bbc television 1983*

porträt einer sängerin/a film by wolf-eberhard von lewinski
saarland television 1985

the south bank show/*london weekend television 1985*

da capo/im gespräch mit august everding/*3-sat television 1986*

schwarzkopf goes west/*bbc scotland television 1987*

die kunst muss aristokratisch sein/interview with christa schulz-rohr
south west german television 1988

musique au coeur/interview with eva ruggieri
france antenne 2 1990

die stimme ihres herrn/*österreichisches fernsehen 1990*

a self portrait/a film by gérard caillat and andré tubeuf/*la sept-arte*
published on vhs and dvd by emi classics

numerous masterclasses which schwarzkopf gave in the 1980s and 1990s
were also recorded for television

appendix c/**selection of radio interviews and documentaries**

mit den ohren singen/im gespräch mit monika steegmann
south german radio 1985

a touch of genius/a portrait by robin ray/*bbc radio three 1979*

her master's voice/a portrait by cathy wearing/*bbc world service 1995*

an elisabeth schwarzkopf evening/4-hour tribute for the singer's nintieth birthday/*bbc radio three 2005*

opernwerkstatt mit kammersängerin elisabeth schwarzkopf/
friends of the vienna staatsoper/*austrian radio 1985*

in conversation with milt rosenberg/*chicago 1982*

seventy-fifth birthday interview with edward greenfield/
bbc radio three 1990

appendix d/**appearances in cinema films**
the german ones were standard entertainment films and not, as has been asserted by at least one commentator, nazi propaganda vehicles: most of these include musical items performed by schwarzkopf, which are therefore included in the discography

das mädchen von saint coeur/germany 1939/directed by bernhard wentzel

drei unteroffiziere/germany 1939/directed by werner hochbaum
schwarzkopf sings title role in a brief extract from bizet's carmen (see discography)

die nacht ohne abschied/germany 1942/directed by erich waschneck
schwarzkopf sings finale of puccini's la boheme with peter anders (see discography)

der ewige klang/germany 1943/directed by günther rettau
schwarzkopf synchronises for olga tschechowa in 2 songs by franz grothe (see discography)

der verteidiger hat das wort/germany 1944/directed by werner klinger
schwarzkopf performs 2 lieder by schumann (see discography)

svengali/england 1954/directed by noel langley
schwarzkopf synchronises for hildegard knef in a cantata by william alwyn and in lieder by brahms and schubert (see discography)

appendix e/**bibliography**

elisabeth schwarzkopf/by bernard gavoty and roger hauert/ *published 1957 by rené kister*

on and off the record/a memoir of walter legge by elisabeth schwarzkopf/*published 1982 by faber and faber*

elisabeth schwarzkopf/by sergio segalini/*published 1983 by fayard*

les introuvables d'elisabeth schwarzkopf/edition of the avant-scene opera magazine accompanying the emi lp record set of the same name/*published 1983*

walter legge/a discography by alan sanders/*published 1984 by greenwood press*

viennese sopranos/discographies by john hunt/*published 1991*

elisabeth schwarzkopf: a career on record/by alan sanders and john steane/*published 1995 by duckworth*

teachers and pupils/discographies by john hunt/*published 1996*

words and music/writings of walter legge edited by alan sanders/ *published 1998 by duckworth*

les autres soirs/memoirs edited by andré tubeuf/*published 2004 by tallandier without the singer's final agreement*

Discographies by Travis & Emery:

Discographies by John Hunt.

1987: From Adam to Webern: the Recordings of von Karajan.
1991: 3 Italian Conductors and 7 Viennese Sopranos: 10 Discographies: Arturo Toscanini, Guido Cantelli, Carlo Maria Giulini, Elisabeth Schwarzkopf, Irmgard Seefried, Elisabeth Gruemmer, Sena Jurinac, Hilde Gueden, Lisa Della Casa, Rita Streich.
1992: Mid-Century Conductors and More Viennese Singers: 10 Discographies: Karl Boehm, Victor De Sabata, Hans Knappertsbusch, Tullio Serafin, Clemens Krauss, Anton Dermota, Leonie Rysanek, Eberhard Waechter, Maria Reining, Erich Kunz.
1993: More 20th Century Conductors: 7 Discographies: Eugen Jochum, Ferenc Fricsay, Carl Schuricht, Felix Weingartner, Josef Krips, Otto Klemperer, Erich Kleiber.
1994: Giants of the Keyboard: 6 Discographies: Wilhelm Kempff, Walter Gieseking, Edwin Fischer, Clara Haskil, Wilhelm Backhaus, Artur Schnabel.
1994: Six Wagnerian Sopranos: 6 Discographies: Frieda Leider, Kirsten Flagstad, Astrid Varnay, Martha Moedl, Birgit Nilsson, Gwyneth Jones.
1995: Musical Knights: 6 Discographies: Henry Wood, Thomas Beecham, Adrian Boult, John Barbirolli, Reginald Goodall, Malcolm Sargent.
1995: A Notable Quartet: 4 Discographies: Gundula Janowitz, Christa Ludwig, Nicolai Gedda, Dietrich Fischer-Dieskau.
1996: The Post-War German Tradition: 5 Discographies: Rudolf Kempe, Joseph Keilberth, Wolfgang Sawallisch, Rafael Kubelik, Andre Cluytens.
1996: Teachers and Pupils: 7 Discographies: Elisabeth Schwarzkopf, Maria Ivoguen, Maria Cebotari, Meta Seinemeyer, Ljuba Welitsch, Rita Streich, Erna Berger.
1996: Tenors in a Lyric Tradition: 3 Discographies: Peter Anders, Walther Ludwig, Fritz Wunderlich.
1997: The Lyric Baritone: 5 Discographies: Hans Reinmar, Gerhard Hüsch, Josef Metternich, Hermann Uhde, Eberhard Wächter.
1997: Hungarians in Exile: 3 Discographies: Fritz Reiner, Antal Dorati, George Szell.
1997: The Art of the Diva: 3 Discographies: Claudia Muzio, Maria Callas, Magda Olivero.
1997: Metropolitan Sopranos: 4 Discographies: Rosa Ponselle, Eleanor Steber, Zinka Milanov, Leontyne Price.
1997: Back From The Shadows: 4 Discographies: Willem Mengelberg, Dimitri Mitropoulos, Hermann Abendroth, Eduard Van Beinum.
1997: More Musical Knights: 4 Discographies: Hamilton Harty, Charles Mackerras, Simon Rattle, John Pritchard.
1998: Conductors On The Yellow Label: 8 Discographies: Fritz Lehmann, Ferdinand Leitner, Ferenc Fricsay, Eugen Jochum, Leopold Ludwig, Artur Rother, Franz Konwitschny, Igor Markevitch.
1998: More Giants of the Keyboard: 5 Discographies: Claudio Arrau, Gyorgy Cziffra, Vladimir Horowitz, Dinu Lipatti, Artur Rubinstein.

1998: Mezzos and Contraltos: 5 Discographies: Janet Baker, Margarete Klose, Kathleen Ferrier, Giulietta Simionato, Elisabeth Höngen.
1999: The Furtwängler Sound Sixth Edition: Discography and Concert Listing.
1999: The Great Dictators: 3 Discographies: Evgeny Mravinsky, Artur Rodzinski, Sergiu Celibidache.
1999: Sviatoslav Richter: Pianist of the Century: Discography.
2000: Philharmonic Autocrat 1: Discography of: Herbert Von Karajan [Third Edition].
2000: Wiener Philharmoniker 1 - Vienna Philharmonic & Vienna State Opera Orchestras: Disc. Part 1 1905-1954.
2000: Wiener Philharmoniker 2 - Vienna Philharmonic & Vienna State Opera Orchestras: Disc. Part 2 1954-1989.
2001: Gramophone Stalwarts: 3 Separate Discographies: Bruno Walter, Erich Leinsdorf, Georg Solti.
2001: Singers of the Third Reich: 5 Discographies: Helge Roswaenge, Tiana Lemnitz, Franz Völker, Maria Müller, Max Lorenz.
2001: Philharmonic Autocrat 2: Concert Register of Herbert Von Karajan Second Edition.
2002: Sächsische Staatskapelle Dresden: Complete Discography.
2002: Carlo Maria Giulini: Discography and Concert Register.
2002: Pianists For The Connoisseur: 6 Discographies: Arturo Benedetti Michelangeli, Alfred Cortot, Alexis Weissenberg, Clifford Curzon, Solomon, Elly Ney.
2003: Singers on the Yellow Label: 7 Discographies: Maria Stader, Elfriede Trötschel, Annelies Kupper, Wolfgang Windgassen, Ernst Häfliger, Josef Greindl, Kim Borg.
2003: A Gallic Trio: 3 Discographies: Charles Münch, Paul Paray, Pierre Monteux.
2004: Antal Dorati 1906-1988: Discography and Concert Register.
2004: Columbia 33CX Label Discography.
2004: Great Violinists: 3 Discographies: David Oistrakh, Wolfgang Schneiderhan, Arthur Grumiaux.
2006: Leopold Stokowski: Second Edition of the Discography.
2006: Wagner Im Festspielhaus: Discography of the Bayreuth Festival.
2006: Her Master's Voice: Concert Register and Discography of Dame Elisabeth Schwarzkopf [Third Edition].
2007: Hans Knappertsbusch: Kna: Concert Register and Discography of Hans Knappertsbusch, 1888-1965. Second Edition.
2008: Philips Minigroove: Second Extended Version of the European Discography.
2009: American Classics: The Discographies of Leonard Bernstein and Eugene Ormandy.

Discography by Stephen J. Pettitt, edited by John Hunt:
1987: Philharmonia Orchestra: Complete Discography 1945-1987

Available from: Travis & Emery at 17 Cecil Court, London, UK. (+44) 20 7 240 2129. email on sales@travis-and-emery.com .

© Travis & Emery 2009

Music and Books published by Travis & Emery Music Bookshop:

Anon.: Hymnarium Sarisburense, cum Rubris et Notis Musicus
Agricola, Johann Friedrich from Tosi: Anleitung zur Singkunst. (Faksimile 1757)
Bach, C.P.E.: edited W. Emery: Nekrolog or Obituary Notice of J.S. Bach.
Bateson, Naomi Judith: Alcock of Salisbury
Bathe, William: A Briefe Introduction to the Skill of Song
Bax, Arnold: Symphony #5, Arranged for Piano Four Hands by Walter Emery
Burney, Charles: The Present State of Music in France and Italy
Burney, Charles: The Present State of Music in Germany, The Netherlands …
Burney, Charles: An Account of the Musical Performances … Handel
Burney, Karl: Nachricht von Georg Friedrich Handel's Lebensumstanden.
Burns, Robert (jnr): The Caledonian Musical Museum (1810 volume)
Cobbett, W.W.: Cobbett's Cyclopedic Survey of Chamber Music. (2 vols.)
Corrette, Michel: Le Maitre de Clavecin
Crimp, Bryan: Dear Mr. Rosenthal … Dear Mr. Gaisberg …
Crimp, Bryan: Solo: The Biography of Solomon
d'Indy, Vincent: Beethoven: Biographie Critique
d'Indy, Vincent: Beethoven: A Critical Biography
d'Indy, Vincent: César Franck (in French)
Fischhof, Joseph: Versuch einer Geschichte des Clavierbaues
Frescobaldi, Girolamo: D'Arie Musicali per Cantarsi. Primo Libro & Secondo Libro.
Geminiani, Francesco: The Art of Playing the Violin.
Handel; Purcell; Boyce; Green et al: Calliope or English Harmony: Volume First.
Hawkins, John: A General History of the Science and Practice of Music (5 vols.)
Herbert-Caesari, Edgar: The Science and Sensations of Vocal Tone
Herbert-Caesari, Edgar: Vocal Truth
Hopkins and Rimboult: The Organ. Its History and Construction.
Hunt, John: some 40 discographies – see list of discographies
Isaacs, Lewis: Hänsel and Gretel. A Guide to Humperdinck's Opera.
Isaacs, Lewis: Königskinder (Royal Children) A Guide to Humperdinck's Opera.
Lacassagne, M. l'Abbé Joseph : Traité Général des élémens du Chant.
Lascelles (née Catley), Anne: The Life of Miss Anne Catley.
Mainwaring, John: Memoirs of the Life of the Late George Frederic Handel
Malcolm, Alexander: A Treaty of Music: Speculative, Practical and Historical
Marx, Adolph Bernhard: Die Kunst des Gesanges, Theoretisch-Practisch
May, Florence: The Life of Brahms
Mellers, Wilfrid: Angels of the Night: Popular Female Singers of Our Time
Mellers, Wilfrid: Bach and the Dance of God

Travis & Emery Music Bookshop
17 Cecil Court, London, WC2N 4EZ, United Kingdom.
Tel. (+44) 20 7240 2129

Music and Books published by Travis & Emery Music Bookshop:

Mellers, Wilfrid: Beethoven and the Voice of God
Mellers, Wilfrid: Caliban Reborn - Renewal in Twentieth Century Music
Mellers, Wilfrid: François Couperin and the French Classical Tradition
Mellers, Wilfrid: Harmonious Meeting
Mellers, Wilfrid: Le Jardin Retrouvé, The Music of Frederic Mompou
Mellers, Wilfrid: Music and Society, England and the European Tradition
Mellers, Wilfrid: Music in a New Found Land: …… American Music
Mellers, Wilfrid: Romanticism and the Twentieth Century (from 1800)
Mellers, Wilfrid: The Masks of Orpheus: …… the Story of European Music.
Mellers, Wilfrid: The Sonata Principle (from c. 1750)
Mellers, Wilfrid: Vaughan Williams and the Vision of Albion
Panchianio, Cattuffio: Rutzvanscad Il Giovine.
Pearce, Charles: Sims Reeves, Fifty Years of Music in England.
Pettitt, Stephen: Philharmonia Orchestra: Complete Discography 1945-1987
Playford, John: An Introduction to the Skill of Musick.
Purcell, Henry et al: Harmonia Sacra … The First Book, (1726)
Purcell, Henry et al: Harmonia Sacra … Book II (1726)
Quantz, Johann: Versuch einer Anweisung die Flöte traversiere zu spielen.
Rameau, Jean-Philippe: Code de Musique Pratique, ou Methodes.
Rastall, Richard: The Notation of Western Music.
Rimbault, Edward: The Pianoforte, Its Origins, Progress, and Construction.
Rousseau, Jean Jacques: Dictionnaire de Musique
Rubinstein, Anton : Guide to the proper use of the Pianoforte Pedals.
Sainsbury, John S.: Dictionary of Musicians. Vol. 1. (1825). 2 vols.
Simpson, Christopher: A Compendium of Practical Musick in Five Parts
Spohr, Louis: Autobiography
Spohr, Louis: Grand Violin School
Tans'ur, William: A New Musical Grammar; or The Harmonical Spectator
Terry, Charles Sanford: Four-Part Chorals of J.S. Bach. (German & English)
Terry, Charles Sanford: Joh. Seb. Bach, Cantata Texts, Sacred and Secular.
Terry, Charles Sanford: The Origins of the Family of Bach Musicians.
Tosi, Pierfrancesco: Opinioni de' Cantori Antichi, e Moderni
Van der Straeten, Edmund: History of the Violoncello, The Viol da Gamba …
Van der Straeten, Edmund: History of the Violin, Its Ancestors… (2 vols.)
Walther, J. G.: Musicalisches Lexikon ober Musicalische Bibliothec (1732)

Travis & Emery Music Bookshop
17 Cecil Court, London, WC2N 4EZ, United Kingdom.
Tel. (+44) 20 7240 2129

© Travis & Emery 2009